On Globalization

Also by Bruno Amoroso

RAPPORTO DALLA SCANDINAVIA

MACROECONOMIC THEORIES AND POLICY FOR THE 1990s (*editor with J. Jespersen*)

SCANDINAVIAN PERSPECTIVES ON EUROPEAN INTEGRATION

WELFARE SOCIETY IN TRANSITION (*editor with J. Jespersen*)

On Globalization
Capitalism in the 21st Century

Bruno Amoroso
*Professor in European Integration and Social Cohesion
 in the Wider Europe (Jean Monnet Chair)
Department of Social Sciences
Roskilde University
Denmark*

© Bruno Amoroso 1998

All rights reserved. No reproduction, copy or transmission of this publication may be made without written permission.

No paragraph of this publication may be reproduced, copied or transmitted save with written permission or in accordance with the provisions of the Copyright, Designs and Patents Act 1988, or under the terms of any licence permitting limited copying issued by the Copyright Licensing Agency, 90 Tottenham Court Road, London W1P 0LP.

Any person who does any unauthorised act in relation to this publication may be liable to criminal prosecution and civil claims for damages.

The author has asserted his right to be identified as the author of this work in accordance with the Copyright, Designs and Patents Act 1988.

First published in hardcover 1998

First published in paperback 2001 by
PALGRAVE
Houndmills, Basingstoke, Hampshire RG21 6XS and
175 Fifth Avenue, New York, N.Y. 10010
Companies and representatives throughout the world

PALGRAVE is the new global academic imprint of
St. Martin's Press LLC Scholarly and Reference Division and
Palgrave Publishers Ltd (formerly Macmillan Press Ltd).

ISBN 0–333–71739–2 hardback (*outside North America*)
ISBN 0–312–21085–X hardback (*in North America*)
ISBN 0–333–93073–8 paperback (*worldwide*)

This book is printed on paper suitable for recycling and made from fully managed and sustained forest sources.

A catalogue record for this book is available from the British Library.

The Library of Congress has cataloged the hardcover edition as follows:
Amoroso, Bruno.
   On globalization : capitalism in the 21st century / Bruno Amoroso.
     p. cm.
   Includes bibliographical references and index.
   ISBN 0–312–21085–X
     1. Capitalism—History—20th century. I. Title. II. Title: Capitalism in the 21st century.
   HB501.A5919 1998
   330.12'2—dc21
                                                97–30923
                                                    CIP

10 9 8 7 6 5 4 3 2 1
10 09 08 07 06 05 04 03 02 01

Printed in Great Britain by Antony Rowe Ltd, Chippenham, Wiltshire

Contents

Lists of Figures and Tables vi
Acknowledgements viii

   INTRODUCTION 1
1 THE DYNAMICS OF SOCIO-ECONOMIC FORMATIONS 7
2 INTERNATIONALIZATION AND CAPITALISM: FROM DUALISM TO MARGINALIZATION 33
3 THE WORLD ECONOMY AND CAPITALISM: THE GLOBALIZATION OF THE ECONOMY AND TECHNOLOGY 50
4 CAPITAL ACCUMULATION IN THE LAST DECADE OF THE 20TH CENTURY – THE END OF DEVELOPMENT 70
5 THE METAMORPHOSIS OF THE FIRM: NATIONAL, MULTINATIONAL, TRANSNATIONAL 84
6 GLOBALIZATION AND EUROPEAN INTEGRATION: EUROCENTRISM AND WESTERNIZATION 104
7 SOCIAL CLASS AND POLITICAL POWER: AUTHORS, ACTORS AND INSTITUTIONS 117
8 ALTERNATIVE POLICIES TO GLOBALIZATION: A POLYCENTRIC VIEW 130
9 TOWARD MEDITERRANEAN CO-DEVELOPMENT 151

   BIBLIOGRAPHY 200

Index 207

List of Figures

1.1	Productions Modes, Institutions and Market Forms	12
1.2	Material Life, Market and Capitalism	16
1.3	The First Diamond of Polycentric Development	28
1.4	The Second Diamond of Polycentric Development	30
1.5	A New Analytical Model of Development and Co-development	31
2.1	The Stages of Internationalization	34
2.2	Worldwide Economic Disparities	47
3.1	Concepts and Economic Realities	51
3.2	Geographic Breakdown of Capital Flow by Provenance	56
3.3	Geographic Breakdown of Capital Flow by Destination	57
3.4	FDI Stock Among Triad Members and Their Clusters, 1993	59
3.5	The Triad of FDI and Its Clusters, 1993	60
3.6	Share of Regional Trade Flows Out of the World Trade of Manufactured Goods	62
3.7	GDP and Employment Growth in Industrialized Countries	63
3.8	Partnership in the Auto Industry	64
3.9	Strategic Partnerships in the Electronics Industry: Europe, Japan and USA	65
3.10	General Motors' Strategic Positioning	66
3.11	Alliances in the Telecommunications Industry Before the CGE and ITT	67
3.12	Automobile Operations of Toyota in Four ASEAN Countries	68
5.1	The Firm's Metamorphosis	87
6.1	Traditional Heartlands and Growth Regions of the Community	106
6.2	Trade Among EU Countries	113
6.3	Trade Relations Among the Baltic Countries	114
6.4	Trade Relations in the Mediterranean	115
7.1	Net Transfers to Developing Countries from Bretton Woods Institutions	119

Lists of Figures and Tables vii

8.1	Regional Scenarios of Europe	134
9.1	Mediterranean Scenario: Agro-food Education Institutions, 1992	171
9.2	Start-up Proposal Outline for Economic and Social Cooperation in the Mediterranean	198

List of Tables

3.1	Inflow of Direct Foreign Investment to Developing Regions	61
9.1	Where They Come From	189
9.2	Resident Permits Issued in Italy as of 31 December 1990 by Region and Reason for Insurance	190
9.3	Reasons for Expatriation, 1990	191
9.4	Estimate of Immigrants Employed in Italy of 31 December 1990 by Region of Residence and Economic Sector	194

Acknowledgements

I should like to thank my friends Pietro Barcellona, Arrigo Chieregatti and Giulio Petti for their patient encouragement in convincing me to take up the labours of the written word. I am in debt to Paolo Maria Ceschel for his scrupulous reading of the manuscript and his painstaking removal of the rust that professional jargon have left upon my writing style. Considerable help to the financing of this research was given by the Department of Social Sciences at Roskilde University, the Jean Monnet Project and the Tempustacis Programme of the European Union. This book is dedicated to Federico Caffè and Ye Jin in the hope they find the time to read it.

Introduction

> Finally, I hope that my frank and uninhibited style, long an inveterate habit, will be endured by my readers on the rationale that progress in the social sciences lies through controversy, which should be sharpened and not veiled.
> Myrdal, 1974, p.VIII

> There is a tendency for all knowledge, like all ignorance, to deviate from truth in an opportunistic direction.
> Myrdal, 1971, p.21[1]

> Now, whenever someone under colonial rule hears a speech on Western culture, the first thing he does is to get out his jack knife, or at least makes sure it's within reach.
> Fanon, 1962, p.10

THINKING ALOUD

This volume offers a reflection upon certain key phenomena affecting our own lives as well as those of communities, nations and states. It is a thinking out loud in the true sense of the term, for it stems from and has matured in the course of my teaching and research activities, and in many encounters with friends and adversaries alike here, there and everywhere – Europe, Africa, America, Asia.

I have turned my thoughts to how we live, feel, express ourselves, make our livelihoods, organize our lives and to how authority, values and the laws of communities are formed. We suffer from a painful dearth of readily perceptible and representational concepts in connection with these processes and activities in that those we do have – culture, development, democracy – are no longer serviceable. Imbued with Western history and culture, these concepts reflect the tragic process of the 'Westernisation of the world' (Latouche, 1996) and are manifestly freighted with all the signs of arbitrary power, abuse of values, manipulation of opinions and ideas.

THE GREAT POLITICO-ECONOMIC EXPERIMENTS

There has been no lack throughout this century, especially during the interwar years, of honest efforts to reinvigorate these concepts by re-animating first and foremost ourselves and our identity. Yet, by the end of the 1980s, despite the energy expended over more than half a century to improve the socialist, welfare and national systems of new nations, these great 'politico-economic experiments' – some already transformed first by the dictates of economic blockade, war and colonialism and then by those of the capitalist marketplace – collapsed.

TODAY'S 'DISCOURSES'

While the talking goes on unabated, it has utterly abandoned in the last few years any claim to language. Meditations on and theories of culture, development and democracy – what in today's academic histrionics is termed *discourse* – are merely ways of seeking control over form wherever it has been lost over values and content – another symptom of the triumph of totalitarianism. These *discourses*, whether of philosophers, economists, political scientists or sociologists, express not so much a reflection as the 'inarticulate and obsessive language of the non-verbal signs' of young people enfranchized in the culture and consumerism so cogently remarked upon by Pier Paolo Pasolini (1975, p.16).

THE TURNING-POINT

The watershed of my own meditations was 1989, the year most pundits hailed as the beginning of a new era, the dawn of an age of greater well-being and democracy. In contrast, I am convinced that 1989 marked the end of the evolutionary path capitalism embarked upon in the mid-1970s and the beginning of a new global force – the *triadic capitalism* of the transnational corporations.

ITS STRATEGIES

The strategies capitalism devised to achieve this goal were *economic marginalization* and *political destabilization*, which led to the destruction of the aforementioned politico-economic experiments and of all forms of resistance to the new world order. The point of departure was the elimination of enemies and in-house opposition. The much vaunted capitalism with a human face that marked all forms of the welfare state had become the most vulnerable, and the Scandinavian model – the foremost among them because of its championing of socialism, solidarity and commitment – was especially troublesome in an era being heralded as the epitome of privatization, individualism and the new world order.

THE SCANDINAVIAN MODEL'S ELIMINATION

This model's main fault was its insistence on applying the principles of the welfare state to international relations. It even went so far as to declare its approach as the third way in East–West relations. As envisaged by Olof Palme[2], the idea was to set up an area of peace and well-being stretching from Scandinavia to Central Europe that could serve as a bridge and sphere of influence *vis-à-vis* Eastern Europe so as to orientate and sustain the latter's efforts towards greater prosperity and a broader participation in the political process of its citizens. Yet, by doing so, the Scandinavian model was directly at odds with the strategy orchestrated during the Reagan era to pursue the collapse of the East.

The Scandinavian approach thus differed from the 'fall-of-the-Wall' strategy and as such was incompatible with blueprints for the new world order that were already being implemented. The tactic chosen to eliminate this first impediment, one often employed in the Third World, was to destroy the political leadership. The physical elimination of Palme himself was the most notable and visible step of this 'surgical operation', which was in any case supported by similar yet less resounding undertakings in Denmark and Norway.

THE ELIMINATION OF THE SOCIALIST COUNTRIES

The socialist countries posed the greatest obstacle and to remove it all the instruments of might at the disposal of *globalization* – the military, the economy and the mass media – were brought to bear, producing as is well known the desired results. The main weapon employed in the conflict was, of course, the textbook one – the economy.

In a rephrasing of the famous pages of Karl Marx's *Communist Manifesto*, it can be asserted that, by the rapid improvement of all instruments of production and by the immensely facilitated means of communication, the *bourgeoisie* drags all nations, even the most *civilized*, down into barbarism.

The cheap prices of its commodities are the heavy artillery with which it batters down all Chinese Walls, with which it forces the barbarians' intensely obstinate hatred of foreigners to capitulate. It compels all nations, on pain of extinction, to adopt the bourgeois mode of production; it compels them to introduce what it calls civilization into their midst, i.e. to become bourgeois themselves. In one word, it creates a world after its own image.

(Marx and Engels, 1968, p.84)

THE ANOMALY OF ITALY

The removal of these major obstacles opened the way to the suppression of all the anomalies of capitalist development created and tolerated during the Cold War. The liquidation of the Scandinavian model in northern Europe was followed by the removal of the southern one – Italy.

Like the Scandinavia of the unreliable Eastern European relations, Italy too posed a reliability problem in its relations not only with the East but, more particularly, towards the Arab states to the South. Italy's post-World War II political system was tolerated so long as its policy of containment *vis-à-vis* Eastern Europe and Italy's communists remained useful. Yet, with the demise of the socialist bloc spelling the end of this policy, the system itself now became expendable. It was liquidated in an operation of political destabilization designed to substitute political and social dialectics with a technocratic-authoritarian form of governance which, entrusted to experts of unquestionable credentials, saw the ship of state's helm placed in the hands of apolitical technicians (bankers, magistrates, high-ranking police officials and university professors).

The Italian anomaly was resolved by cutting back the funds of the welfare state – the *Mezzogiorno* (the 'South') economic development legislation, the public-sector companies and general budget expenditures. These were the same financial policy instruments that had ensured legitimacy and electoral support for the political parties as well as nurture the economic aspirations of the citizenry in the postwar years, when an unrealizable capitalist modernization (stubbornly recycled at the end of the Cold War) was launched.

While the dust storm stirred up by the war on waste concealed an attempt to sell an image of capitalism's honesty and efficiency, capitalism was in fact the laboratory from which the criminal activities of the new mafias are issued and are managed – financial speculation; the destruction of the genetic and environmental heritage of extensive areas of the world; the manufacture of and trafficking in arms and drugs.

The drain on employment and the income fluctuations generated by these policies, not to mention the stark scenes of unemployment and misery they generate, carry the risk of linking up political and social destabilization, thereby initiating an unresolvable vicious circle in the Italian crisis. The events of the past year – events that continue to unfold – indicate that the success of the structural adjustment (*economic marginalization*) and of institutional normalization (*political destabilization*) decreed by the interests of *triadic capitalism* is pushing Italy towards an Algeria-like situation.

RETHINKING THE TASK

These considerations induce, or rather compel, us to further reflection and thought – to take a closer look at the processes and contradictions so as to glean a bit of hope and, in a way, to stand aside momentarily from the much-ado-about-nothing that almost invariably goes on behind false, if not altogether non-existent, heroes and objectives. Theodor Adorno's (1951) aphorism to the effect that in a world where everyone is running heedlessly hither and thither even those who stand still or move in the opposite direction seem to be fleeing, is just as true today as it was when first pronounced. This makes such a rethinking even more difficult, especially for any one who wants to take up the challenge and the search by beginning with ideas and a rereading of the facts.

The optimists – some can always be found among the scholars in the social sciences – come to the task as if looking for precious stones to be acquired in the luxury boutiques of European culture (the universities and renowned research centres). They marshal erudite citations and no less distinguished references in reconstructing an interpretation of a social reality that is not necessarily true but is paraded out to assure maximum effect. Others, less optimistic but more pragmatic, go diligently to the supermarket of the academic world, borrowing or purchasing whatever is most useful and choosing the best quality at the lowest price through sophisticated evaluation methods of the quality-cost ratio.

Ever mindful of caution, I like to recall how Federico Caffè taught us to be more modest, likening our task to that of the archaeologist moving about among the ruins of the past and searching the various layers for the pieces of puzzle necessary to reconstruct the theories we need today. As his pupil, I feel somewhat removed from the archaeologist and more akin to the vagabond who inhabits the outskirts of capitalism's metropolises. I prefer this more modern 'symbol of man' that searches through the rubbish heaps, whether steaming or frozen, of what the world's wealth has left behind. For these are the shards and tatters which, though having lost their original function, enable one to survive and to continue looking in the midden for the rest of the pieces and theories which have escaped the suffocation that consumerism and cultural opportunism have heaped on top of them.

NOTES

1. Myrdal's classic work on objectivity in the social sciences is Myrdal, (1953). This contribution was anticipated by Myrdal, (1958) and followed by Myrdal, (1969).
2. Olof Palme, the 59 year-old Prime Minister of Sweden was assassinated in 1987 on his way home from the cinema with his wife. Who the assassin was may never be known.

1 The Dynamics of Socio-Economic Formations

> We now come to 1972. That September I was in the city of Isfahan, the heart of Persia. As the horrendous saying goes, an underdeveloped country that, no less horrendously, is in full boom.
>
> Pasolini, 1975, p.14

THE ISSUE OF DEVELOPMENT

The Dual Interpretative Polarities of Development

Must a civilized society adapt to the needs of industry or must technology respect the needs of human communities?

Development is to be found among the most closely watched issues. Indeed, the continuum of field reports and analyses, the variety of studies and approaches – from the most academic to the most politically orientated – abound (Sachs, 1995). The literature and the political designs of the last 30 years can be grouped into two large blocs, the first undoubtedly being the dominant one.

i) Studies that are designed to promote the adaptation by local communities, regions and entire countries to the continually new demands of integration and industrial innovation. They start from the assumption that human communities are the dependent variables and industrial needs the equation's fixed given.

ii) Studies that seek ways to adapt integration processes and technological innovation to the development needs of communities. They are posited on the assumption that the latter are the given and the industrial processes are the dependent variables.

Both positions, despite their diversity, assume as facts the substance and direction of development and appear optimistic about the benefits of modernization. The first holds that adaptations of human communities to industrial exigencies merely derive from the processes of world development, processes in which one must strive for as large a role as possible. The second, though evincing concern about the risks of social exclusion and unacceptably high costs, holds that the risks as well as the costs can be overcome by the appropriate policies.

Yet I prefer a third line of inquiry, one that starts from a study of the needs each community or society expresses as a result of the growth of their production systems. This approach takes into account the cultural dynamics and social bonds these needs have generated and derives therefrom the policies and postures towards market-forming processes, economic integration and the technologies to be adopted. The substance, or contents, of development and modernization is thus to be sought and defined in consonance with the historical trajectory and the specific needs of each community. My objective is therefore to achieve an overall representation of how socio-economic formations work and the conflictual relationship these latter have today with the capitalist mode of production.

Capitalism's Revision of History

The issues implicitly embodied in the concept of development constitute a kind of 'Ur' sign, or better of original sin, and mirror the basic cultural matrix from which capitalism arose. Yet its history in all the contemporary manuals is made to begin with the Industrial Revolution, thereby denying *de facto* any evolution as well as the great revolutions of mankind. The ongoing, daily, multi-millennial evolution of the human species, which stretches from the discovery of the upright position to that of fire, the wheel, the map, navigation, and has forged the transformation of our fundamental production systems from nomadic hunting and gathering to the first agricultural settlements, is overshadowed and cast into a twilight zone of prehistory and barbarianism.

Agriculture, the cradle of every evolution, revolution and emancipation, is labelled as a pre-industrial phase or 'the idiocy of rural life'. The process of innovation and progress wrought by everyday changes, at once invisible, indivisible and collective, is counted null and history rewritten – History, Development, Science, Inventions, Patents, Genius, Competition all begin with the Bourgeoisie. The vast areas of world civilization that saw the birth of history and that for millennia have been its main laboratory – the Middle and Far East, the Americas, Africa – are relegated to the attention of anthropologists, ethnologists and archaeologists and banished to the realm of the 'non-technological primitiveness' of collectivism, of religio-philosophical thought, of thought and systems related to being rather than having (Fromm 1976). The 'History of Mankind' thus becomes the history of a few hundred years and few thousand individuals, its principle trait being the self-appropriation of existing knowledge and its aim the exercise of power and dominion through an escalating vortex of violence and environmental and social pollution, to devastating effect on the entire planet.

This has, of course, not gone unnoticed. The social protest against this cultural genocide[1] has found powerful, if unheeded, voices. How can one not recall the violent words of Leo Tolstoi against the socialist and liberal theories which the bourgeois *intelligentsia* imported into Russia in the expectation of educating people to the truth?[2] And how can one forget the need of writers like Marguerite Yourcenar, of historians like Fernand Braudel and of economists like Gunnar Myrdal to steep themselves in the experience of peoples and civilizations off the beaten and chokingly narrow path of eurocentrism?

Capitalism's Success is Built on the Partitioning of the Interactions of Human Societies

With respect to other forms of social and economic organization, to previous socio-economic systems and to those still extant in areas of the world beyond its dominion, capitalism's success has been achieved through a process that splits up the basic components in the life of every community.

One of many fine pages written by Enrica Collotti Pischel, a distinguished scholar of Asian societies, reminds the reader that 'the interaction of the environment, production, population and culture' is the basic element of Chinese civilization and explains, for the past as well as the future, its greater talents for survival and resilience (1979, p.XVI). Such interaction is found to varying degrees in all socio-economic formations, and it is only through the splitting of its complex patterning that capitalism has been able to triumph and impose its supremacy on communities, nations and regions the world over.

The degree of this operation's success – greater and more extensive in colonized countries though significant even in others where capitalist modernization has gained a strong foothold – determines the extent of the disintegration of a given society or its chances of regaining its autonomy. The origins of capitalism's rise to prominence lie in the city-states of the Middle Ages. Here the bourgeois citizenry engaged in a struggle to become the mercantile patriciate and bankers and, with the power that money confers, managed to take over the cities, turning them first into the *signorie* of the Renaissance and then into the ruling class of the Enlightenment's absolute monarchies. As Fernand Braudel puts it:

> In the process, capitalism destroys certain bastions of upper society, but it does so in order to reconstruct to its own advantage other bastions that are equally solid and durable.
>
> (1977, p.70)

The first step in this struggle aimed, as Machiavelli's aphorism that 'the end justifies the means' makes perfectly clear, to separate ethics, economics and politics. The second stage proceeded to consolidate this fragmentation by consciously separating the powers of the state into the legislative, executive and judicial branches. Thus, by eliminating the unity of the human point of view and hence any overall appraisement about the facts of life, it led to the pre-eminence of the means – money, and its coincident power – over the ethico-politico-economic (in that order) ends. The culture of separation consolidated itself in the course of capitalism's development by feeding upon the fragmentation of roles and powers and convincing us in the end that Culture (humanist) is an accessory category distinct from that of production systems and technology.

Academia has passively reflected the political demands of certain elites and social classes in its curricular development. Whence the rise of disciplines, which originate in a political need for control and not in an objective need for specialization. The historian David Noble has collected a wealth of documentary evidence on how the bourgeoisie deprived workers of control over the production process (in cultural terms even earlier than in trade-union or policy terms) through the organization of the workplace and the division of labour. The relationship of technology and society is paradigmatic:

> Thus, a stock device of recent social analysis is to view modern technology as though it had a life of its own, an inner dynamic which feeds on the very society that has unleashed it. Propelled

The Dynamics of Socio-Economic Formations 11

according to its own immanent logic and operating through witting and unwitting human agency, it ultimately outstrips the conscious activities that gave birth to it, creating a society in which people are but functional parts of the mechanism. There is a core of truth in the view – a common theme in modern mythology – that human creations tend to assume an existence independent of their creator's will. Problems arise, however, when, in a more or less subtle way, the metaphor is substituted for history, when the rich complexity of the social process is reduced to the inexorable logic of formalistic technology. Artificially abstracted from the world in which people actually live, such a conception distorts both technology itself and the society which gives it meaning.

Unfortunately, such facile explanations of history do enjoy wide currency, and are daily reinforced by the common conceptual habit of distinguishing between 'technology' on the one hand and 'society' (or 'culture') on the other, as if the two were made of altogether different stuff.

(1977, p.xviii)

Critiques like those noted above are a big help in attempting to devise an analytical method for and a theory of *socio-economic formations* which is capable of examining how capitalism first influenced and then took over the economy and society up to the current stage of *globalization*.

CAPITALISM AND SOCIETY: SEVERAL HYPOTHESES

Production Modes, Institutions, Market Forms

The history of *socio-economic formations* has evolved as a transformation of the relationship between man, with his organization into social classes, and nature. The various factors of this evolution can, by simplification and grouping, be summarized as production modes, institutions and market forms.

The diagram (figure 1.1) enables us to examine and highlight certain symmetries and asymmetries along its axes, which plot the causes of the equilibria, and the imbalances, of socio-economic formations, and to posit on their basis general rules of interpretation.

12   On Globalization

Figure 1.1   Production Modes, Institutions and Market Forms

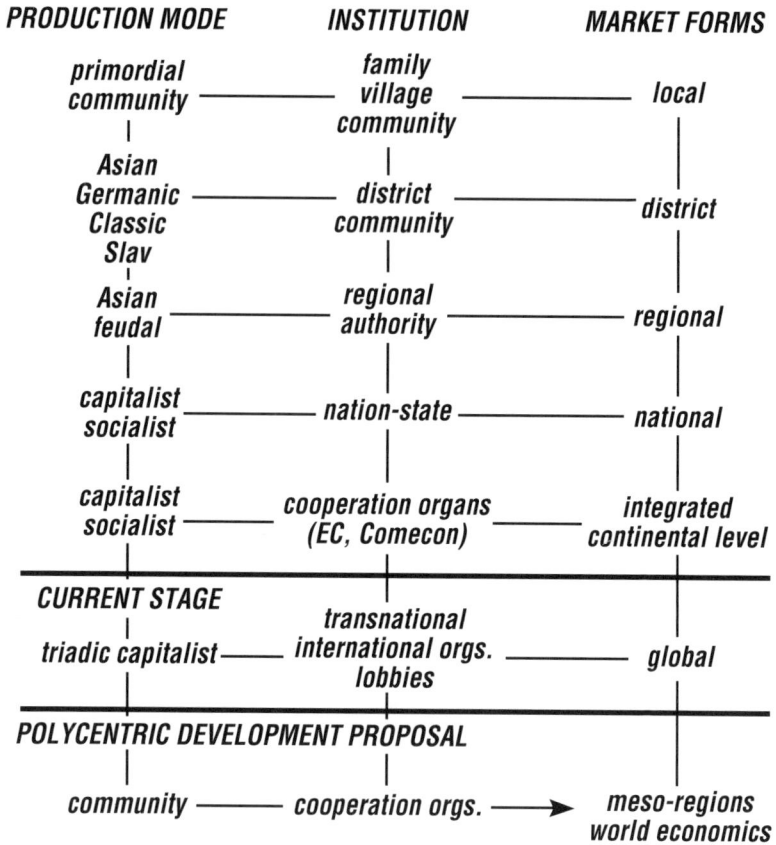

Transformations Along the Vertical Axes

Let us note at the outset that any excessive asymmetry between elements along the vertical axes, say between a national market and regional institutions, would indicate a clash of interests. The ensuing predicament could only be resolved by moving both elements to a common ground of reference, that is to the horizontal axis. For example, if the asymmetry resulted from an attempt to organize a national market upon the incipient formation of the national state – in the presence of local, regional or even merely district institutions – the outcome would be either the coalescing of the state or the failure of the national market.

The multi-ethnic or colonial empires witnessed throughout the course of history have given rise to forms of domination that have wiped out certain socio-economic formations either by incorporating them or by colonizing them. This has resulted in the establishment of institutional bonds that have destroyed, whether temporarily or permanently, what until then had been symmetrical interactions.

The same can be said for the interrelatedness of production modes, institutions and market forms wherever the capitalist mode of production has been able to trigger the destruction of institutional forms and participatory governance incompatible with the exercise of its own functioning. There are cases, of course, in which the given institutional make-up and market forces, through their preponderant influence over the accumulation process, have impeded or limited the territorial expansion of capitalism and given rise to other models of development.

Correlations to the Horizontal Axes

The globalism we have postulated, that is the existence of triadic capitalism, readily makes possible a cogent analysis of the crisis nation-states find themselves in today and its implications. It is obvious that the global consolidation of the production mode currently being espoused by the triadic capitalism of the transnational corporations threatens the very existence of all forms of national organization in that the former tends to eliminate, or at least supercede, the socio-economic formations nurtured and protected by the latter.

Without trying to posit rigid guidelines of proportionality regulating the interaction of production modes, institutions and market forms, it can be asserted that wherever an exaggerated asymmetry intervenes in these three factors, it generates tensions and the need for them to recoalesce upon a higher common ground. The examples below highlight the pressures at work among the various factors involved in a given socio-economic organization during the process of reciprocal adaptation.

Take the case of communities with a sparse population spread out over a fairly wide area of arid lands, a situation often encountered in the Mediterranean hinterland. Here production systems are strongly rooted in a nomadic way of life consonant with an extensive model of land use. The techniques adopted to exploit the land's resources appropriately can be seen in the kinds of livestock selected, type of diet, local customs, religious beliefs and so on. The defining lines of education, health and habitat gradually integrate with these ways of life, with the institutional and political make-up reflecting this situation through a decentralized and highly autonomous organization.

Now let us look at the socio-economic structures rooted in smaller but wetter areas with extensive mountain formations and a numerous population. Here, too, the production systems have adapted themselves to the context by developing appropriate technologies and innovations, their output and work cycles being linked to the climate and terrain, with matching dietary regimens, ways of living, dwellings. The evolution of production techniques is geared to intensive land use, inevitably entailing high labour-input processes. The forms of property ownership cannot but be coherent with these organizational structures, having developed into family-managed holdings and cooperatives with strong institutional bonds throughout the area. Yet should inappropriate technologies, institutional structures and housing designs of alien countries and production systems be introduced into either of these two examples, they would ineluctably generate not further growth but decline and demise because they are incapable of working the miracle that transforms into sustenance the basic factors of life – water, climate, soil and demography.

Development: Conclusions

Similarly, endogenous attempts to preserve forms of government or management that have come into conflict with the development needs of their production systems and their matching ways of life will also generate crisis phenomena. It is no accident that external intervention and internal preservation are in many countries often joined together in a symbiotic embrace.

National market capitalism has destroyed many of these socio-economic formations via two approaches:

i) colonization, the imposing of backward social systems and authoritarian forms of administrative control, and
ii) modernization, arresting the development of so-called backward

communities through the overlapping of exogenous social relationships and giving rise in many instances to the cultural genocide mentioned by Pier Paolo Pasolini in summing up Italy's postwar development.

Thus, because the process of transforming production systems affects a society's entire structure and its ways of life, it should unfold over the course of generations and in the necessary historical time. If not, it will prevent a gradual evolution of socio-economic formations, and the time needed for assimilation, and quite simply determine their collapse. A good case in point is the modernization of the indigenous people in the Amazon River Basin or the Lapps in northern Europe – a modernization that has led to the destruction of the ways of life of both these cultures and peoples.

SOCIO-ECONOMIC FORMATIONS AND CAPITALISM

The Analysis of Fernand Braudel

Fernand Braudel's analytical model of the traits marking production systems and the processes of capital accumulation in today's societies introduced a very useful tool for their understanding. It is grounded in three basic concepts – material life, the market economy and capitalism.

The broad outlines of this interpretation of capitalism, which has received the attention of numerous critics and sparked as many illuminating debates,[3] are shown in Figure 1.2.[4]

Material Life
Material life includes the *structures of everyday life*, that is 'the informal other half of economic activity, the world of self-sufficiency and barter of goods and services within a very small radius' (Braudel, 1981, vol. I, p.24). This facet is surely the largest and most significant in the existence of every socio-economic formation and retains, even in the most advanced countries, all the interactive traits of the dynamic factors mentioned above. Its disappearance would ensure the same fate for the given socio-economic formation and, as noted *supra*, can only be caused by its incorporation in another like formation or by its colonization.

Figure 1.2 Material Life, Market and Capitalism

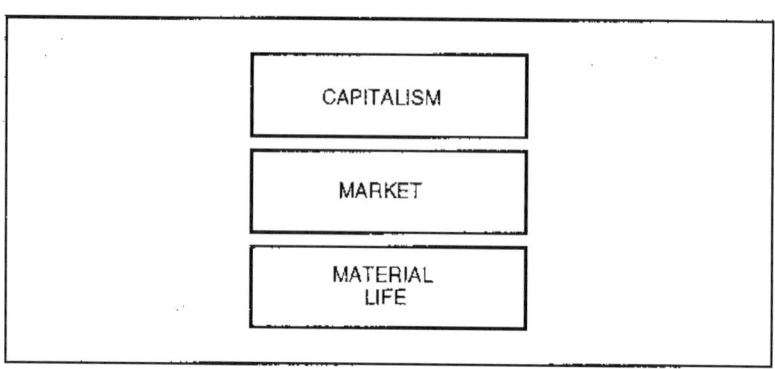

Aside from the life of the family and the community, material life subsumes such key economic functions as the gift, barter, the direct exchange of services and the natural and simple mercantile economy. Despite being the most significant sector and the basis of all extant societies, it is deemed by economists and politicians alike as a residual one. The material life share of Gross Worldwide Product is not even recorded, and it is completely ignored by capital in all investment and technology development plans. Attention is drawn to material life only when it is mentioned in relation to crime (by the police), tax evasion (by politicians), the underground economy (by business leaders) and black labour (by the trade unions). Yet the fact must be realized that it is the only sector based on self-sufficiency and polycentric development, and as such it is the indispensable cradle and permanent safety haven of civilized society.

The Market
The origin of markets in socio-economic formations stems from increasing exchanges – between villages, towns, cities – and from the forms of organization and specialization of production. Markets arise from the need to establish rules for production, trade and competition, their extent or range varying from age to age, society to society.

Along with market growth and evolution, social needs bring forth and breathe life into public services in spheres of activity proper to material existence – education, health, justice, self-defence and so on. Both the market and the state are thus stimulated to growth by the new demands of society which are either not immediately met by material existence or which take over areas and roles of material existence so as to ensure criteria of equity and efficiency. The market and the state introduce criteria of openness and behaviour codes, which they try to apply and administer in the public interest. This is true in both liberal systems, where the market is governed by profit and prices, and in socialist ones, where the market is regulated by targets and central planning.

Capitalism

The market and the state rapidly become important instruments of power by virtue of their role in establishing and administering the rules of the economic and social commonwealth. The idea of power's neutrality with respect to vested interests arises from concrete and worthy concerns, though it has never been applied in real life. Even those who have couched it in words and theory, from the liberal thinkers of the Enlightenment onwards, have used it to serve other ends. Indeed, at first they proclaimed the primacy of free competition and individual choice to undermine the political power of the Church (secularism as principle) and of the social classes of the old order (the principle of equality). Then, once the heights of the state had been scaled, they proclaimed the primacy of policy and the national interest to undermine the power of guilds and social classes. Since gaining control in the present epoch of the levers of economic power on a worldwide scale, they now assert the primacy of the economy and of globalization. Such is the evolution which capitalism has grafted onto the market and the state, prevailing in the end over both.

Capitalism's extraordinary talent for moving between economic sectors and countries has been highlighted by both Marxist analysis and by historians. As Fernand Braudel notes:

> Capitalism is essentially conjunctural, that is, it flourishes according to the dictates of changes in the economic situation. Even today one of capitalism's greatest strengths remains its ability to adapt and to change.
>
> (1981, vol. I, p.61)

For in order to lay firm foundations for its fortune and its power, capitalism successively or simultaneously depended upon local

trade, upon usury, upon long-distance trade, upon the venal administrative office, land ... and upon society itself.
(1981, vol. I, p.69)

Capitalism thus thrives in a market economy and in a liberal political system, although once it gains control of the levers of power it distorts the roles of strengthening, efficiency and openness proper to socio-economic formations. Once successful, capitalism tends to shed the integument covering it at birth and to occupy those sectors of the market and of material existence that further its own ends and to rid itself of the others. In other words, capitalism embarks upon the path to development by increasingly distancing itself from the needs of the socio-economic formation to which it had grafted itself. Warnings to this very effect had already been sounded by both bourgeois and marxist economic studies.

Gunnar Myrdal on Developed Countries

As an exponent of bourgeois economic scholarship, Myrdal has voiced strong doubts on numerous occasions as to whether economic science, or the social sciences in general, can formulate objective, and hence neutral, judgments about differing political and moral ideals.

This implicit belief in the existence of a body of scientific knowledge acquired independently of all valuation is, as I now see it, naïve empiricism.

(1971)

Contrary to orthodox economic theory, he begins with a critical examination of the central concept of gross national product (GNP) and its inadequacy to account for the dynamics of capitalist economies. His critique unfolds along two lines that are logically, though not necessarily chronologically, successive. Based mainly upon the cases of developed countries and the welfare state, he first introduces the distinction between the concepts of economic growth and development (Myrdal, 1957; and 1973, pp.182–96). Economic growth, as measured by GNP, is linked to economic factors whereas development stands for another and much broader category that includes non-economic factors, or as he puts it:

I understand development as the movement upward of the whole social system. In other words, not only production, distribution of the produce, and modes of production are involved, but also levels of living, institutions, attitudes, and policies. Among all the factors in this social system there are causal interrelations. Even in developed countries, the coefficients of the interactions among the various factors in the social system are largely unknown and, in any case, not available in precise form. For this reason alone, the possibility of working out an index of development in this sense is not within sight.

(1973, p.190)

That the numerous problems of measurement and calculation needed for the integrations mentioned by Myrdal are unresolved has proved lethal to the experience of the welfare state. Recourse to the paradigm of market imperfections brings the basis of calculation back to the capitalist market, so that the outcome contrasts with the stated objectives. This has resulted not in the humanizing of the market's operating rules but in the market's integrating and, hence, dehumanizing the governing rules of those sectors of economic, social and political life that had remained outside it. What was presented in programmes as an attempt at decommodification in important sectors of production became transformed instead into its opposite. The well known limits and insufficiencies in the application of this approach – in cost-benefit calculations or in social planning – bear eloquent testimony to it.

Gunnar Myrdal on Underdeveloped Countries

The critique's second line of inquiry derives from Myrdal's increasing contact with underdeveloped countries, for which, as he notes, 'all the critical points raised above are pertinent, some more so than others' (1973, p.194). The type of analysis Myrdal advocates here is 'an institutional approach' that includes not only the means of production, output and distribution of goods but also 'modes and levels of living and attitudes and institutions'. He concludes by raising doubts about the very 'modernization ideals that have been used as value premises' in studies of underdeveloped countries. (1968, vol. III, pp.1834–5)[5]

This line of thought falls within what has become the rich vein of the *Autocritica dell'economista* ('The Confessions of an Economist' Caffè, 1975; 1977). Yet, when it comes down to recommendations of economic policy, it is surprising how this self-flagellation of bourgeois economic thought does not spur those in the know to greater heights of theoretical advancement. Myrdal himself provides an example in his (master)piece, *Asian Drama: An Inquiry into the Poverty of Nations*, where in the appendices of the third volume he notes:

> Even if this point is conceded, it is possible to doubt whether the modernization ideals that have been used as value premises in the present study are appropriate to the purpose. In particular, it can be argued that these ideals, which gradually developed in Europe, matured to a high degree of explicitness in the era of Enlightenment, and thereafter determined the main ideological structures of the developed Western and Communist countries, are foreign to South Asia. Admittedly, the choice of value premises is, to an extent, a volitional decision, and the criteria of relevance and significance allow for arbitrariness, particularly when one is studying countries where popular valuations are as diverse and as difficult to ascertain as in South Asian countries.
>
> (pp.1834–5)

Coming at the end of his vast study, this insight led Myrdal to the heart of the crucial issue of development, that is that capitalist modernization and Western culture are extraneous to the countries of the Third World, and to draw conclusions that I would term weak and contradictory *vis-à-vis* his initial propositions:

> There were two main reasons for choosing the value premises applied in the present study. First, the modernization ideals are those actually proclaimed by the political and intellectual leaders in the regions; they are implicit not only in the plans but also in the policy discussions in all the South Asian countries. As was pointed out in Chapter 3 (Section 1), the traditional valuation cannot be used as a basis for comprehensive policy planning, and this gives the modernization ideals a strategic position. The second, and even more compelling argument for choosing these value premises was that the South Asian countries, and particularly the bigger and poorer among them, have passed the point of no return. Given the present and foreseeable rate of population growth, the choice of remaining traditional societies is no longer open. Only by a fairly vigorous application of the

modernization ideals – the internal coherence of which I have demonstrated in several contexts – can they hope to avoid not only stagnation, which might be bearable, but actual impoverishment with increasing misery of the masses.
(1968, vol. III, p.1871)

The importance of Myrdal and the Scandinavian School in the critique of neoclassical economics lies in their attempts – not without some success in the battle against market imperfections – to apply these analytical tools to economic policy. Yet loyalty to the reformist-functionalist approach (functional socialism) robs the message of its radical cultural contents which, by being trapped in the net of capitalist economics even at the best of times in the history of this approach, are jettisoned as foreign bodies in the 1980s and 1990s. What eviscerated the Scandinavian School was that it remained bound, despite Myrdal's warnings about the interrelations of the various factors involved, to an institutional model of development. Its proponents had taken the separation of policy and economics, of ethics and politics, as fact and not as ideological construct. In other words, it had assumed that the idea of progress was based on the myth of welfare and technology.[6]

William Kapp and Capitalism

The social cost approach, which Myrdal had defined as too eclectic, has proved to be a notably potent tool affecting the analysis of and intervention strategies in the market economy. Starting from motivational factors and employing an approach grounded in the noted concept of externalities and in pragmatic and often detailed analyses of external economies and external diseconomies, it has led to radical changes in our understanding of certain factors. In many cases, its effects have not been limited to policies of containing and offsetting social costs themselves but have even pointed an accusing finger at structural elements of capitalism's own *modus operandi*.

The core concept of K.W. Kapp's thought defines capitalism 'as an economy of unpaid costs', that is those which are not paid by businesses but shifted 'onto third parties or the community'. It raises serious doubts about what has always been considered the strong point of such an economy's dynamics and legitimacy – efficiency and productivity (1950, p.231).[7]

John Maynard Keynes on Capitalism

Keynes, who observed at first hand and studied the Great Depression, deliberately tackled the problems of development and anticipated many recent issues – the growing deformation of capitalism caused by its symbiosis with finance capital, the devastation of nature, the separation of the economy and the environment: 'The same rule of self-destructive financial calculation governs every walk of life. We destroy the beauty of the countryside because the unappropriated splendours of nature have no economic value. We are capable of shutting off the sun and the stars because they do not pay a dividend' (1982, vol. XXI, p.242); the impossibility of market mechanisms to ensure an equitable redistribution of income, labour and wealth: 'The most glaring defects of the economic society in which we live are the inability to provide full employment and the arbitrary and iniquitous distribution of wealth and incomes' (1946, p.372); the need to socialize investments: 'I conceive, therefore, that a somewhat comprehensive socialization of investment will prove the only means of securing an approximation to full employment' (p. 378); the need to integrate institutional reform with the new economy based on the concept of 'economic democracy', and the awareness that economic and social accumulation is a single process (Kregel, 1983, pp.28–50).

Keynes repeatedly stressed his idea of bringing the production system's factors into line with the needs of employment and of bringing all citizens into the same production system – an idea opposed to the wishful thinking, current even today, that the various sectors of the economy, the productive and the unproductive, can be managed by different criteria.[8] The illusion here is created not by the intentions, which are good, to promote the non-profit sectors of human endeavour but by the belief that there is room for their autonomous growth. The demise of 'real reformism' and of 'real socialism' is proof that no such room exists. Thus, to advocate that these sectors are to be strengthened in the age of globalization, or even to propound economic growth in countries outside the Triad, leads directly to a clash with the latter, with the institutions and the governments which represent it.

It was over these cardinal points that a split occurred between bastard Keynesianism, the school that wanted to bring Keynesian economics under the bridle of the capitalist market, and radical Keynesianism, which was ready to go beyond it. Conclusively, it can be stated that all the foregoing theories of the various bourgeois schools of economic thought have failed. The Scandinavian and the social cost schools succumbed in spite of the modest ambitions of the theoretical and policy reforms they enunciated and pursued because they followed the logic of the capitalist market and were unable to effect significant changes in that market system. The Keynesian school failed in spite of its very ambitious theoretical and policy reforms, which sought to bring about too significant a change in the workings of the capitalist market and the power structure. These approaches are thus no longer tenable today without a substantial reworking that takes into account capitalism's new *modus operandi* and the disappearance of those agents that were the social forces upon which rested the political and economic experiments of the bourgeois school of economics.

Marxist Economists on Capitalism

The contributions of Marxist scholars have also dealt with development. Their proponents realized, though not without wrenching internal conflicts and divisions which never quite healed, that the explanation for the apparent paradoxes and contradictions was to be sought in a more detailed analysis of ongoing processes and the intervening changes in capital accumulation (Sofri, 1979; Melotti, 1977). The Marxist debate is notable for the two major themes briefly expounded below.

The Theoretical Construct Designed to Elucidate the New Forms of Post-War Capitalist Accumulation – Pitting the Needs of Capitalism's Growth Against Those of Society
What emerged as new here is that the fundamental conditions which made capitalism a form of development, albeit a particular one, for society and the productive system (yet keeping it within their orbit) no longer exist. Much evidence supporting this change had already come to light during the stage of monopolistic capitalism, so that the need for a theoretical reworking of Marxist thought became clear.

Paul Baran and Paul M. Sweezy took up this challenge in the 1960s, reassessing the importance of the distinction between capitalist surplus value and society's economic surplus (Baran and Sweezy, 1966; Baran, 1973). Quite apart from the numerous discussions their theoretical postulate fuelled (Botta, 1971), it clearly anticipated the newly emerging mode of both capitalist accumulation and the interrelationship of capitalism and society that has become so topical in the current stage of triadic capitalism. The insight here was the increasing lack of the basic conditions that had made capitalism a distinct, albeit but one, form of society's development and the capitalist model of production an efficient and self-reproducing system.

If one leaves aside all considerations of distribution and realizes that under competitive conditions capitalism can make an optimum use of resources, then the value added which accrues to the capitalist expresses a society's output potential and measures the real amount of the available means (the surplus). The slowing down of these mechanisms and the tendency of the unproductive side of its character to grow, its rediscovery of parasitic roles and of rent positions which it had fought against at its beginning, and the breakdown of all links between the use value and the exchange value make capitalism a system that first smothers the very market economy that had cradled it (from competitive capitalism to monopolistic capitalism) and then turns development into its opposite through triadic capitalism (the end of development) in both the industrialized societies and the rest of the world.

Studies of Socio-Economic Formations Elucidating the Historical Interrelations of Socio-Economic Formation, Production Mode and Production Systems
These studies are driven by the need for theoretical elucidation, a need that in turn is fuelled by the weakening of the most original and strongest insights that Marxist scholarship brought to the study of the interaction of society's constituent factors – the identification of categories of productive forces and social relations – and that is rooted in the influx to Marxism of scholars and currents of thought with a bourgeois derivation. The errors Marxism incurred with economicism and subjectivism (that is the primacy of the economy, of culture and of politics) are the result of the permeation of this bourgeois interpretation into the history of Marxism.

The most pertinent reference point here is the debate initiated in Italy by Emilio Sereni in the 1970s. He posited the need to reassess, once again, such key Marxist concepts in the study of societies as socio-economic formation and production mode (Sereni, 1970, pp.29–79).[9] At the heart of Sereni's contribution, which re-evaluates the importance of the concept socio-economic formation *vis-à-vis* production mode and the growing need to keep them distinct, is his emphasis on the turning point that the rise of capitalism represents in the history of mankind. Whence the perception of a new dualism pitting capitalist modernization against the modernization of society, which Sereni cogently applies to Italy's development. Significant in this connection was the debate centering on the capitalist modernization of Italy's agriculture in the 1960s that pitted Emilio Sereni against Manlio Rossi-Doria and Rosario Romeo, the latter two being supported by the Marxist scholar Camillo Daneo and the union leader Vittorio Foa.[10] Whereas Sereni propounded the importance of a rural development based upon the peasant family, production and consumption systems appropriate to the character traits (natural, cultural and social) of a given area (Sereni, 1956; 1961),[11] Rossi-Doria and Romeo advocated the need for the capitalist modernization of agriculture via the models adopted by other countries (the United States and central-northern Europe), maintaining that it was enough to separate the 'bone' from the 'meat' so that all could reap the resulting benefits (Rossi-Doria, 1958; Romeo, 1959).[12]

The latter position was subsequently embodied in the agricultural policies of the then European Communities (EC) now the European Union (EU). The ensuing results are well known: the 'bone' was thrown away and along with it the conditions ensuring the livelihood of millions of peasant farmers who found themselves forced to emigrate or face poverty, and the 'meat' was exported to the central-northern European countries, thereby enabling the artificial re-establishment of competitive production conditions *vis-à-vis* Mediterranean products. Italian agriculture and the small-farm family soon became residual factors of development.

Whereas in all former historical epochs, and even today in those societies as yet untouched by capitalism's great transformation, the mode of production has represented the very nucleus of society, generating and fuelling all its functions, and can be taken as identical to social and economic formation (which is why Marx usually employed the two terms synonymously), capitalism introduces a time-widening gap between production mode and socio-economic formation, the result being that the success of the former dictates the extinction of the latter, the development of the former the underdevelopment of the latter.

These theories were not without reverberations in Italy's postwar policy debates. Their significance is to be sought in the fact that they made it possible to contest, though not to put an end to, the rush towards capitalist modernization by exponents of Marxism and the political left. Indeed, some of the latter were to be found among the most ardent supporters of economicism and technological determinism, having been induced to chose Shumpeter's brand of Darwinism over Keynesian humanism.

TOWARDS A THEORY OF POLYCENTRIC DEVELOPMENT

Recent Contributions

The events of the last two decades have convinced the political and institutional establishment of the need to revise the concept of development so as to make it fit differing economic and production systems. One of the efforts in this direction has included finding an alternative to GNP as an indicator of a country's socio-economic level. There is also the concept of sustainable growth, which stems from the simple yet important realization that the concept of development has no provision for environmental protection and today has even been extended to include the need to reunite the forms and functions of the community. Another step in the same direction is the UNDP's introduction in 1990 of the idea of human development, which is based on an index including life expectancy, level of education and standard of living. Yet it is my conviction that the theoretical limits of these concepts reside in the presumed universality and objectivity of the analytical criteria and standards they subsume, all derived obviously from the experience of Western countries and, hence, in contrast with the need for the polycentric approach advocated herein.

Towards a Polycentric Model of Development

My initial theoretical efforts in formulating a *polycentric model of development* date to the study in the 1970s of the features that evolved in the various European societies during the course of industrialization. The reasons behind their diversity, which has given rise to various *development models* (for example the Scandinavian, the South European, the German, the French), were traced to the variously interlocking strands represented by *forms of industrialization*, *political-institutional structures*, the *history of social classes* and *national cultures*. Useful in the comparative analysis of socio-economic systems,

The Dynamics of Socio-Economic Formations 27

this early theoretical groundwork has recently been developed into a framework for the analysis of individual societies by appropriately linking the basic analytical grounding to the institutional one by identifying policies and agents.

A polycentric development system implies the realization that the models of industrialization and economic growth introduced into certain European countries under certain historical conditions (for example colonialism, imperialism) cannot be retained. The issue thus becomes how to find a way out of the vicious circle of growth without development rooted in a Eurocentric model and embark upon a virtuous circle of *co-development*.

From Cooperation to Co-development

Polycentrism's *co-development* is not to be confused with Eurocentrism's *cooperation*. Eurocentrism introduces forms of cooperation between regions or states without altering the *status quo* relations between the partners involved, thereby retaining dependency and barring any new forms of global economic dynamics from reaching out towards new forms of productive specialization. Through trade relations between regions and meso-regions, co-development tends to increase overall product volume and achievable social benefit while enabling various forms of specialization, which match differing forms of social organization, freely to develop.

> Co-development means that the social groups, cities and countries which are the members of an integrated region, or one on the way to integration, share common development objectives in the general interest of the region's population and adopt rules, institutions, mechanisms and resources needed to achieve the objectives.[13]
>
> (Petrella and Saussay, 1993, p.39)

Achieving co-development requires the concatenation of the factors necessary to the life of a society in which the criteria of equity and efficiency are not just felicitously interwoven but are the scaffolding of polycentric development.

The First Diamond of Polycentric Development
The concept of the *First Diamond* as rendered graphically in Figure 1.3 it places at its centre the need to ground production

Figure 1.3 The First Diamond of Polycentric Development

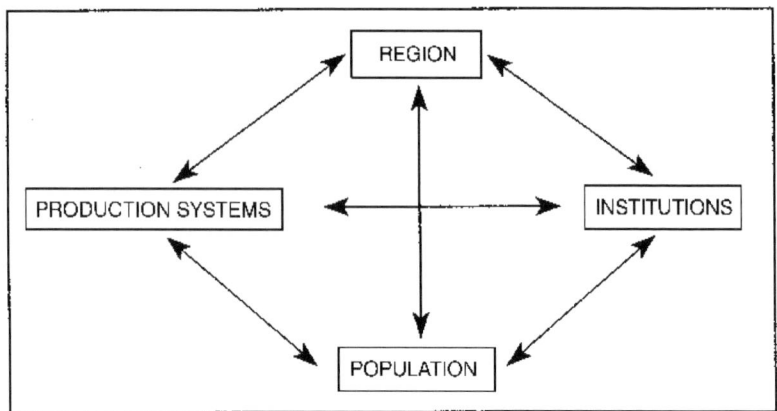

systems in a given region and in the populations inhabiting it. The diamond[14] form symbolises the indivisible unity of the four factors presented. Thus, unlike current theories that confine themselves to introducing environmental considerations or externalities into economic growth, *polycentric co-development* brings back to the fore the interaction of these four factors and their indispensable unity. It is widely known that the central feature of triadic globalization is the separation of production systems from a given region, from populations and from institutions – a separation held to be one of the essential pre-requisites for efficiency. The definition of *polycentric development* as intended here is the exact opposite in that it retrieves, on the structural and not the terminological plane, the unity of forms and contents.

The weight of the factors within the diamond can vary as the relative weight of one or more of them increases. Yet the absence of one from the model, or its pronounced weakening, will trigger a disconnecting that voids the possibilities of achieving the desired goal – the very conditions of a society's life.

The Second Diamond of Polycentric Development:
Co-determination as a New Form of Government
New forms of development call for new forms of government at greater levels of participation than those with Eurocentric cooperation. This is why *co-development* has to be matched by *co-determination*

The Dynamics of Socio-Economic Formations

at the level of regional units and among the various regions throughout the world.

Co-determination means that the system works on the basis of complex and diversified forms of popular participation in the decision-making process of planning development priorities, allocating material and intangible resources and assessing the results of the actions and policies undertaken.
(Petrella and Saussay, 1993, p.39)

The public-sector representatives are not just the local communities involved or government agencies. It is essentially a matter of bringing together training, public education and research institutions, and all the authorities responsible for the management and development of these sectors. Mobilizing the private sector, such as businesses and their affiliates, economic development organizations, local associations, is one of the requisite conditions for the project's success.

The strategy being put forth here goes beyond the perception these various agents have of the issues involved. It is designed to point these agents towards a community concept of polycentric development orientated around concrete projects of partnership, cooperation and exchange. The meso-regional dimension is to act as an institutional framework for the safeguarding and evolution of the various forms of existing productive systems.

The guiding concept is that only through an economic and social planning consonant with the principles illustrated in the *First Diamond of Polycentric Development* is it possible to achieve a solid basis for a projected sustainable development of environmental, human and productive resources.

The institutional features of co-development are shown in the *Second Diamond of Polycentric Development* (figure 1.4). The institutional, that is government, approach opted for here is linked to the most advanced concepts of territorial planning, whose main features are the following:

i) It is implemented from below and across the board with respect to the areas and sectors involved.
ii) Its government capability is interwoven with the complexity of the issues and the pluralism of the agents.
iii) It works across the board of sectors but, within the framework of its specific targets, is focused on the given territory.

Figure 1.4 The Second Diamond of Polycentric Development

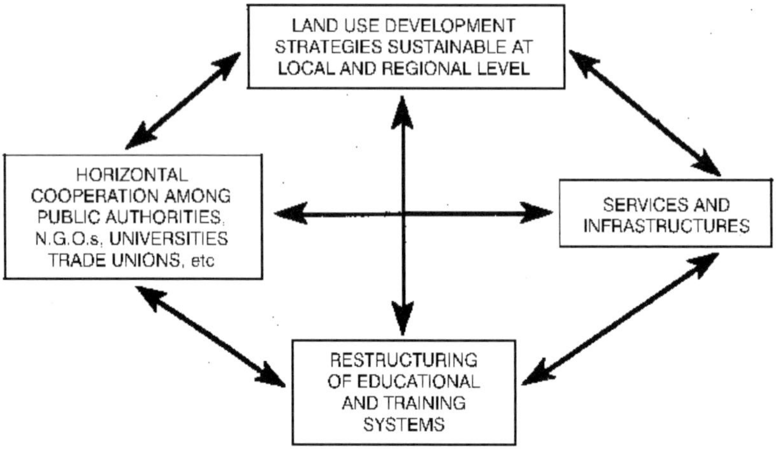

```
                    LAND USE DEVELOPMENT
                    STRATEGIES SUSTAINABLE AT
                    LOCAL AND REGIONAL LEVEL
                              ↑
   HORIZONTAL                 |
   COOPERATION AMONG          |                SERVICES AND
   PUBLIC AUTHORITIES,    ←———+———→            INFRASTRUCTURES
   N.G.O.s, UNIVERSITIES      |
   TRADE UNIONS, etc          |
                              ↓
                        RESTRUCTURING
                        OF EDUCATIONAL
                        AND TRAINING
                        SYSTEMS
```

The meso-regional area is an appropriate level for consideration and intervention for several reasons.

- It enables the public and private sectors to mobilize for development into a partnership endeavour while making possible broader-based synergies to match the new demands for the use of strategic technologies in the safeguarding and development of local production systems.
- It is conducive to the construction of specific, sustainable-development projects by combining the economic, social, cultural and environmental dimensions.
- It can act as a support to local planning conceived within a participatory framework.
- It combines both exogenous and endogenous dimensions of development in a co-developmental project.

Achieving the two diamonds of co-development requires radical changes to the dominant economic paradigm, which is based on the principles and priorities of the capitalist market. The following illustrates a summary view (figure 1.5).

Figure 1.5 A New Analytical Model of Development and Co-Development

"Market" Economy Model	Development and Co-development Model

– Independent variables
   production systems
   • capital
   • technologies
– Dependent variables
   needs
   • employment
   • welfare system
   • migrations
   • natural resources
	– Independent variables
	   needs
	   • employment
	   • welfare system
	   • migrations
	   • natural resources
	– Dependent variables
	   production systems
	   • capital
	   • technologies

The needs and levels of the rich & technologically advanced nations define the world "market". Its "triadic" nature derives from the yard-stick measuring the efficiency of results in the competition among the EU, Japan and the USA. This is a Eurocentric model relying on the growth of high-tech industries.	The needs and levels of the meso-regions define the "market"; technology development & innovation are guided by meeting them. Its polycentric nature derives from the yard-sticks measuring the efficiency of results in cooperation and co-development between diversified areas and meso-regions. Polycentrism concerns both means (the forms of productive organisation & participation in co-development) & objectives (development models, of which in Europe there are at least four: the Baltic, Mediterranean, Central Europe & EU).

NOTES

1. The term genocide to express the effects of the modernization process is here taken from Pier Paolo Pasolini: Cf. his 'L'articolo delle lucciole', in Pasolini (1973) 1975, p.163.
2. For an informative summary of Tolstoi's contribution to the critique of Western capitalist modernization see Rolland (1913) 1921.
3. Let one example suffice for all: 'The Fernand Braudel Worskshop' held at Châteauvallon on 18–20 October 1985; the proceedings are published in the volume *Fernand Braudel (1986)*.
4. See *Braudel (1977)* for a brief, highly informative introduction to his work.
5. For a more detailed study of Myrdal's approach and propositions, see the appendices in vol. 3
6. Gunnar Myrdal often alluded to his intellectual kinship with the broad outlines of bourgeois and Enlightenment thought. About his brief encounter with Marxism, he wrote: 'all my roots are embedded deep in the soil of Enlightenment philosophy yet the first French and English

socialists held a much more powerful sway over me. Unlike Marx, the "utopian" socialists were planners ... I should perhaps add that my attachment to the Enlightenment's fundamental ideals and values – peace, liberty, equality and brotherhood – have never waivered,' in the Foreword to the 1972 Swedish edition of his *The Political Element in the Development of Economic Theory*.

7. For a detailed review of this topic see Caffè (1981) p.39–65.
8. This illusion also embodies generous attempts to promote the third sector or volunteer work (Archibugi, 1993), and the many proposed solutions to the problem of unemployment based on socially useful work (Lunghini, 1995).
9. The subsequent debate included, among others, Valentino Gerratana, Maurice Godelier, Philippe Herzog and Georges Labica. For a brief review, see Sofri (1979).
10. For their respective positions, see the *Atti del convegno economico* dell'Istituto Gramsci, *Tendenze del capitalismo italiano*, vol. 1, Editori Riuniti, Roma (1962), e *Daneo (1964)*.
11. A more recent work inspired by Sereni's approach is Gomez y Paloma (1995).
12. For a more detailed view of this debate, see Sereni (1959) reissued in Sereni (1966).
13. The concept of co-development has been elaborated and politically emphasized by the European Economic and Social Committee. See Amato (1993).
14. The form of the diamond to represent interdependences has already been employed to good effect in a work by Michael Porter on the *Competitive Advantages of Nations* (1990). Mine is an alternative use (or better, opposite) to Porter's, although it employs the same graphic means.

2 Internationalization and Capitalism: from Dualism to Marginalization

THE STAGES OF INTERNATIONALIZATION

The Historical Forms of Industrialization

The concept of *internationalization* is usually employed to convey a positive connotation of its meaning – the nature of the economic, political and cultural relations that a community or country establish with others. Depending on the forms these relations take, internationalization can be mercantile or trade (exchange of goods), productive (foreign investments), financial (capital movements), technological (technology transfers), cultural (cultural relations) and movements of people (migrations).

The theoretical framework of internationalization can thus be defined as the exchange between two or more communities that enhances areas of their potential complementariness, thereby resulting in an advantage for each and an increase of the overall social product. Yet comparing the concept's theoretical basis to real processes reveals important deviations. As shown in Figure 2.1, applying the exchange theory to two countries or areas would lead in the long run to reciprocal advantages along the bisecting line, which is obviously the optimization indicator of parity exchange. Each stage of the internationalization process would thus be matched by an equal partition of advantages between North and South, or between two countries. Integrating the theoretical framework with the forms the internationalization process has taken on throughout various historical ages highlights a deviation from the bisector that is proportional to the extent of the inequality of the real exchange.

Noteworthy among the phenomena of internationalization in Europe are *mercantilism* from the 15th to the 17th centuries and the *slave trade* from the 16th to the 19th centuries, the latter placing the movement of people on the level of goods. Both evince a

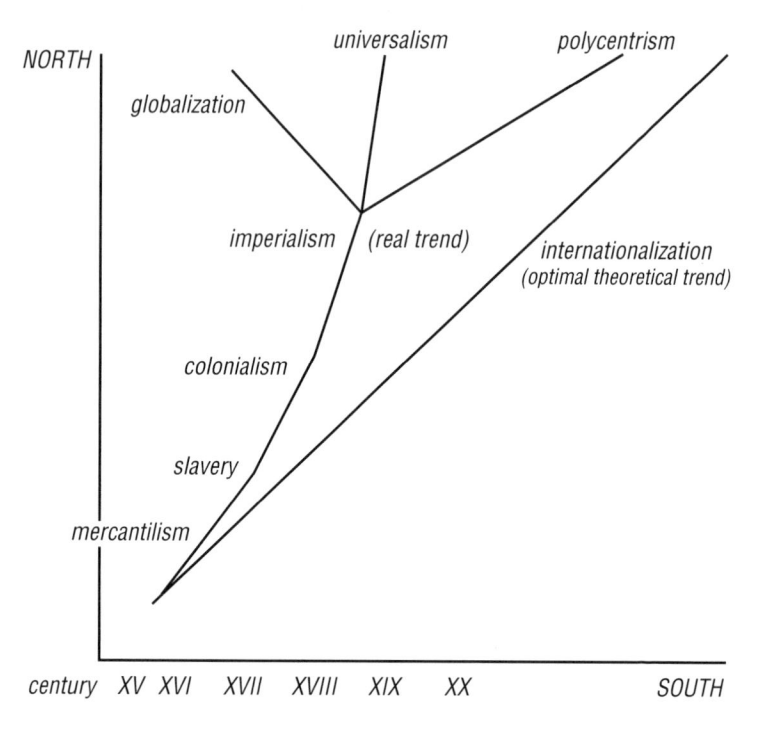

Figure 2.1 The Stages of Internationalization

```
NORTH |         universalism      polycentrism
      |  globalization
      |
      |       imperialism  (real trend)   internationalization
      |                                   (optimal theoretical trend)
      |
      |    colonialism
      |
      |   slavery
      |  mercantilism
      |_____
        century XV XVI XVII XVIII XIX XX              SOUTH
```

prevalently predatory character, so that in the diagram they generate the same asymmetry in terms of benefit distribution. *Colonialism* during the 18th century is the just as predatory, if not more so, continuation of both these forms of internationalization in the new context of the Western empires and of the possibilities afforded by the then new transport and military technologies.

Imperialism of the 19th century represents the adaptation of these relations and functions to the new context of monopoly capitalism and nation-states, its nature becoming increasingly more predatory by the changes introduced by the so-called industrial revolution into the structure and range of the markets and production systems. To take a more detailed look at the features of the current stage of capitalist development – globalization – and its relation to internationalization, it is a good idea to recall the forms it has taken on in the post-war years: the *dualism* of the *national monopoly capitalist* phase led to the *marginalization* of the current *trans-national triadic capitalism*.

THE ORIGINS OF DUALISM

The Issue of Inequality

Inequality in capitalism's development has caught the attention of many scholars in the course of its history. Their focus has been above all on the distributive features rather than on the forms taken by the production system. Yet Marxian economists have continued to support the link between inequality phenomena and the process of capital accumulation, although their thesis was couched in terms too obvious to satisfy the demands of academia for sophisticated and complicated analyses.

The Two Economies: the Orthodox and the Keynesian

Even economists belonging to bourgeois schools of thought have not failed to notice, and to raise, the issue. Keynes himself, in the midst of the Great Depression, worked out a radical critique of the neoclassical paradigm of general equilibrium, thereby giving rise to two types of economics, the classical or orthodox and the Keynesian. 'The Keynesian move from one to two economic theories was crucial: the ice of mono-economics had been broken' (Hirshman, 1981, p.6).

Gunnar Myrdal and the Vicious Circle of Poverty

Myrdal's contribution here rests upon his oft-repeated conviction that understanding the causes of inequality in the world economy requires first of all jettisoning the distinction between economic and non-economic factors. This distinction, which he considered illogical and misleading, should be replaced by that between significant and insignificant or even more significant and less significant factors. The real point, as Myrdal himself stressed, was that:

> A theory of under-development and stagnation which works only with 'economic variables' is for logical reasons doomed to be unrealistic and thus irrelevant.[1]
>
> (1957, p.162)

Recalling the work of other scholars (C.E.A. Winslow, R. Nurkse), Myrdal focused on the vicious circle of poverty, by which he meant the relations between two or more factors that reciprocally affect one another so as to worsen the position of countries (or social groups) which are already disadvantaged. While economists have demonstrated the cumulative effect of a development process (cumulative circular causality), they have proved far more reserved when it came to noting that the opposite can also be true. Unlike the widely held theory of *stable equilibrium*, Myrdal pointed out that the changes which take place in an economic system generate forces that push the system towards changes in the same direction – towards a process that all too soon becomes cumulative and irreversible. The idea that a spontaneous shifting towards an automatic re-equilibrium via forces which tend to move in the opposite direction is thus, according to Myrdal, unfounded.

The Historical School's Critique of Walter Rostow's Monoeconomics

It is worth recalling at this juncture the contribution of the historical school of economics. Along with Alexander Gerschenkron, it distanced itself from Rostow's theory of stages by showing how the problems of *catching up* made it impossible for countries at differing levels of development to repeat the textbook model of English industrialization (Hirshman, 1981, p.11). It is a known fact that their studies, though stemming from various roots, were rescued from oblivion by official economic science which, by setting them apart as particular case of a unique and unchanging general orientation, overturned the results they had achieved. Studies of the dynamics of economic systems resumed after World War II but the focus was now more on structural problems and long-term fluctuations, although the approach was a fundamentally ahistorical one.

A glance at Europe's economic history shows that there were three main waves of industrialization – the first in England (the classical model), the second in the Netherlands and Belgium, the third in Germany and certain regions of France – with a fourth in the countries of late industrialization like those in Scandinavia and southern Europe. These waves have been seen as a spreading of the classical model to new countries and regions, the differences being viewed more as a matter of timing and direction rather than form.[2] This has resulted in the literature taking on a prevalently economistic-orientated and unilinear character which has prevented the development of policies appropriate to the issues at hand. Particularly noteworthy in the post-war years have been the theoretical efforts directed at combining the analysis of the forms of industrialization with that of institutional and policy changes. Two stages can be distinguished, though not in chronological order. The first is marked by the theories of dualism that turn on the relationships between the dynamics of industrial systems and such socioeconomic variables as wages, trade unions, demand, government policies. The second concerns the concept of development models and seeks to explain the overall dynamics of the economic and social system by focusing on the interrelations of production systems, forms of consumption and institutional factors.

THE PROCESS OF ACCUMULATION AND DUALISM

The Genesis of Dualism Theories

New theories of dualism in the postwar years found fertile ground for reflection and experiment in Italy and, generally, in southern Europe. Their genesis in these countries can be traced to the study of the origins of capitalist industrialization processes and the rise of national markets featuring:

a) Original imbalance in the industrial facilities between North and South.
b) Original imbalance in agriculture between North and South.
c) Lack of complimentariness between the economies of North and South.
d) Disparities in the level of the infrastructures needed for industrial development in both areas.

Italy's second wave of industrialization in the boom years between the 1950s and 1970s generated a number of studies aimed at assessing its impact on dualism.

Lewis's Model

W.A. Lewis (1954) was the first to propound a model dealing with the growth process of a dual economy featuring a modern sector and a traditional one, the latter being marked by marginal productivity, backward techniques, subsistence wages and a high degree of under-employment. Yet the traditional sector absorbs the surplus labour from agriculture and the unemployed, who find in it a source of income, albeit very low. All these factors make possible a growth of profits and increased production investments.

The modern sector is characterized by a high level of technology and output but wages pegged to the level of marginal production (a bit above those of the marginal sector). The model shows that employment can rise because of the labour surplus in the traditional sector and that this will result in higher profits and investments. Overcoming this dualism is possible through a mechanism inherent in the model itself, which ensures growth in both sectors. By contrast, the model grinds to a halt as the shrinking of the labour supply generates a set of obstacles to growth concerning the interrelations of wages-prices-profits (wage increases, rise in demand for consumer goods, decreased profits) and investment trends (dwindling investments, increased capital intensity, greater dependency on foreign sources for development).

Klinderberger Model

The effects of export-led growth on the development of Italy's economy have been analyzed by C. Klinderberger (1967). The virtuous circle of increases in imports, in national income and in industrial investments will continue so long as agriculture and unemployement allow it to do so. In this stage industry will be able to increase output and expand exports. However, once the effects Lewis describes begin to make themselves felt, the result is a drop in investments, a lessening of international competition and a deficit in the balance of payments.

Lutz's Model

Vera Lutz (1958) studied the application of these models to dualism. She focused her attention exclusively on the role of trade unions in determining a situation in which the normal growth mechanism comes to standstill because of the high wages in the modern sector, which prevent further growth there and maintain the system's dual structure.

Graziani's Model

A number of Italian scholars have dealt with the effects of internationalization and the industrial structure on dualism. Augusto Graziani (1972) analyzed the influence exerted by the export-led growth model on Italian society at three levels, which generate three forms of dualism – demand, output and consumption.

Demand dualism regards *foreign* and *domestic demand*. The former spurs the production of goods with high-technology input and stimulates the dynamic sectors of the economy towards export. With output levels comparable to those of the more industrialized nations and large-scale, capital-intensive industries, these sectors are able to attract investments, pay higher wages for productivity increases and generate an imitative process of consumption.

Domestic demand is largely met by the backward sector, which is marked by the production of staple commodities, the prevalence of small-scale industry characterized by outdated technology, low productivity and a high employment rate of the labour force. The low wages here generate a different form and level of consumption with respect to the primary sector. This brings about a new form of dualism resulting from the distortion of private consumption. As Graziani noted in the debates that came in the wake of his analysis, factors such as the trade unions and the level of conflict alter this landscape.

Other Contributions: Dualism and Production Structure

While Graziani was bringing his analytical skills to bear on the relations between production structures and demand, other scholars were concentrating on the production structure as seen from the interrelations of its various parts (Paci, 1975). The dual model generally hinges on a division between the modern sector (large-scale industry) and the backward one (small-scale industry), the component businesses of the latter being conceived as uniform.

To explain the survival of small-scale businesses in the process of capitalist modernization, various types of functional relations that arise between large- and small-scale industry, between the modern and backward sectors, are analyzed. Three types of small industry were singled out on the basis of their functional structure within the industrial system:

40 On Globalization

- *buffer*, which runs counter to the economic cycle and acts mainly as a labour pool for large-scale industry,
- *lung*, which acts as a production decentralizer in periods of economic boom for large-scale industry, and
- *cog*, which acts as a support to large-scale industry in times of inevitable transitional or economic changes in production resulting from internal restructuring.

What emerges as the key to survival in all three of these cases is the greater flexibility of the small-scale enterprise – as to wages, layoff capability, work shifts and so on. It also turns out that the small business, though far from being an autonomous production system, is closely linked to the system of mass production. A number of new factors concerning the existence and roles of the small-scale industries have also been pointed out – policy options and strategies, (Salvati, 1974) technological innovation, (Blair, 1972) and management strategies (Vianello, 1975).

Fuà's Analysis of Lagged Development

The contribution of the Italian economist Giorgio Fuà fits in with the dual-economy theories despite the new insights and greater attention his work displays *vis-à-vis* economic policies devoted to a different kind of development (1981). His study of the 'problems of lagged development in Europe', which starts from the dual-economy factors separating Greece, Ireland, Italy, Portugal, Spain and Turkey from the countries of earlier industrialization (EDCs), indicates that the former evince *today* certain features similar to the past experience of the EDCs[3] and markedly different ones not only from the present but also from the past experience of the EDCs.[4]

The weak competitive position in the world market of these six countries is laid to three mechanisms:

i) the technology gap
ii) the demonstration effect, and
iii) the organizational and entrepreneurial capacity available at firm level (the 'E-O Factor').

Fuà used this groundwork to build up a different conception of the development process for the countries of lagged development and, with an approach similar to Myrdal's, highlighted the irreversibility of historical development. He also stresses the gradual nature of industrial development, of the spread of new technologies and of innovations in the countries of early industrialization. The situation is entirely different in the countries of lagged development. These latter are lacking both an industrial vocation and industries capable of exploiting new technology, and their output development is too restricted to absorb the available labour supply. Sectors evincing unemployment and a black labour market enable the survival of low-technology businesses with matching low output and incomes. All this results in a dual structure for production, incomes and the labour market. This kind of development generates conflicts that are escalated by the demonstration effect of European consumer models made popular by the mass media, advertising campaigns and tourism. The upshot is that aspirations grow at a faster pace than the capability to organize and produce.

Fuà concludes his study by noting that:

> There is a general reason for expecting that the structural evolution of the lagging economies will not be an exact replica of the evolution of the economies which have preceded them. Even if the endogenous forces of development were equal in both cases (a far-fetched hypothesis, indeed), the milieu with which these forces interact has been modified, if only because of the development which has taken place meanwhile in the advanced countries.
> (1978, p.133)

New development conditions call for new strategies and economic policies.

> An appropriate development policy for lagging economies cannot be modelled either on the one valid for the advanced economies or even for those of yesterday, but calls for *ad hoc* reflection. Such reflection has so far been lacking.
> (Ibid.)

This lack of thought about the peculiarities obtaining to the development of the countries that came late to industrialization is, Fuà maintains, the main reason for the many errors made in delineating their economic policies. Repeating the modernization model of the advanced nations means a rush to sprawling urbanization with the concomitant internal migration, destruction of agriculture and waste of resources. The economic and industrial policies implemented in the industrialized countries are uncritically reproduced, thereby giving priority to highly capital-intensive production yet without dealing beforehand with the issue of labour supply. Industrial policy promotes big business to the detriment of small business despite the fact that the latter would be capable of creating jobs while its greater and more balanced geographical range would better equip it to counter the adverse effects of a rapid concentration of people. These approaches to economic policy prevent a gradual modernization of the overall production system in countries that have come late to industrialization. Nor is that all. They also promote the spread of backward forms of exploitation and organization like the black economy and so forth. Fuà believes in the end that economic policy cannot eliminate income and productivity differences but that it can contribute to attenuating their more undesirable effects.

INDUSTRIALIZATION AND DEVELOPMENT MODELS

These represent differing strands of study that, at least in part, stem from opposite assumptions. The dual-economy approach started from an analysis of the structure and needs of industrial systems in an effort to define their effects on the social structure and to identify appropriate policies to remedy them. Development models start instead by assaying the needs and features (natural and human) of socio-economic formations to arrive at an evaluation and a choice of production systems.

The Myth of Economic Growth: The Alternatives of Manuela Silva

The worldwide economic recession of the 1970s helped, according to the Portuguese economist Manuela Silva, to debunk the myth of economic growth by bringing to the fore critiques of economic development, of its complex nature and of the various paths it can take. The Mediterranean countries evince a number of common features with respect both to the forms development takes – *la croissance appauvrissante* – and to the specific conditions which make it possible to move to a different style of development.

The concept of *croissance appauvrissante* denotes a development marked by a high rate of economic growth but accompanied by a significant impoverishment of the society in which it occurs. Its causes include

> The flight of human resources (labour export), deepening inequalities, strengthened foreign dependency, vulnerability to emerging crises, the transfer of values underestimating labour, the spread of numerous dysfunctions (slums, unemployment, urban congestion, pollution, desertification of rural areas, etc.).
>
> (Silva, 1983)

As an alternative to this kind of development, Silva propounds that the specific features of the Mediterranean countries be reassessed on the basis of their common cultural and historical traditions and on the many similarities of their economic and social structures. She singles out among these traits the marked openness of the economy of these countries: their rich yet poorly exploited agricultural resources; their qualified yet under utilized work force; a consumer model that wastes resources because of too individualistic an administration; a demographic profile skewed towards the young; and values of popular culture inspired by a real concept of time that promotes social contact, solidarity and life's aesthetic features. These traits are often perceived in a negative light, as though too restrictive, with respect to development. Silva points out instead that they should be viewed in a positive way *vis-à-vis* a development strategy that can meet, better than the current one, the needs of these countries. She goes on to espouse a policy shaped by the needs which, in her view, can give rise to a new style of development, one more consonant with these societies.

Silva holds that a new style of development should take into account the concrete obstacles posed by the strong reliance of Mediterranean countries on other ones. The primary objective ought to be freeing the Mediterranean countries from these fetters and strengthening their ability to opt for alternatives that better meet the needs of the people. She then proceeds to enumerate the most important of these goals.

1. A balanced relation between demands and resources, which can only come about by according priority to essential needs and the broadest use possible of national resources.
2. A more balanced distribution of labour and creation of new jobs.
3. An agricultural development designed to better the quality of consumption, of output and of diet through environmental protection

and a better use of the necessary technological resources.
4. An industrial development that safeguards the environment and moves to a better use of local resources and a decreasing reliance on other countries.
5. A local decision-making process that involves the people directly affected.
6. Enhancing the content of job tasks as to both individual and social values.

Silva's change in values between the modern and traditional sectors is to be accompanied by a change in the existing relations between the central and the local powers that be. The political institutions must be made responsive to the new style of development. It is not hard to see that Silva clearly anticipated the uncertain and contradictory theories which 20 years later were repropounded under the revised heading of human development or sustainable development.[5]

Many of the topics raised by Silva recall the themes advocated by Fuà in his study of the late-developed western European countries. The major difference between the two lies in the final goals pursued. Fuà stresses the need to accept the existing pluralism in the organization of these countries' production systems – even for a lengthy period – as the final objective is the modernization of the overall economic and social system along the lines laid down by the economy's advanced capitalist sector. Silva sees the issue instead as revitalizing the values and resources found today in the traditional sector to create a radically different society from the existing one. Both the old centre (modern sector) and the old periphery (traditional sector) must undergo a change of roles and relative importance as each is part of the re-organization of the economic and social relations.

THE MEDITERRANEAN AND EUROPEAN INTEGRATION

Giulio Querini

The enlargement of the then European Communities (EC) to include Greece, Portugal and Spain in the Mediterranean area is the departure point for Giulio Querini's analysis of the developing relations between the EC's North and South within the planned European integration (1982). He asserts that by ignoring the marked differences between *Mitteleuropa* and Mediterranean Europe, EC policies aggravated rather than improved this situation, delaying development of the countries in both areas.

Querini's study addresses the quality of the factors that stimulated economic growth over a 30-year period. The growth of international demand was the engine driving the economy but its weight was behind the production of luxury goods. The demand itself came from the marked differences in income and property ownership, whereas the investment strategies were informed more by the desire to cut the cost of wages and curb the power of the trade unions than by bolstering the evolution of the production system in the various countries. According to Querini, the main reason in the last few decades for transferring part of the industrial output of the wealthy advanced countries to those in southern Europe lies in these considerations. This was a development that benefited the latter countries only to a very limited extent as they were caught between the investment policies of the rich countries and competition from Third World countries in manufacturing activities that held out for them good development potential.

Like Silva, Querini stresses the disproportion in extensive social strata between forms of consumption and needs. That the branches of activity which eluded the recession are those meeting the demand of the wealthy for luxury goods is a dramatic counterpoint to the failure to meet essential needs, public and private, throughout the countries of southern Europe. This contrast is not just the subject of rather obvious ethical and political considerations but has a high-profile economic importance for future development. The lack of jobs, of schools, of decent housing and health services, especially in the EC's southern areas, generates a deterioration of the social networks, throws up hurdles to sector changes and leads to social conflicts. The productive branches of these countries are thus largely limited by diseconomies resulting from the lack of social services.

Querini's analysis leads him to espouse a greater complementariness in development between the EC's northern and southern countries. He holds that exploiting a greater freedom in economic policy with respect to the current organization of the world's trade system should make it possible to introduce a development model that breaks with traditional EC thinking on growth and that promotes the quality aspects of development, which should focus on how better to meet social needs.

FROM DUALISM TO MARGINALIZATION

Dependence And Exclusion

The very brief overview *supra* of the most recent studies of comparative development in the EU's northern and Mediterranean countries indicates that the disparities denote a relationship of dependence under dual-economy conditions between the backward and modern sectors – a link that is also functional. Dualism is thus the form dependence takes on during that process of industrialization marked by 'monopolistic national capitalism'. It is a dependence that also explains why in this stage it is possible to reach a social compromise by providing for the transfer of incomes and employment (by the public sector) from rich to poor regions (between North and South in Italy and with regional development policies in the EU).

The concept of marginalization is the harbinger of a new phenomenon that permeates all aspects of economic and social life. Marginalization differs from dualism in that the latter is to be viewed as a new form of dependence on capitalist development and the former an expression of *exclusion* and *discarding* by the triadic centre. Paradoxically, this delinking from the capitalist countries, which had been foreseen by theories of Marxist and Third-World scholars (Amin, 1965), is being implemented today through globalization as a delinking of triadic capitalism's three poles from the rest of the world.

Economic marginalization, and its ensuing political destabilization, constitute the globalization of the economy and technology that are consonant with the triadic capitalism centred in the United States, Japan and the European Union, that is they constitute the new form of the internationalization process. Since the 1970s, the globalization of the economy and technology has exhibited in many guises the effects on society of economic marginalization and political destabilization. The most significant of these phenomena are the dismantling of the welfare state in Western Europe, the 'great transformation' of the centrally planned socialist economies into capitalist market ones, and the demoralization of the Third World's efforts to introduce development models based on the principles of self-sufficiency and social justice. The end of that functional dependence *qua* link that existed under dualism also leads to the end of the matching national and EU social policies of regional

Internationalization and Capitalism 47

Figure 2.2 Worldwide Economic Disparities

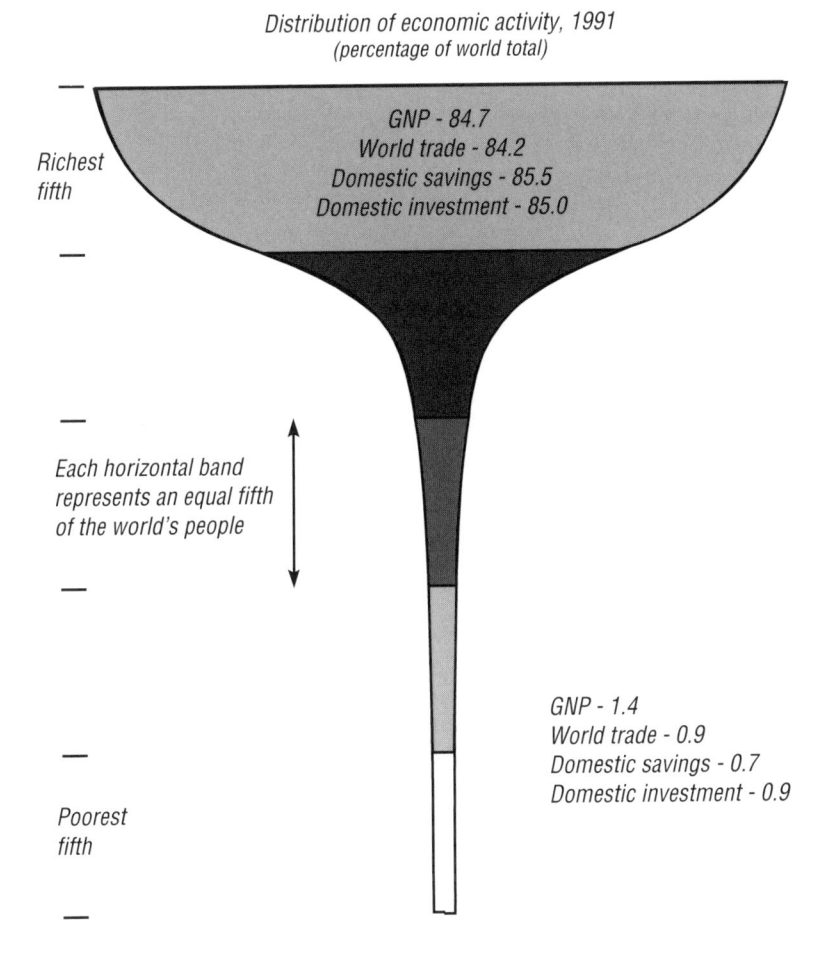

Distribution of economic activity, 1991
(percentage of world total)

Richest fifth

GNP - 84.7
World trade - 84.2
Domestic savings - 85.5
Domestic investment - 85.0

Each horizontal band represents an equal fifth of the world's people

GNP - 1.4
World trade - 0.9
Domestic savings - 0.7
Domestic investment - 0.9

Poorest fifth

Source: UNDP 1994, 'Human Development Report' (Oxford University Press, Oxford) p.63.

development. Once that functional (even dependent) link to the centres of production is broken, the EU's social and regional policies lose their legitimacy.

Political Destabilization And Worldwide Apartheid

The most troubling and dangerous aspect of economic marginalization is the generating of social reactions which turn nationalistic and xenophobic in manifest attempts both to escape it and to control these flashpoints through *political destabilization*. The result is that:

> The new world order taking shape in the world today is not the one imagined by obsolete statesmen of the Cold War era – that of nation-states weighing in on a new global balance of power. Quite the contrary. Rather, a high-tech archipelago of affluent, hyper-developed city-regions is evolving amid a sea of impoverished humanity. Transnational business firms, in their ceaseless pursuit of new customers, are creating these networks, which bypass the traditional nation-state framework. By placing science and technology solely in the service of the market objectives of these companies, nation-state governments are not only hastening their own demise; they are also accomplices in a global development strategy that excludes most of the world's population.
>
> (Petrella, 1993, p.5)

Explaining the cause for this ongoing change – this irresistible tendency to create a 'worldwide *apartheid*' (figure 2.2) – cannot but start with a description of the phenomenon of globalization, its depth, its taking root in the production and distribution system and its power.

NOTES

1. For a more recent and radical treatment of these issues, see Orati (1996).
2. There have been many attempts to provide an overall synthesis of the dynamics of industrialization's processes: Paul Rosenstein-Rodan's 'big push', Walter Rostow's 'take off', Alexander Gerschenkron's 'great spurt', Harvey Leibenstein's 'minimal critical effort', Albert O. Hirshman's 'backward and forward linkages'.

3. Fuà (1981) pp.11–12: '(a) low GDP per capita and low average productivity of labour; (b) low stock of capital per head; (c) high share of agriculture and low share both of industry and of services in total employment and total production; (d) low share of manufacturing and correspondingly high share of construction in industrial employment and production; (e) low share of fabricated metal products in manufacturing employment and production; (f) high share of self-employment in total employment; (g) high proportion of small-sized firms; (h) strong productivity differentials between agriculture, industry, services (highest); (i) high share of private (and total) consumption in GDP; (j) high share of food in total consumption; (k) strong movement of population from rural areas to towns, and especially large towns; (l) high inequality in personal income distribution and in regional income distribution, though the statistical basis for comparisons is quite weak'.
4. Fuà (1981) pp.13–14: 'First, the Six show very strong productivity differentials not only between industries and between regions (which is not without precedents in EDCs), but also between firms inside any given industry and region ("dualism"). Second, the Six have a poor performance in finding regular employment for their potential labour supply, in the sense that all these countries' participation rates – at least as reported in official statistics – are either very low, or falling very rapidly, or in most cases both ("employment slack")... Third, the Six suffer from above-the-average proneness to price instability and to government deficit, and from a special fragility of their balance of payments'.
5. For a recent reworking of these issues, see *Perna, 1995*.

3 The World Economy and Capitalism: The Globalization of the Economy and Technology

> In a society such as ours, which long ago abandoned social purpose to the automatic mechanism of the market, and attributed to things a supremacy over people ('things are in the saddle and ride mankind', wrote Emerson), technology has readily assumed its appearance as the subject of the history.
>
> Noble, 1986, p.IX

THEORETICAL TOOLS AND REAL PROCESSES

Attempts to describe and analyze such pronounced and complex changes like the ones which have occurred in the last 20 years, to account for the similarities and differences of the various ramifications of the phenomenon analyzed and, often, of the complex weave linking them, have been made by resorting to concepts and definitions that can gradually help us to determine the extent of our understanding and the insight achieved.

As always happens when the thought processes and ideas are no less tumultuous than the phenomena being described, certain concepts like internationalization and globalization have been inflated by various meanings bestowed upon them by different, and even the same, authors. Other concepts have been introduced to make necessary distinctions yet without giving adequate emphasis to the specificity of the meanings, universalization (mondialization) and meso-regional integration among them. It is thus my intent to make clear the use of the concepts mentioned heretofore by reiterating the description expressed in Chapter 2 (see figure 2.1). The distinctions are important because they establish the link between each concept or definition and the specific matching phenomenon (there would be no reason to introduce new concepts were this not the

Figure 3.1 Concepts and Economic Realities

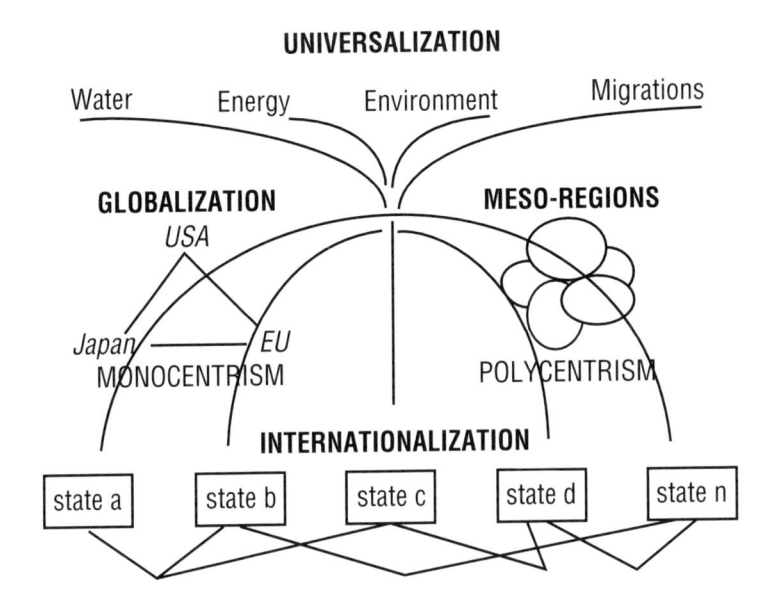

```
                    UNIVERSALIZATION
   Water      Energy     Environment      Migrations

   GLOBALIZATION                    MESO-REGIONS
        USA

   Japan         EU
     MONOCENTRISM              POLYCENTRISM

                 INTERNATIONALIZATION
  state a  | state b | state c | state d | state n
```

case). Different too are the *authors* and *actors* to be taken into account to arrive at an analysis of the dynamics of the issues and eventual options or policy alternatives.

I have just introduced the distinction between *authors* and *actors* into the development process. By authors I mean the roles and non-preset functions, that is those which are being formed, so that they are the active part of the transformation (whatever its direction may be), or those who plan, decide and support new orientations. The actors on the other hand are those whom we traditionally define as passive agents of development. They play a role in the administration and implementation of functions already determined elsewhere by others. The actors, as the term is used here, are those who assimilate and faithfully reproduce previously written text. The four concepts being used here are shown in Figure 3.1.

Universalization

It means the nexus of issues with universal impact which can only be resolved by cooperation among nations. The environment, water resources, the planet's atmospheric pollution and protection, migrations, energy resources are but a few of these problems. Because of their worldwide import, they can only be adequately addressed and resolved through the creation of international, worldwide or mesoregional bodies which, by dint of their unquestioned legitimacy or by the authority vested in them by all the world's national states, are capable of applying and enforcing solutions in individual countries. These issues are the most vital and urgent for the earth's survival and their resolution requires a broad consensus of peoples, extensive cooperation among states and unswerving ethical commitment.

As Figure 2.1 in Chapter 2 indicates, universalization tends to grow along the unequal line of development traced by preceding historical stages and is unable to stray very far from it. The *authors* are non-governmental organizations (NGOs) and some national states; the *actors* are international organizations with weak power like the International Labour Organization (ILO), UNESCO, UNICEF, UNDP.

Globalization

By this term is meant the new forms taken on by the process of accumulation in the world of triadic capitalism (USA, Japan, the EU). In its current form, globalization is the means being used to control the market and available resources so as to increment worldwide profits. It is rooted in a strong cohesion among social classes and privileged groups of power which exploit to their own advantage principles of planning, coordination, centralization and authority. The ideology of competition and a free market is employed as a tool to exercise ever greater power over citizens and workers or to penetrate without the constraints of bureaucratic red tape the weaker parts of the global system.

Globalization (see Chapter 2, figure 2.1) marks an important turning point in the historical trend towards the continuation of unequal development and becomes the 'end of development'. For the first time in history there is a rapid acceleration in the growth of capitalism accompanied by a notable shrinking of the areas and social groups involved. As we have seen, the strategies for domination are *economic marginalization* and *political destabilization* of the social groups and nations excluded from the triadic system.

An altogether new ethos of competition (flexible specialization) and competitiveness among nations (the competitive advantages of nations) and regions (industrial districts) has been knowingly orchestrated to these ends by the 'mandarins of capital', and found its echo in the opportunism of academia (the paladins of capital).[1] The strategies of transnational firms are designed to maintain high levels both of economic competition among states and the three poles of the triadic system, so as to increase the overall output of the economic system in which they operate, and of planning and political control, so as to restrict the subversive reactions which processes of this scope inevitably arouse.

The *authors* are the industrial and financial transnational firms, and the *actors* the agencies of cooperation (aid) and coordination of the industrialized countries (for example, G7, the Trilateral) and the international organizations charged with managing this system of world domination (World Bank, International Monetary Fund (IMF), World Trade Organization, OECD, the federal governments of the three poles of globalization).

Meso-Regional Cooperation: The World-Economies

The term world-economies means the phenomena of reaction and response to triadic globalization by the countries and areas excluded from it. The attempt of these latter countries to fend off the economic marginalization and political destabilization enacted by globalization has given rise to various forms of economic and political cooperation among those states. In other words, there has been a rediscovery of world-economies, that is the value of the historical bond linking production systems, the meeting of the needs of individual areas and trade flows. Economic, cultural and scientific cooperation are the traits peculiar to these structures, and the major threat to potential competition among them comes from destabilization.

It is no accident that the institutions of globalization continue to opt for bilateral relations with individual countries instead of establishing ties of cooperation in other areas and their eventual internal specialization. Like globalization, meso-regional cooperation also marks a turning point in the historical trend of unequal exchange, but in the opposite direction – towards the principles of internationalization and trade parity.

The *authors* are business groups and workers hit by economic marginalization, political and national power groups that reject the role of dependent bourgeoisies or *compradoras*, political, cultural and religious movements that retain a critical attitude towards forms of modernization dictated by the system of globalization. The *actors* are the bodies of cooperation (cultural, university, economic, social) at the meso-regional level and the institutions of regional cooperation (for example the AMU in the Mediterranean countries and ASEAN in Southeast Asia).

Internationalization

This old concept stands for the trade relations between countries. It assumes the existence of states or other regional bodies capable of independently establishing regular exchanges and is based, in the interpretations of the classical economists, on objective criteria of cooperation and reciprocal benefit (comparative advantages) rather than on criteria of competition.

Internationalization has always been considered a process through which two parties (two cultures) reciprocally exchange their goods, thereby promoting the specificity of their respective production systems, forms of consumption, ways of life and, hence, their own identities. The *authors* of internationalization are the regional or national economic, social and political groups; the *actors* the economic, political and state organizations.

CAPITALIST GLOBALIZATION

Triadic Capitalism

World economic development since the 1970s has been marked by an increasing concentration of growth and economic power in the three poles of the world's economy – the United States, Japan and the European Union. The concept of triad was introduced at that time by scholars with ties to the big transnational corporations as well as by international observers and European research centres.[2]

At the core of the system are 37 000 transnational corporations (TNCs) that control over 200 000 affiliates throughout the world and that have again privatized the world economy at varying levels by destabilizing every national system opposed to their logic of growth. Two-thirds of these transnationals (26 000) come from 14 of the most industrialized countries.

The influence of the largest TNCs on output, employment, demand pattern, technology and industrial relations should not be underestimated: the world's leading 100 TNCs, ranked by foreign assets, held US $3.4 trillion in global assets in 1992, of which about 40 per cent were assets located outside their home countries. The top 100 control about one-third of the world FDI stock.
(United Nations, 1994, p.xxi)

The UN's Study Centre noted in its 1988 report on the power of transnational corporations:

They reach beyond national borders and the biggest TNCs have sales which exceed the aggregate output of most countries. The foreign content of output, assets and employment in many of them is large, ranging from 50 to over 90 per cent. All told, adding their home-country output and their production abroad, they account for a significant proportion of world total output. It is estimated, for example, that the largest 600 industrial companies account for between one-fifth and one-fourth of value added in the production of goods in the world's market. Their importance as exporters and importers is probably even greater. For example, between 80 and 90 per cent of the exports of both the USA and the UK is associated with TNCs. TNCs also loom large in international capital flows. Transnational banks (TNBs) and other non-bank financial companies account for the bulk of international lending. Moreover, owing to the transnational character of their operations, non-financial TNCs hold liquid assets in several currencies and, in recent years, they have become important participants in world financial markets. And, of course, TNCs are responsible for the vast majority of foreign direct investment (FDI) and production abroad.
(United Nations, 1988, p.16)

The data published annually in the UN reports provide reliable evidence for and enables a check of

1. the decline of national capitalism,
2. the obsolescence of the perception of an alleged conflict between speculative and non-speculative capitalism based on the mistaken idea of the co-existence of industrial and financial capitalism,

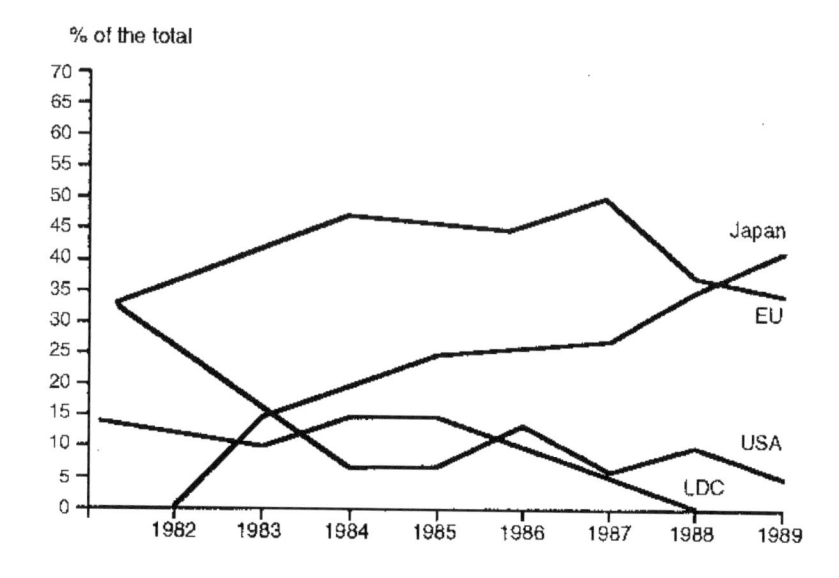

Figure 3.2 Geographic Breakdown of Capital Flow by Provenance

% of the total

[Line chart showing Japan, EU, USA, and LDC shares from 1982 to 1989]

Source: Muldur Ugur, *Les formes et les indicateurs de la globalisation*, FAST, EU, Brussels (1993).

3. the high degree of flexibility that the TNCs are capable of attaining in using and, at the same time, determining technological development, and
4. their appropriation and monopolization of many advances through the system of patents.

The effects of globalization on the world economy can be detected by analyzing its impact on a series of such key phenomena as foreign direct investment (FDI), world trade, the relation between economic growth and employment, the organisation of science and technology, industrial systems and the processes of meso-regional economic integration.

Figure 3.3 Geographic Breakdown of Capital Flow by Destination

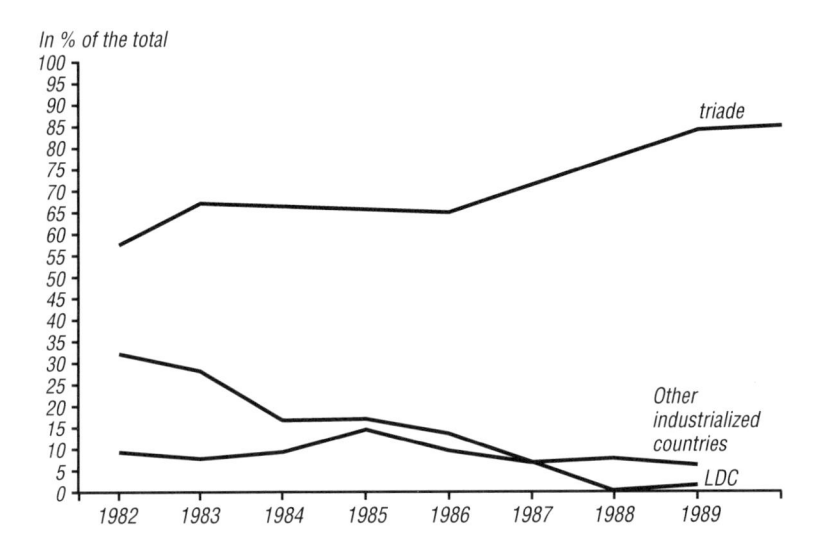

Source: Muldur Ugur, *Les formes et les indicateurs de la globalisation*, FAST-CE, Brussels (1993).

Foreign Direct Investment

Foreign direct investment has registered a strong upswing since the 1980s. Its volume and the strategies that have determined its direction make possible several summary considerations. The last 20 years have seen the consolidation of the trend towards a strengthening of the triadic structure of the world market. The data show that both the provenance of FDI and the recipients are increasingly represented by the Triad's transnational corporations. FDI abroad stems mainly from the most industrialized countries, whose share is in the order of four-fifths of the total flow. The Triad also receives 70 per cent of capital flow. In both cases, the share earmarked for Third World countries is in sharp decline. Africa is losing ground to Asia and, although the share of Latin America has remained stable, it is being concentrated in a few countries (Argentina, Brazil and Mexico) (see figures 3.2 and 3.3).

These UN studies of foreign investment lead to the conclusion that the TNCs have concentrated on those countries that have already crossed the border of development and have done nothing for the world's 50 poorest countries. Indeed, the former have created many problems for the latter by placing restrictions and burdens on economic policy that stifle any further chances of development and, in any case, subordinate the latter to the objectives of the former (United Nations, 1988, p.125).

Similar effects have been found in European countries because of disparate attempts to wrest control of their markets and economies. The governments have been caught in a trap between the need to ensure employment and development in backward areas and the need to attract investment projects from the TNCs. The central, regional and local governments – even cities – of each country have established their own lobbies so as to gain a competitive edge in courting the transnational corporations, the result being a destabilization of the political system and its delegitimation. Government action thus becomes a function of objectives laid down by the TNCs, which in turn feel no responsibility whatsoever for the environment, the social inequalities within the Triad, the development of the Third World and, in the end, world peace. The make-up of *direct foreign investments* in the Triad is shown in Figure 3.4.

To elucidate the nature of the expansionist strategies of triadic capitalism, it is useful to look at the geographic orientation of *foreign direct investments* by large area outside the Triad (figure 3.5). What emerges is the core position of the Triad's poles in the broad areas of origin (that is Latin America for the United States, Europe and Africa for the European Union, Asia for Japan). A non-aggregate analysis for the Third World countries shows the historic trend of decline in share of investments earmarked for these countries (see figure 3.6 below).

Note that the most favourable trend for certain countries in Asia (China and South-East Asia) is due not to the transnational corporations but, prevalently, to major shifts of capital from one Asian country to another (excluding Japan) and of Chinese capital to within Asian areas. Noteworthy too is that the recurrence of flash booms (economic miracles) in several Latin American countries fails to alter the overall picture. Rather, it helps better to define the quality traits of the predatory forms of the internal resources of these countries and of the distortions in income distribution they involve.

The World Economy and Capitalism

Figure 3.4 FDI Stock Among Triad Members and Their Clusters, 1993

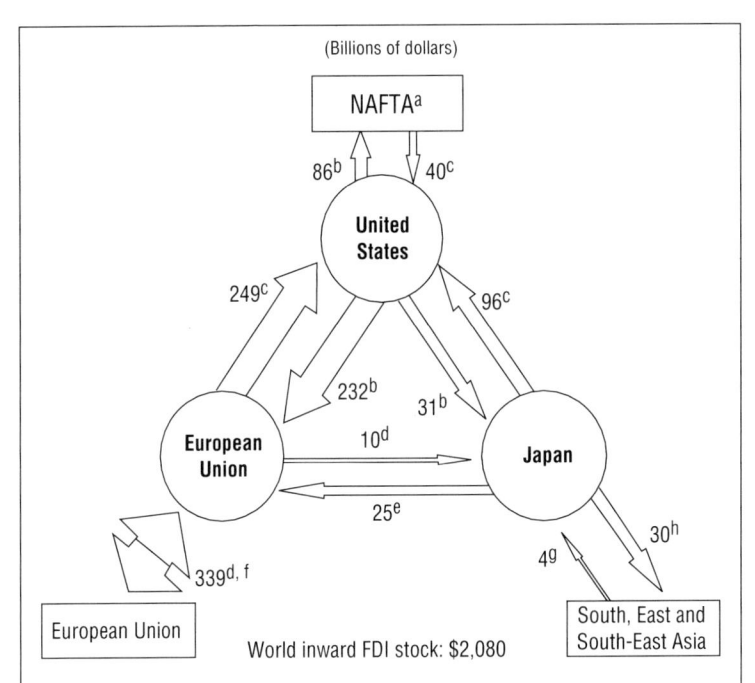

(Billions of dollars)

NAFTA[a]

86[b] → United States ← 40[c]

249[c] ← United States → 96[c] (to Japan)

232[b] European Union → Japan 31[b]

10[d] European Union → Japan

25[e] Japan → European Union

339[d,f] European Union

4[g] Japan → South, East and South-East Asia 30[h]

World inward FDI stock: $2,080

Source: UNCTAD, division on Transnational Corporations and Investment, FDI database.

a Canada and Mexico.
b United States outward FDI stock.
c United States inward FDI stock.
d Outward FDI stock of Austria, Finland, France, Germany, Italy, Netherlands, Sweden and the United Kingdom. Data for Austria are for 1991 and data for France and the Netherlands are for 1992.
e Data from inward FDI stock of Austria, France, Germany, Italy, Netherlands and United Kingdom. Data for Austria and France are 1991 and data for Italy and the Netherlands are for 1992.
f For Sweden, the data reflect FDI to and from all European countries. Intra-European Union FDI, based on inward stocks, is $225 billion.
g Data are based on approvals/notifications and represent those from countries other than those in North America and Europe.
h Estimated by multiplying the values of the cumulative flows to the region according to FDI approvals by the ratio of disbursed to approved/notified FDI in developing countries.

Source: United Nations, *World Investment Report. Transnational Corporations and Competitiveness*. New York and Geneva: United Nations Conference on Trade and Development. Division on Transnational Corporations and Investment. 1995, p.11.

Figure 3.5 The Triad of FDI and Its Clusters, 1993

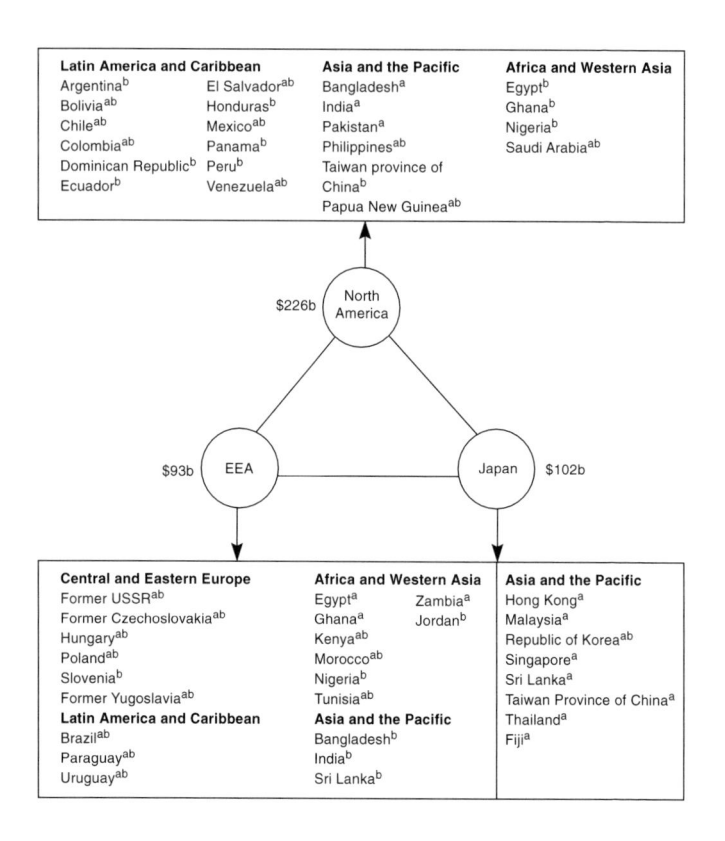

Latin America and Caribbean		Asia and the Pacific	Africa and Western Asia
Argentina[b]	El Salvador[ab]	Bangladesh[a]	Egypt[b]
Bolivia[ab]	Honduras[b]	India[a]	Ghana[b]
Chile[ab]	Mexico[ab]	Pakistan[a]	Nigeria[b]
Colombia[ab]	Panama[b]	Philippines[ab]	Saudi Arabia[ab]
Dominican Republic[b]	Peru[b]	Taiwan province of China[b]	
Ecuador[b]	Venezuela[ab]	Papua New Guinea[ab]	

$226b — North America

$93b — EEA   Japan — $102b

Central and Eastern Europe	Africa and Western Asia		Asia and the Pacific
Former USSR[ab]	Egypt[a]	Zambia[a]	Hong Kong[a]
Former Czechoslovakia[ab]	Ghana[a]	Jordan[b]	Malaysia[a]
Hungary[ab]	Kenya[ab]		Republic of Korea[ab]
Poland[ab]	Morocco[ab]		Singapore[a]
Slovenia[b]	Nigeria[b]		Sri Lanka[a]
Former Yugoslavia[ab]	Tunisia[ab]		Taiwan Province of China[a]
Latin America and Caribbean	**Asia and the Pacific**		Thailand[a]
Brazil[ab]	Bangladesh[b]		Fiji[a]
Paraguay[ab]	India[b]		
Uruguay[ab]	Sri Lanka[b]		

Source: United Nations, *World Investment Report. Transnational Corporations, Employment and the Workplace*, United Nations Conference on Trade and Development. Division on Transnational Corporations and Investment. United Nations. New York, 1994, p.132.

Table 3.1 Inflow of Direct Foreign Investment to Developing Regions

Recipient regions and economies	% share of total FDI 1980–4	1988–9
Developing countries	25.2	16.9
Africa	2.4	1.9
Latin America and Caribbean	12.3	5.8
Far, South and S-E Asia	9.4	8.8
Less developed countries	0.4	0.1
10 highest DFI economies	18.1	11.1
Argentina	0.9	0.6
Brazil	4.2	1.5
China	1.1	1.9
Colombia	0.8	0.2
Egypt	1.1	0.8
Hong Kong	1.4	1.2
Malaysia	2.3	0.7
Mexico	3.0	1.4
Singapore	2.8	2.0
Thailand	0.6	0.8

Source: UNDP, *Human Development Report*, Oxford University, Oxford (1992) p.52.

World Trade

Another indicator is the trend in *world trade* shown in Figure 3.6. The triadic structure this trade has taken on provides additional, confirming, evidence for the data *supra* on direct foreign investments.

Economic Growth and its Impact on Employment

A third indicator is globalization's impact on employment. A survey of the economies of several of the most industrialized countries confirms the trend 'toward a divorce between economic growth employment underscored by a number of scholars in various contexts'. (Figure 3.7)

This is borne out by the fact that in the period 1960–87 the very strong GNP surge in France (+268), Great Britain (+183), Germany (+222), the United States (+217) and Japan (+379) was matched by employment rates that were negative in France, Germany and

Figure 3.6 Share of Regional Trade Flows Out of the World Trade of Manufactured Goods, (in % of total world trade) 1970 and 1990

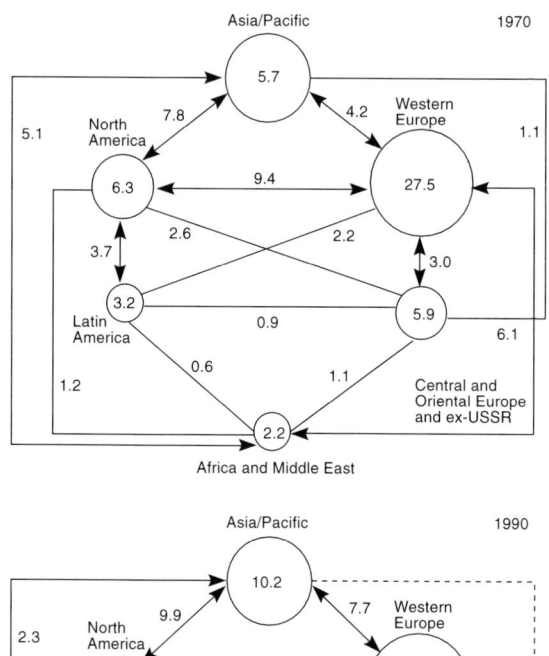

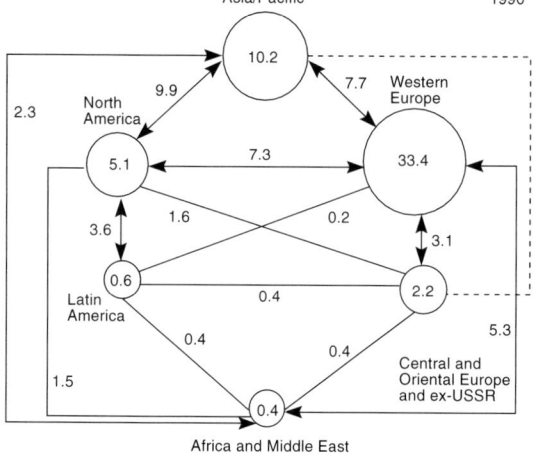

Source: Muldur Ugur, Les formes et les indicateurs de la globalisation, FAST, Commission of the European Communities, Brussels (1993).

The World Economy and Capitalism 63

Figure 3.7 GDP and Employment Growth in Industrialized Countries, 1960–87

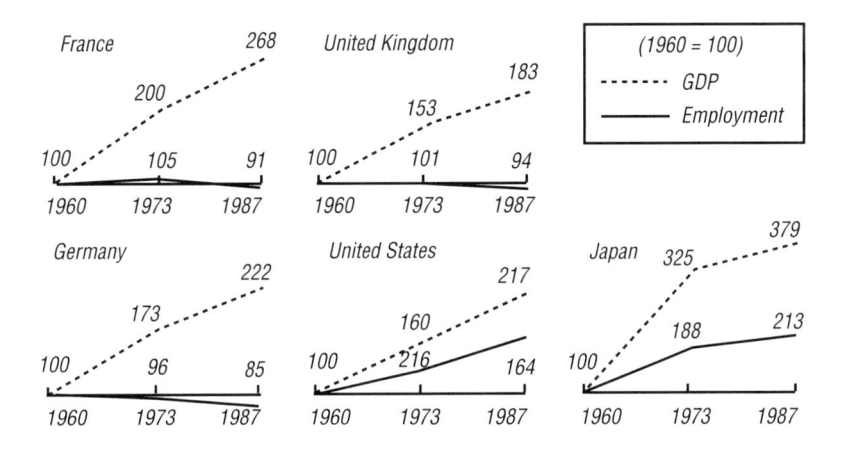

```
France          268        United Kingdom                (1960 = 100)
         200 ..--''                         183           ------ GDP
       ..--''              ..--'' 153 ..--''             ———— Employment
100 .--''  105    91       100 ..--'' 101     94
└──────┴────┘              └──────┴────┘
1960   1973   1987         1960   1973   1987
                                                                           379
Germany                    United States          Japan   325 ..--'' ..--''
                    222                 217            ..--''
       173 ..--''              160 ..--''          ..''  188        213
100 ..--''  96    85       100 ..--'' 216   164   100 ..''
└──────┴────┘              └──────┴────┘          └──────┴────┘
1960   1973   1987         1960   1973   1987    1960   1973   1987
```

Source: UNDP, *Human Development Report*, New York (1993).

Great Britain and far below the economic growth rates in Japan and the United States (Petrella, 1995, pp.39–40).

Globalization and Industrial Organization

It is instructive to take a look at the new organizational forms adopted by big business in strategic growth sectors over the last two decades.

The scholars who have undertaken this task chose the key sectors of industrial development, whether traditional or new (for example automobiles, electronics, new materials, biotechnology), ascertained the extent and forms of their worldwide integration and charted their geographic locus by large area to determine whether there was a triadic form of development even for industrial organization and territorial position.

These graphs, taken from the far more detailed studies under the general editorship of Riccardo Petrella, provide a clear-cut answer to these questions. Those for the automobile (figure 3.8) and electronics (figure 3.9) industries are excerpted here. Comparable results are shown by examining the stable links each transnational corporation has with other businesses. Figures 3.10 and 3.11 below, which analyse General Motors, IBM and the web of alliances

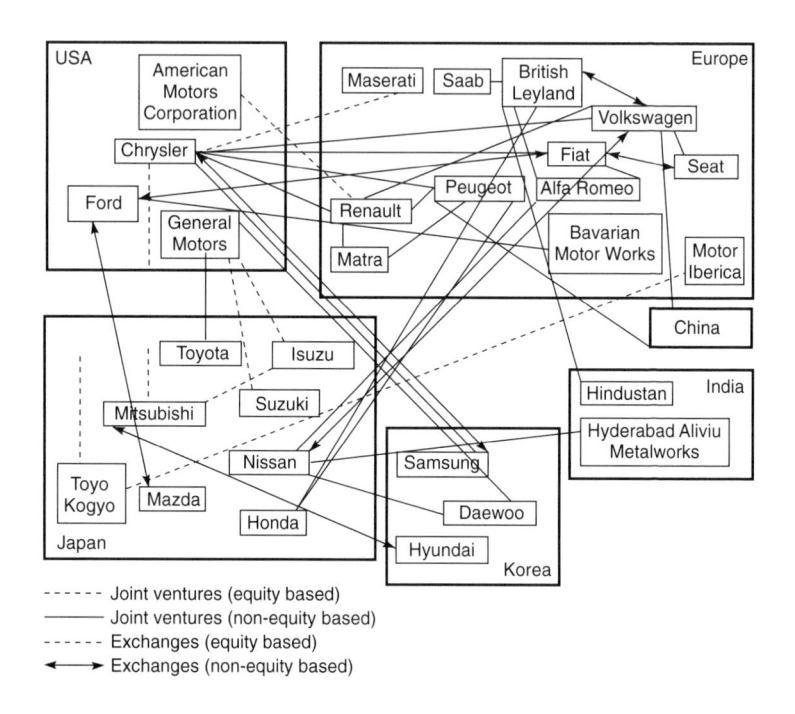

Figure 3.8 Partnership in the Automobile Industry

```
USA          American                                              Europe
             Motors          Maserati   Saab    British
             Corporation                        Leyland
                                                        Volkswagen
       Chrysler                                    Fiat
  Ford                                Peugeot  Alfa Romeo    Seat
             General          Renault
             Motors                            Bavarian
                              Matra            Motor Works   Motor
                                                             Iberica

                                                             China
             Toyota      Isuzu
                                                   Hindustan    India
       Mitsubishi    Suzuki
                                                   Hyderabad Aliviu
                     Nissan          Samsung       Metalworks
  Toyo
  Kogyo   Mazda                      Daewoo
                     Honda
  Japan                              Hyundai
                                              Korea
```

- - - - - - Joint ventures (equity based)
────── Joint ventures (non-equity based)
- - - - - Exchanges (equity based)
◄────► Exchanges (non-equity based)

Source: Riccardo Petrella, *Four Analyses of the Globalisation of Technology and Economy*, Monitor-Fast, Brussels (1991), p.5.

in the telecommunications sector, confirm both the *triadization* and the new nature of *transnationalization* with respect to the multinational corporations.

All the studies cited *supra*, and many others besides, inequivocably and definitively evince that the strictly national character of big business, and thus national capitalism, belong to the past. They also make evident that, as a result, the national state is linked no longer to national capitalism – a tie of that same past – but to transnational capitalism – a tie that is becoming ever more consolidated.

Figure 3.9 Strategic Partnerships in the Electronics Industry: Europe, Japan, USA

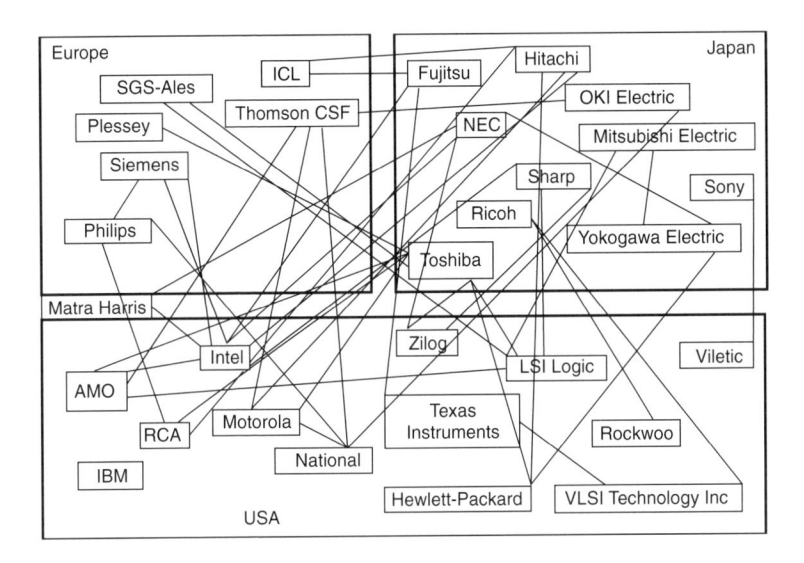

Source: Riccardo Petrella, *Four Analyses of the Globalisation of Technology and Economy*, Monitor-Fast, Brussels (1991), p.7.

Production Organization, Specializations and New Technologies

It is also worthwhile taking a look at the new *forms of production organization adopted by the transnational corporations*. The view here is focused on how countries and areas of the world are integrated into the production process by estimating labour costs, ready access to energy sources and raw materials, or even to promote policy measures in support of political systems or governments. These new forms were made possible by the horizontal decentralization of production and by the new information and telecommunications technologies.

The horizontal decentralization of production obviates the need to shift production sectors to various regions or countries (for example textiles, chemicals, the manufacture of certain products) since each product is simply broken down into so many components (for example a car can be broken down into 26 000). The individual parts can

Figure 3.10 General Motors' Strategic Positioning

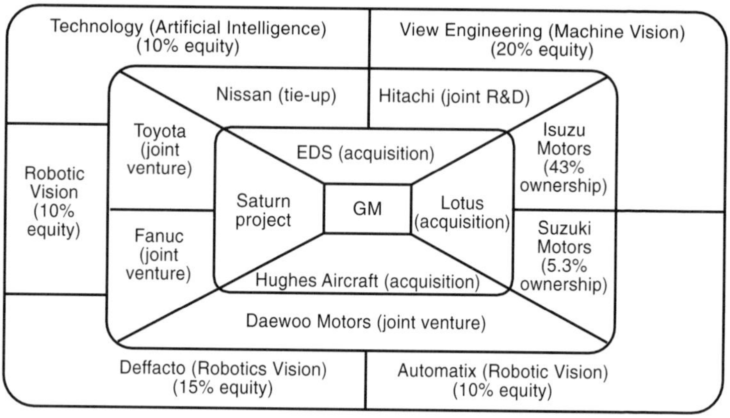

```
┌─────────────────────────────────────────────────────────────────┐
│  Technology (Artificial Intelligence)  View Engineering (Machine Vision) │
│             (10% equity)                      (20% equity)              │
│          ┌─────────────────────┬──────────────────────┐                │
│          │   Nissan (tie-up)   │  Hitachi (joint R&D) │                │
│  Toyota  ├─────────────────────┴──────────────────────┤   Isuzu        │
│  (joint  │        EDS (acquisition)                   │   Motors       │
│ venture) │                                            │   (43%         │
│ Robotic  │   Saturn  │          │       Lotus         │   ownership)   │
│ Vision   │   project │    GM    │   (acquisition)     │                │
│ (10%     │           │          │                     │   Suzuki       │
│ equity)  │  Fanuc    │          │                     │   Motors       │
│          │  (joint   │                                │   (5.3%        │
│          │  venture) │   Hughes Aircraft (acquisition)│   ownership)   │
│          ├───────────┴────────────────────────────────┤                │
│          │          Daewoo Motors (joint venture)     │                │
│          ├─────────────────────┬──────────────────────┤                │
│          │ Deffacto (Robotics Vision) │ Automatix (Robotic Vision) │   │
│          │       (15% equity)         │      (10% equity)          │   │
└─────────────────────────────────────────────────────────────────┘
```

Source: Riccardo Petrella, *Four Analysis of the Globalisation of Technology and Economy*, Monitor-Fast, Brussels (1991), p.7.

thus be manufactured in different geographical areas chosen for the relative advantages each offers. Low-wage areas for parts requiring high labour input, low-cost ones for manufactures requiring raw materials or energy inputs, local markets with skilled labour forces for specialized tasks are a few examples. Yet none of this would be possible without a system of industrial planning, data communications and quality control that is so efficient as to make any of the socialist planning systems blush with shame. Figure 3.12 shows the textbook example of organization – the Toyota production plants located in four South-East Asian countries.

Horizontal decentralization is possible because of the new systems of data transmission and remote production control, the passive subordination of the various production units and workers in the various sectors, and firm control of the various systems of government through destabilization pressure brought to bear against the risk of surprises.

That the new industrial systems and political destabilization go hand in hand may seem paradoxical and misleading. But that is the case. Political destabilization and the civil war in Somalia have not proved the slightest obstacle to the business dealings of the

The World Economy and Capitalism 67

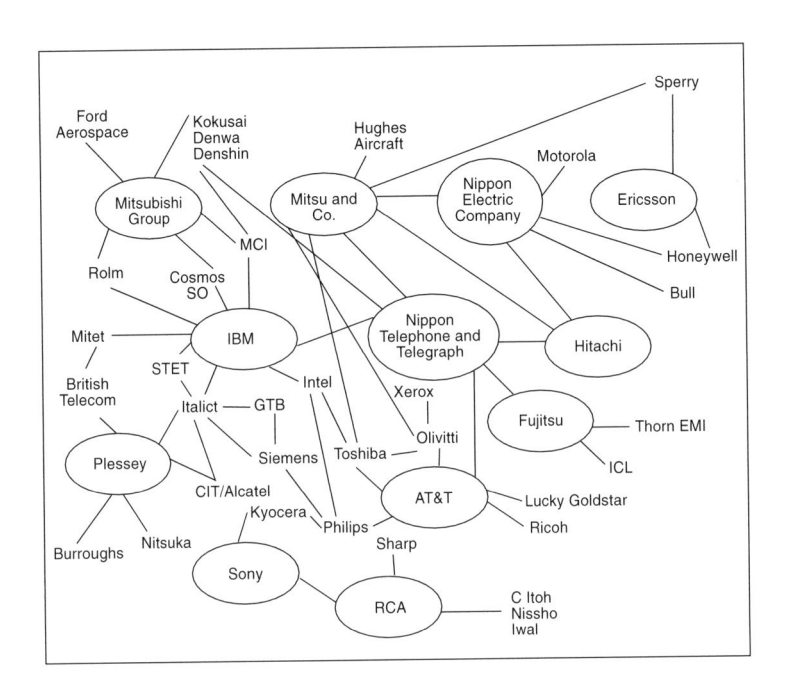

Figure 3.11 Alliances in the Telecommunications Industry

Source: Riccardo Petrella, *Four Analysis of the Globalization of Technology and Economy*, Monitor-Fast, Brussels (1991) p.8.

big banana companies, which continue to operate unhindered with their own communication systems, airports and so on. The oil drilling in the areas of northern Iraq 'protected' by American aircraft and destabilized by the conflict involving the Kurds, the Turks and the Iraqis goes on undisturbed. In the very midst of the Cambodian tragedy the plunder of the country's rich forest and mineral resources continues unabated by the Thai, Cambodian and other armies acting on behalf of the transnational corporations and protected by the destabilization of the area that the United States finances. And, despite the civil war now bathing Algeria in blood, the big oil companies proceed unperturbed with their investment plans for the transport of oil and natural gas to the European Union's industrial

Figure 3.12 Toyota's Automobile Operations in Four Asean Countries

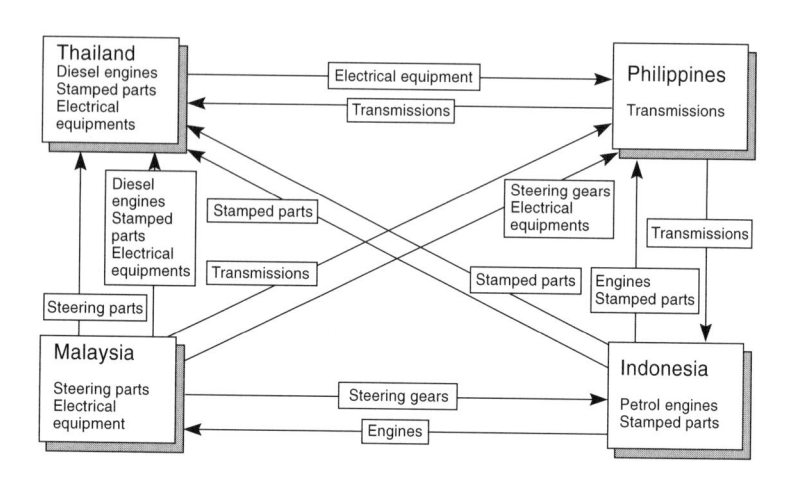

```
┌─────────────────┐                              ┌─────────────────┐
│ Thailand        │                              │                 │
│ Diesel engines  │──── Electrical equipment ───▶│ Philippines     │
│ Stamped parts   │                              │ Transmissions   │
│ Electrical      │◀─── Transmissions ───────────│                 │
│ equipments      │                              │                 │
└─────────────────┘                              └─────────────────┘
         ▲                                                ▲
         │   ┌──────────┐                ┌─────────────┐  │
         │   │ Diesel   │                │ Steering    │  │
         │   │ engines  │ Stamped parts  │ gears       │  │
         │   │ Stamped  │                │ Electrical  │  │  Transmissions
         │   │ parts    │                │ equipments  │  │
         │   │ Electrical│ Transmissions │             │  │
         │   │ equipments│               │ Stamped parts│ Engines
┌──────────┐ │          │                │             │ Stamped parts
│ Steering │ │          │                │             │
│ parts    │ │          │                │             │
└──────────┘ └──────────┘                └─────────────┘
┌─────────────────┐                              ┌─────────────────┐
│ Malaysia        │                              │                 │
│ Steering parts  │──── Steering gears ─────────▶│ Indonesia       │
│ Electrical      │                              │ Petrol engines  │
│ equipment       │◀─── Engines ─────────────────│ Stamped parts   │
└─────────────────┘                              └─────────────────┘
```

Source: 'Part Exchange' in *Far Eastern Economic Review* (21 September 1989) p.73.

centres, and, because they can produce at low cost thanks to the low prices paid for the oil and gas, further confine to the margins the economies of Algeria and the other countries of the Mediterranean Basin.

NOTES

1. The expression 'mandarins of capital' is the title of a book on the subject by Samir Amin, whereas 'paladins of capital' is my coining for those academics (Beccattini, Salvati and so on) who, by distorting the historical importance of such signal experiments in cooperation and polycentric development as 'industrial districts', advocated in Italy the ideology of 'competition', 'innovation' and 'flexibility' propounded by American scholars (Piore and Sabel, Michel Porter) in relation to the new forms and demands of industrial organization stemming from that country and from transnational corporations. See also Amoroso, 1994.
2. Of these let us recall Kenichi, 1977, and the reports on World Investments of the UN Centre on Transnational Corporations which in the

last five years have provided documentary evidence of the triadic trend to which I shall hereafter refer. The 1991 report is devoted to 'The Triad and Direct Foreign Investments'. Also worthy of note is the outstanding contribution to the study of this phenomenon by the FAST Programme, headed by Riccardo Petrella, of the EU's DG XII on Science and Technology.

4 Capital Accumulation in the Last Decade of the 20th Century – The End of Development

> A race of wolves that has well organized plans for hunting in packs is likely to survive and spread; because those plans enable it to catch its prey, not because they confer a benefit on the world.
>
> Marshall, 1919, p.175

THE END OF HISTORY?

The Crisis of the Socialist Countries and the 'End of History'?

The political events in the countries of Eastern Europe in the late 1980s have claimed far more attention than that usually reserved for the news highlights of an entire decade. The failure of these countries' political systems to achieve their objectives, that is to replace capitalism with a more just and equal social system, is widely recognized and numerous interpretations have been proffered to explain it.

The prevailing theory does not essentially differ from the one advanced for the crisis of the welfare state in Western Europe. These experimental political systems were held to be a deviation from what was supposed to be the end point of human history – capitalism and liberal democracy. Thus the demise of the last historical anomaly – totalitarian communism – is supposedly the final victory.

Lester Thurow's Theory: The Duration of Capitalism has Hitherto Been Insignificant

The American economist Lester C. Thurow has remarked that all the statements about the 'ending of human history' reveal a thorough ignorance of mankind's development. All those who have sought to reach it – whether the longer-lived attempts of the ancient Egyptians, Greeks and Romans or the shorter-lived ones of Nazi Germany – have been swept away by the tide of history.

> Democracy as we know it has only 200 years of life and Capitalism 150 years. As the years roll by they have still to demonstrate their validity in the long run. Slavery, feudalism, and absolute monarchy have lasted much longer.
> (Thurow, 1990, p.1)

The history and the crisis of the socialist countries are the result of not very different factors from those we have had to deal with in the capitalist countries. Both systems in the past have exhibited remarkable vitality. Soviet society from the 1920s to the 1970s evinced a very pronounced dynamism and an ability to mobilize. The same can be said for countries like Sweden. What, then, changed in the 1970s? Thurow's answer to this query is that:

> The socialists in the 19th century believed in the possibility of creating a new human being capable of giving higher priority to social rather than individual goals. But in practice nobody has ever succeeded in producing this new human being.
> (1990, p.1)

Since the 1970s this has probably stood in the way of both the socialist countries and the welfare states. Yet the history of events continues its march. The crisis that afflicted these countries is also showing up, albeit in different guises, in the capitalist countries with development models based on individualism and liberal democracy.

The rate of productivity growth in the United States during the last two decades is higher than the one in Eastern Europe but is much lower than the one in Japan's and of the countries in the Pacific area. Furthermore, without government intervention, finance capitalism as is practiced in the United States would today be collapsing at the same speed as socialism is disintegrating in Eastern Europe.

(p.2)

The Crisis of the Nation-State

It can thus be stated that the issue common to just about all countries today, regardless of whether they are in the East or the West, is to redefine their forms of economic and political development so as to deal with the process of worldwide economic globalization and integration. It should also be noted that, as a result, insufficiencies in redefining national economies with respect to regional economic globalization and integration will highlight the crisis of the nation-state – a crisis that will involve the entire system of economic and political institutions erected around it. Paradoxically, this is precisely what is occurring just as the countries of Eastern Europe seem to be rediscovering its values and virtues.

The Second Great Crisis of the 20th Century

The second great crisis of the economic and political systems of our century – the first being the Depression in 1929 – is the result of these processes. Both Communism and Socialism's revolutionary utopia and the reformist one of a possible civilization have suffered a great deal from it in the last two decades. The Italian liberal philosopher Norberto Bobbio has termed the events in Europe of the late 1980s the 'upturned utopia':

> The unprecedented sense of drama in the events of the last few days events lies in the fact that they have not involved the crisis of a regime or the defeat of great, invincible power. Rather, and in a seemingly irreversible way, the greatest political utopia in history (I am not talking of religious utopias) has been completely upturned into its exact opposite.
>
> (1989, p.37)

> The conquest of the freedom of the modern world – if and insofar as it is possible – cannot but be the starting point for the countries of the upturned utopia. But to go where? I ask this question because the founding of the law-based liberal democratic state is not enough to solve the problems which gave birth to the proletarian movement of the countries that embarked upon a savage form of industrialisation and later among the poor peasants of the Third World [to] the 'hope of revolution'.
>
> (Ibid., p.38)

It does not appear to me that the questions posed by a liberal thinker like Bobbio can raise doubts of interpretation. 'Do we really think', he goes on, 'that bourgeois democracy and the market system can be the reply to the aspirations of revolution and justice in the world? Can consumerism be a realistic and desirable alternative to Communism?'

The introduction of the capitalist market and liberal ideology have already given rise, at least in our part of the world, to a growing and dangerous exclusion of large segments of the population from the welfare economy. The expression 'the two-thirds society' was introduced into the debate by Peter Glotz, a leading proponent of West German social democracy (Glotz, 1985). He details the crisis of the welfare state and its transformation from a model of social and political rights universally valid for all citizens to one where political and social power is concentrated in the majority; 'the two-thirds of the citizenry to the exclusion of the remaining third'. The Italian economist Riccardo Parboni pointed out in conversation that this interpretation too was far from realistic as even in the most efficient welfare systems power is concentrated in the upper third of the two-thirds society.

Attempts to Overcome the Crisis of the Nation-State

We have already abandoned the welfare state for the two-thirds society, in which the privileged two-thirds rule and prosper with nothing to fear from the excluded poor third. The destructive effects of this kind of development on the quality of our lives are evident. Yet the excluded third, which today is controlled and exploited by and through the abuse of the political-economic powers that be (which also enlist the mass media's manipulation of ideas), will soon grow until becoming four-fifths or even nine-tenths because of globalization and economic integration. This kind of development catches us at a moment in which, as Bobbio notes, we lack the wherewithal to deal with problems that in turn have given rise to Communism and humanist welfare utopias.

Attempts to break out of this situation seem headed towards both an open market economy, which currently appears to be supported by the major political groupings in Europe and, at the same time, timid looks in the direction of the social democratic model, especially the Scandinavian. It would thus seem that in terms of ideas there is an acritical return to the drawing board of the 1920s.

Yet, precisely because this approach appears to be acritical, it is well worth reflecting on the historical experience that has accrued in the last half-century.

GLOBALIZATION AND NEW TECHNOLOGIES

Market Economies in the 1990s

Many of the opinions propounded about the crisis of the Eastern European countries seem to converge on the assumption that there is a substantial difference between the reasons behind this crisis and those behind the crisis of the Western European countries. Western models of production and consumption and their matching political and institutional counterparts can thus be held out as solutions to the Eastern countries' dilemma, albeit with the necessary adjustments.

My own thoughts on the subject are predicated on the opposite assumption. In other words, Eastern Europe's economic marginalization and political destabilization are the end-phase of a general breakdown of European development models which is traceable to the systemic crisis of the welfare state.

Overview of the Historical Process Leading to the Crisis of the European Countries

The main bone of contention in the clash between Europe's social and political forces over the last 50 years has been the forms that the processes of industrialization and modernization are to take. The struggle has been exasperated by the contrast between development models based on a growing commodification and decommodification of economic and social relations. The histories of the different systems of the welfare state in Europe, including the more successful Scandinavian ones, represent even in their sometimes contradictory courses the concrete realization of a political project whose goal was to 'free man's survival from the need to work and the uncertainty of the marketplace' (Paci, 1988, p.22).

Karl Polanyi notes that the historical roots of this process are grounded in 200 years of uncertainty about the conditions of material existence and of capitalist exploitation:

The congenital weakness of nineteenth-century society was not that it was industrial but that it was a market society. Industrial civilisation will continue to exist when the utopian experiment of a self-regulating market will be no more than a memory.[1]

(1971, p.250)

Elaborating on what subsequently became part of reformist strategy, he stated:

Much of the massive suffering inseparable from a period of transition is already behind us. In the social and economic dislocation of our age, in the tragic vicissitudes of the Depression, fluctuations of currency, mass unemployment, shifting of social status, spectacular destruction of historical states, we have experienced the worst. Unwittingly, we have been paying the price of change.

(Ibid.)

Yet this change spelt problems for the welfare state, and they have been mounting since the 1970s. A widely held explanation attributes these difficulties to a dysfunction of the market system caused by welfare institutions: political behaviour is in conflict with the sound principles of capitalist accumulation and the welfare ethos has undermined its competitiveness (Lindbeck, 1977). All of a sudden the very democratic institutions that had previously been praised have now become a problem. What had been held up as a happy marriage between the market system and democracy has now become an incompatible union because, it is now alleged, the market itself is democracy and the relative autonomy of the state *vis-à-vis* such a democracy cannot but be entirely illegitimate.

It will therefore come as no surprise that in the face of such conditions all the theorists of liberal democracy and neo-corporativism have tried to survive by reworking the concept of legitimacy as market legitimacy and downgrading the political process to a passive reflex of market rationality. 'While for many centuries a political conception of economics has prevailed, today an economic conception of politics is fast gaining greater currency.' (Bobbio, 1989, p.1). Game theory has thus entered the political arena, putting all institutions and organizations on an equal footing and reducing the strong social character of Scandinavia's political tradition to a system of an indistinct negotiated economy.

Another Explanation for the Change: Growing Incompatibility of the Market and Democracy

A different line of inquiry detects the reasons for the crisis of the welfare-state's systems in the market's inability to provide a satisfactory response to the demands of a developed society (Caffè, 1986, pp.13–24; Hirshmann, 1980, p.133 foll.) and in the growing incompatibility between the market and democracy (Bobbio, 1989). The pursuit of profit *qua* primary objective of a company and business ethics *qua* code of conduct are particularly pernicious in a society where economic and political power are closely interwoven. Indeed, through this very pattern, capitalists soon learned to use the levers of social compensation set up by the welfare state as a way to socialize losses. These bookkeeping practices transfer the social costs of business to the government's budget in the form of public expenditure that has to be paid for by higher taxes. The discontent of the citizenry is thus channelled against the state, not the market. This is why Federico Caffè ascribed the crisis of the welfare state not to its realization and senescence but, rather, to its unfulfilment (Caffè, 1986).

The End of the Social and Political Contract

The social and political contract upon which the modern European democracies were founded after World War II was officially rescinded in the 1980s. This breakdown came in the wake of the acceleration of the processes of capital concentration throughout the world, which resulted in severe restrictions of social and political rights and was accompanied by a technocratization of a political system increasingly operating in accordance with mathematical models based on economic restraints and principles of accounting and rationality compatible to these choices.

It is beyond doubt that advanced technology is the driving force behind the processes of capitalist restructuring and the major cause behind the deterioration of the existing social equilibrium at every level. It has made possible the miracle of *growth without development*, which has turned capitalism from an *extroverted* system, pointed towards expansion to win over new markets and new consumers, into an *introverted* one, its aim being to raise profits by exploiting the world's resources for increasingly restricted elite markets and increasingly wealthier consumers.

The critique of the Marxists and the left held that up to the 1970s capitalism's rate of expansion was too slow and the direction in which it was expanding too imbalanced geographically, although it had no doubts that capitalism was by nature expansive, directed towards the conquest of new markets and consumers. When the 'end of development' (Club of Rome) was first mentioned in the late 1960s, reference was made to emerging external limits (energy, raw materials, environment) that posed problems of a more rational use of existing resources and of development models capable of curtailing waste.

The End of Development

Globalization, the historical form of the paradox of capitalism's growth and, coincidently, of the underdevelopment of societies, derives from the capitalists' discovery of rising production waste, the result of management problems involving large facilities (both technical and political management problems), and the awareness of the increasing difficulties in gaining access to the raw materials and natural resources needed for a broad-based rise in consumption. New technology provided the solution.

> When economists realised how much easier it was to halve a product's lifetime rather than double the number of consumers, there ensued a flurry of some pretty wild ideas, like the watch to be thrown away instead of being repaired (actually produced) or the throw-away car ('throw-away' insofar as a good number of easily replaceable parts are concerned).
> (Giarini and Loubergé, 1978, pp.11–2)

The technical solution was easy – restrict the number of consumers and increase the consumption capacity of the wealthiest ones. Yet two problems remained:

i) how to weaken the power of the organizations and institutions linked to the preceding model so as to exclude socially the poorer ones; and
ii) how to ensure continuous, cheap supplies of raw materials and energy found in vast areas of the world that would be marginalized by globalization.

The Social Side of the Market Solution: the Theories of Innovation

The technical and the social solutions are, of course, inseparable. Implementing the technical one aimed at the market required overturning the logic of both social and Keynesian policies. Whence the revival of the innovation theories which, it should be noted, concern not just techniques but even institutions and behaviour.

It is worth noting that this concept of innovation, broader than that of technological innovation, was introduced in the 1970s by those who thought that doing so would lead to their exerting a social and cultural influence on development and the introduction of new technologies. The innovation theories of the 1980s and 1990s turn this approach upside down: the main problem is how to permeate every aspect of social and political life with the organizational logic of the transnational corporations via the new technologies.

Evolution leads from industrial democracy – *locus* for the pursuit of values, the quality of development, the appropriate technology for existing production systems and community needs – to the constraints deemed necessary for a rapid introduction of existing technology and the production system linked to it – competition, flexible specialization, new organizational and communication techniques. The latter become the new jobs, the new professional profiles for the many researchers who have quickly recycled themselves from the *liaisons dangereuses* they had fallen into in the 1960s and 1970s.

Types of Technological Innovation: of Process and Product

Our discussion of technology distinguishes between process innovations and product innovations. Process innovations are designed to cut output costs through the decentralization of production units and the concentration of control. Small is beautiful and flexible specialization, demands already called for by critics of capitalist industrialization, are recycled by big business to its own advantage. This result is a breakdown in the system of worker representation and participation in production and a contraction of the productive labour pool to a qualified few. Big business even takes over the historical forms of organization. The industrial districts are a prime example. Having arisen as regional experiments designed to promote polycentric, endogenous systems of production and consumption, they are now held up as access vehicles to the rich markets, the upshot being that they are uprooted from their indigenous areas.

Product innovations induce the acceleration of the forms and frequency of consumption for the wealthy consumers, thereby assuring high profits at lower risk. Product innovation is, of course, very expensive as to inputs of energy, research and new materials, so that it must be assured access to energy sources as well as to control of innovation systems.

The great demands for capital accumulation required to meet the investments needed by these new production systems leave nothing to government budgets and autonomous commitments to culture, solidarity and protection. This insidious drive to profit and the reorganization of production systems is defined as a war on waste and justified as a legitimate moral initiative. Whence the need for the political destabilization of national states and of all forms of resistance, as these innovations are the spearhead aimed at assuring the stability of a new, overall economic organization within the framework of a *worldwide apartheid* system.

Globalization: Economic and Technological Choice, Not Necessity

The 'end of development' mentioned in these pages derives from the course charted for globalization in Chapter 2, figure 2.15. It originated not from limits or external constraints but from an internal choice about the role of capitalist accumulation. It thus derives not from restrictions placed on the model but from its full deployment and success.

A technological explanation of the major causes of globalization and of the new guises taken on by the accumulation process is possible so long as it is predicated on the assumption that technology is not the fruit of inscrutable events of human destiny but the result of deliberate choices that social classes and strata make as to instrument of domination. The well-known technology gap has been widening dramatically since the 1970s. The number of countries and industries capable of sustaining the evolutionary pace of the new technologies is getting smaller and smaller, with devastating effects on the production systems within and without the orbit of the Triad. Simultaneously, the decision to promote a market model premised upon a shrinking output base and upon a concentration on wealthy consumers results in the elimination of important basic industries (for example steel, construction, agriculture) that are necessary to create infrastructures and to meet primary needs. This elimination not only causes unnecessary joblessness but prevents primary needs being met – while millions of people continue to exist below the threshold of a decent standard of living.

The de-industrialization areas of the European Union mentioned *supra* are the result of this decision and not, as is often alleged, of bad investments or political corruption. With the economic, social and political destabilization that comes in the wake of these processes, the de-industrialized areas cease to be useful as markets. Their ties to the Triad are retained only because of their eventual strategic importance in gaining access to raw materials.

Globalization and the New Colonization

There is in fact very little 'global' and nothing international to globalization. The relations between the Triad and the periphery are fast becoming colonial in form. Yet the nature of this colonization is colliding with other factors and phenomena that have worldwide significance (for example migration, environmental protection, energy and water conservation) and, thus, require greater concord and cooperation among national states (see universalism in Chapter 3, figure 3.1). Globalization's attempt to gain control over these phenomena can be seen in its replacing the old concrete walls by the new electronic walls, thereby turning the peripheries of capitalism into the *townships* of globalization. All of this is being accomplished in the flag-waving name of our common future, of universal principles, values and rules set down and administered by none other than the Triad. NATO's supplanting of the UN in resolving regional conflicts can be seen in this light.

AMERICANISM AND REFORMISM

The Monetarist Counterrevolution

The qualitative change that occurred in the 1980s was duly recorded by some and denied by others. Recalling the contributions of Stuart Holland and Riccardo Parboni:

The privatisation of world industry, the dismantling of the Welfare State, the increasing concentrated control of the economy, the re-assertion and institutionalisation of the separation between equality and efficiency (whose unification had been one of the most signal achievements of European culture), all are the expression of world capitalism's new strategy. The world's bourgeoisie no longer needs the national states and has begun turning monopolistic state capitalism into world capitalism.

(Amoroso, 1994, p.193)

James Tobin had no qualms in speaking about a 'monetarist counter-revolution' designed to weaken the influence of national governments over both business and markets (1982). Federico Caffè noted in his assessment of the same phenomena:

Fifty years have proved enough to forget (or to pretend to forget) the intrinsic inability of the market to determine, with its own spontaneous forces, both an unacceptable level of employment and a less inequitable wealth and income distribution than it is in those countries calling themselves industrially advanced'. The same span of time was enough on the other hand to have to record the deep-seated disappointment about the ability of government intervention to plan development rather than barely administering a frustrating situation of *stag-flation*. Nor in times of pronounced interference by multinational corporations and dizzying movements of capital can one seriously think about or have confidence in decentralised initiatives, in activities on a human scale, in the solidarity of cooperation and self-management. More to the point would be an argument that reforges a link to the 'institutional' creativity promoted in the United States by the upheavals of the Great Depression and, in general, by the intention to prevent their recurrence.

(1990, p.160)

By the late 1980s the total commodification model had taken hold in the Eastern as well as Western European countries, spreading to areas and sectors of the economy which until then had been unaffected. The aggressive nature of this capitalism, which up to the 1970s had been limited to the commodities market, a few areas of the service sector and the private labour market, is today regaining ground as a component of a new hegemonic order postulated on the ideology of individualism, on the core position of the firm as both economic and social leader of community life, and on the ideology of the market as independent and self-reliant regulating element (Barcellona, 1990; Cantaro, 1990).

Interrelation of Equality and Efficiency

The turning point of the 1980s was marked by the dissolving of the link between equality and efficiency – the relation of economic growth to redistribution which had provided the basis for all post-war agreements and political hegemony. The virtuous circle had run its course, and many studies provide conclusive evidence of the deterioration of the condition of workers and their organizations. An accurate reconstruction of the relations between modernization and reformism in post-war Europe notes that

> There is too the collapse of a rather widespread and consolidated set of values and attitudes in economic policy that from 1945 to 1979 in Europe had been the acme of antithesis and resistance to the processes of Americanisation.
>
> Even the final step in the creation of a unified European market scheduled for 1992 looms in many ways as the completed edifice of America's vision of Europe as an interdependent network whose cornerstone was laid by the Marshall Plan. It is hard not to believe that the new development processes, which almost certainly will benefit from a further mobility of all production factors, do not also imply an extension of the market's powers and, accordingly, a restriction of government's range of intervention, which had been the essential fulcrum of reform policies for an entire historical era. At a time when everything points to a development of capitalism that runs markedly counter to the safeguarding of social needs, the reformist programme as charted in the years of the Depression and the Second World War appears increasingly destitute of credibility and efficacy.
>
> (Paggi, 1989, pp.xviii–xix)

The advent of a single European market as of 1992 and the directions imprinted on the process of European integration are fundamental features of the new situation in Europe today, which is defined by Leonardo Paggi as the realization, under the pressure

Capital Accumulation in the Last Decade 83

of 'American civilization', of the *pax americana* begun in 1945 under the Marshall Plan.

NOTES

1. For a more detailed account of Polanyi's analysis, see Polanyi, 1977, and Polanyi, 1968.

5 The Metamorphosis of the Firm: National, Multinational, Transnational

GLOBALIZATION AND THE CAPITALIST FIRM

A transformation process of the extent reported and analyzed herein can hardly not regard the first tier of the accumulation process – the capitalist firm. Research into and the debate engaging business have developed along the vertical axis of historical dimension and the horizontal axis of both comparative studies and national case-histories. Yet extending these studies along both axes has generated not a cognitive organic system but a compartmentalizing and separation of knowledge. Following in the footsteps of these disciplines by heading off along their respective trails is misleading, so it is necessary and justified to attempt a synopsis of their findings.

Let us begin with the issues related to property and then go on to those dealing with management and organization. The aim of this discussion is to document the changes that have taken place in the structure of economic power and bring to the fore their influence on the working structure of the corporation, on social class relations and on the role of the trade unions.

OWNERSHIP AND MANAGEMENT

The point of departure here is the fact that, while the economic power structure has remained unchanged, the working structure of the corporation, the relations of the social classes and the role of the unions have undergone a number of metamorphoses. Considerable effort has been expended over the last 30 years to show that the socialist bid to link ownership to efficiency was groundless. Indeed, it has been pointed out that the modern business enterprise is marked above all by the separation of the roles of management and ownership

– a critique often wielded against the prevailing trend which at the time was in favour of nationalizing or placing under government control the means of production. Lumping together ownership and management was supposedly the reason for the stagnation of the socialist economies. If we look at the prevailing trends over the last decade and apply the same analytical approach used by the proponents of this critique, their prior findings get turned upside down. For it is a well-known fact that since the 1980s, which saw the capsizing of political systems and alliances, the first measure enacted by the new bourgeois governments of these countries was privatization, which was adopted as the cornerstone of the strategy of transformation. Yet, to be coherent with one's position, the first step undertaken should have been to reform the management of the state concerns and cooperatives. So, why privatization?

All this attests to the fact that capital remains the core of capitalist power and that the functions derived presuppose ownership. It is no accident that the defeat of both real socialism and functional socialism was accompanied and followed by private capitalism's reappropriation of capital.

THE FIRM'S FUNCTIONAL STRUCTURE

The Origin of the Firm

The firm arises within a given society over the course of a historical process of economic, social, political and cultural sedimentation which constitutes the umbilical cord for both production and consumption needs (supply and demand). While distinct from the others, each firm is part of the productive fabric surrounding it. It is out of this original historical phase, that is that of the medieval workshop, that the *industrial districts* arise. The firm's activities at this stage are conducted in a context combining both the informal (family, exchange of services, uncompensated labour) and the formal (the market, commercialized relations, hired labour). The functions of production are met by local resources and labour, based on community customs and rules, and directed towards local needs.

Stage One: The Local Capitalist Firm

The key to the success of the local capitalist firm at this initial stage is the changing to its advantage of the market's rules and the commodification of the relations governing output and need fulfilment through consumption. The formal sector now comes to dominate the informal one, which becomes residual and leads to an overturning of importance and influence as roles and the division of labour become increasingly distinct.

Yet this type of firm continues to remain a traditional activity and retain its links to the milieu – the local market – from which it stemmed. There are, of course, forms of exchange (capital, labour, goods and technology) that reach beyond the given community but they are marginal and play no part in defining the roles involved. The firm's structure revolves about the capitalist entrepreneur and encompasses within its walls management, the innovations of research and development (R&D), production, distribution and finance (figure 5.1).

Stage Two: The National Capitalist Firm

This second stage, the emergence of a national capitalist firm, is the result of the long and painful formation of national markets – a process that determines the first radical split between community life and production systems. Yet the rhetoric of the national market and the nation needed to legitimize the birth of the nation-state fails to cover up the artificial nature of this extension of the national market. The national community hardly hides the fact that the enlarging of markets generates a separation between production systems and local communities. Rather than promoting the parallel growth of local markets, this extension, which in theory is supposed to produce an advantageously rich fabric of synergies, leads instead to the invasion of local markets (whose competitive edge depends largely on how strong their influence is with the political powers that be in establishing the rules of competition, standards and forms of consumption) by firms that are both internal and external to them. The formation of the national state in Great Britain and Italy is a clear-cut example of these processes.

The ideology of competition, efficiency and modernization accompanies the triumph of the national company and results in all the local communities embodied in the national market having to

Figure 5.1 The Firm's Metamorphosis

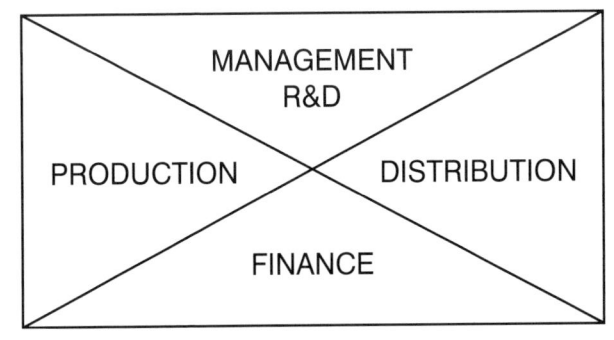

```
          MANAGEMENT
             R&D
PRODUCTION        DISTRIBUTION
            FINANCE
```
Stage 1: Firm at local level

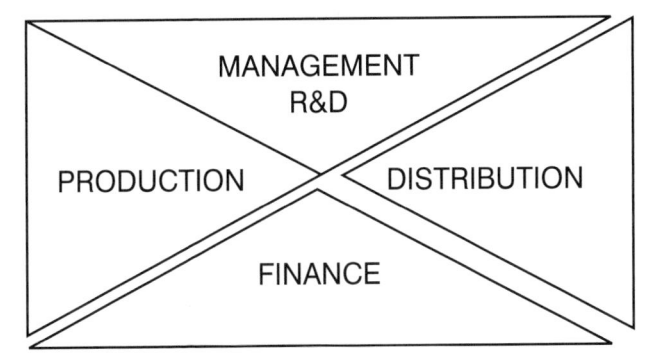

```
          MANAGEMENT
             R&D
PRODUCTION        DISTRIBUTION
            FINANCE
```
Stage 2: Firm at national and international level
Distribution and finance externalized

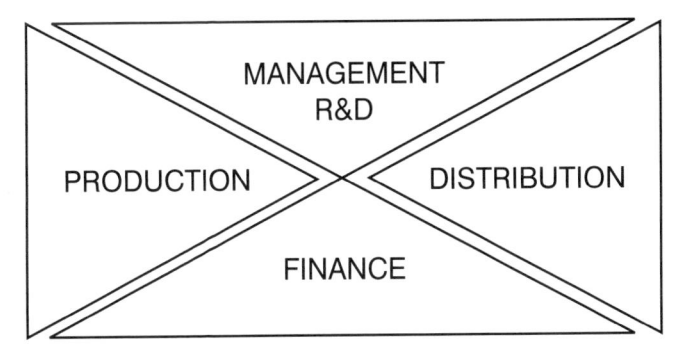

```
          MANAGEMENT
             R&D
PRODUCTION        DISTRIBUTION
            FINANCE
```
Stage 3: Transnational firm level
Production and distribution externalized

comply with the economic and institutional (and hence cultural) tenets which are held to be advanced and coincident with the dominant companies (and communities). Whence the rise to prominence of the principle that has dominated the interpretation of history since the 1500s – that might makes right. The national company develops rapidly by expanding production, distribution and consumption throughout the national market in the direction of monopolies, industrial alliances and political privileges, which just as rapidly place limits on competition. The same also holds true for the securing of the necessary resources (capital and labour). What thus remains within the national market's confines is a fiction of community that business uses to accumulate resources from all areas and to exploit consumer markets.

A national company is marked by an output prevalently geared to a domestic market and, hence, influenced by the latter's culture, customs and habits. Exports to other countries and markets in this phase do not account for a large share of total output (one-fourth to one-third) and coincide with national traits. In other words, the exports are the *surplus* produced for the domestic market and sold abroad, for example, as typical Italian, Spanish, Dutch goods. The success of national exports leads to the opening of production branches abroad, which because they become national companies of the given export market, though external to it in origin, they tend to acquire a growing independence from the parent company. The product remains the original, typically national one but begins to undergo adaptations.

This marks the rise of the multinational corporation, which is still distinguishable by its national origins, that is it is still seen as a German, Italian or Japanese company, yet to growing extent imports new customs and ways into the country of origin. This is followed by a further impulse towards a separation of production systems from the original markets and a fragmenting of both raw material sources and sales outlets. Organizationally, while management, R&D and production of the multinational remain in the hands of the parent company, distribution and the financial system are externalized. The commodification of production reaches its peak and the division of labour is reflected in the organizational forms of production (Chapter 3, figure 3.12).

Stage Three: The Transnational Corporation

This is the stage of the transnational corporation; here it is important to stress that this phase marks the definitive separation of territory, production systems, institutions and population. The TNC can no longer be distinguished by community or country of origin. Its producers and consumers can be found anywhere, and its product introduces forms of consumption and life styles modelled along class lines – of the wealthy societies – whose behaviour and consumer patterns are copied by all communities. The same holds true for production and the institutional systems accompanying it. As we shall soon see apropos of globalization, this universality is in fact quite limited and derivative of the behaviour and interests of a very small part of the world and no longer linked to a given community or country but entirely to the corporate culture of the transnational firm.

The organization of this type of corporation involves the separation of management, R&D and finance on the one hand, which now become the centre of power of this new industrial system, from production and consumption on the other, which are externalized with respect to the corporation's structure. Control of the strategic technology and capital finance sectors thus becomes the TNC's centre of gravity and tool of domination. Its sources of profit now derive from the commodification of both technology and finance capital, whereas production and distribution are forced into the background. This results in the almost complete breakdown of the institutional set-up encompassing the organization of the production systems, worker participation and social control by the state in which production plants are located (see Chapter 3, figure 3.12).

STATE AND INSTITUTIONS IN THE WEST

An initial line of inquiry verges on the history of the state and social institutions in Western societies – a topic widely discussed in numerous seminars and studies on the development of European societies. Noteworthy in these studies is their otherwise successful attempt to provide an historical and national framework to the development of the Western countries and the various institutional forms the capital–labour relationship has taken. Less convincing, and in part contradictory to the historical view taken, are the results achieved by imposing on these analyses concepts like liberalism, corporatism, democracy, which are taken as constant values and forms in relation to the seeming variable that history represents. This is not to say that every generalization or periodization of development is arbitrary, nor is it intended to discourage comparative approaches, which make up an important part of my own work. Yet it is my conviction that the level of generalization appropriate to the drawing of comparisons, especially in historically orientated approaches, should always be such as to make possible critical distinctions between the qualities of the subjects being discussed. Placing the analytical framework of an institutional development that occurred at a given time in a given country around all societies ends up forcing their development patterns into the same moulds. It carries with it the risk of defining a camel (for example the Scandinavian or Italian model) as a badly made horse (taking the German or French model as the horse). The often criticized monolinear approach to development thus rears its head in the guise of the corporate or liberal one.

The *fallacy of generalization* is frequently accompanied or followed by the *fallacy of extrapolation*. This occurs when conclusions concerning development in a given sector (information technology, labour organization), or a societal specific function (service activities) or institutional form (negotiation, organized interests) are used to define the general paradigm of society (the information society, service society, negotiated economy).

THE ENDLESS HISTORY OF CORPORATISM

From Feudal Guild to Modern Trade Unionism

The concept of corporatism is a special case of the ability to survive. It has been employed to describe almost everything, unencumbered by limits in time and space. The professional organizations of the Middle Ages were called guilds. Yet, despite the considerable changes these underwent during the formation process of national markets and capitalist industrialization, the basic concept of the guild remained intact − from the industrial system of the city-states with its guilds to the corporative trade unions of the industrial age.

Marx rightly saw in the modern syndicalist movement the

expression of new interests and ideologies, new historical organizations, the emergence of a new class and the beginning of the struggle for control of the state. The concepts of class and class struggle, which 'popes and tsars, Metternich and Guizot, the French radicals and German police vainly fought against' (Marx and Engels, 1968, p.78) were eclipsed a century later by institutionalism, which once again dusted off the concept of corporatism with an historical interpretation capable of shifting the spotlight away from events and the dramatic defeats of the great reform movements (catholic, socialist, communist) and the workers movement of the 1920s and 1930s. Capitalist society became the corporate state, the classes the social parties. The juridical fiction devised to legitimize the Fascist regimes in Europe is well known. The triangular structure of corporate power (state, capital, labour) is like the Catholic Church's mystery of the Trinity, three in one – the state is the capitalist state, the unions are the state unions and capital controls both.

Postwar Neo-Corporatism

Class conflict became very acute in Western Europe during the 1970s, and the socialization of the means of production via economic democracy was introduced into the programmes of Scandinavia's social democracies. Any interpretation of a corporative nature for this development should be considered misleading. Yet, against all odds, the ghost has reappeared.

> Corporatism can be defined as a system of interest representation in which the constituent units are organised into a limited number of singular, compulsory, non-competitive, hierarchically ordered and functionally differentiated categories recognised or licensed (if not created) by the State and granted a deliberate representational monopoly in exchange for observing certain controls on their selection of leaders and articulation of demands and support.
> (Schmitter, 1979, pp.13–15)

By the late 1970s this approach encountered increasing difficulties because of the new liberal-conservative wave. The dominant theoretical view was aimed at rehabilitating concepts of pluralism, democracy and the market that were even older and more compromised than corporatism. The process of the Americanization of

European society even took hold of the social sciences, resulting in the concept of democracy being changed from a set of values typical of European culture to one of procedures.

It was in this context that the need resurfaced to rethink the interrelations of the economy, policy and institutions so as to define the new trends through new analyses. While many scholars prefer to characterise this situation as disorganized capitalism, a few see in it the further development of a capitalism consonant with the globalization of the world's economy in the guise of 'triadic capitalism' (Petrella, 1989; Parboni, 1988), which has been brought about by the structural and market changes of the meso-economies and meso-institutions (Holland, 1987a; Holland, 1987b; Parboni, 1988; Amoroso, 1994, pp.189–214). Once again, with the aid of the new prefixes, the concept of corporatism rears its head.

Postwar neo-corporatism is defined as meso-corporatism, meaning the new forms of sector integration between the state and interest groups; micro-corporatism means the same relations within the corporation. Corporatism's existence requires distinct agents – the state, the trade unions and the capitalists. If we take pre-fascist society as corporative, we cannot then define Fascism as corporative because these agents are missing. If we take Fascism as corporative, assuming the mere juridical form as an expression of reality, we cannot apply this concept to postwar Italy since it would presuppose an arbitrary underestimate of its labour movement, of the significance of its new democratic institutions and of its constitution.

The current situation, which is marked by globalization, is witnessing the success of international capital in the economy within the Triad's strong meso-regions and in politics with the process of a new worldwide colonization. Again, the political institutions and the trade unions either cannot achieve these levels or are shadows of the preceding forms. Reducing this new situation to mere class struggle would be an over-simplification; interpreting it as an enlarging form of democracy is false; and forcing it into the straitjacket of corporatism is simple nonsense.

INTEREST GROUPS AND POLITICAL EXCHANGE

Another line of inquiry has taken a more marked institutional and organizational approach. It deals with interest groups as political exchange (Lehmbruch, 1979) and/or forms of organization (Offe and Wiesenthal, 1980; Schmitter and Streeck, 1981) in capitalist societies and seeks to explain the asymmetry between labour and capital in political negotiation and collective bargaining. The scholars involved in these studies stress that income policies have always attempted to influence and control labour but not capital gains. Similarly, collective bargaining has never questioned the right of capital to direct and organize labour.

It would only be reasonable to expect that so radical a view of the history of social classes and political organisations in Western societies – radical because it neglects the multi-directional efforts mounted over many decades by the Keynesians and labour organizations – end up by drawing just as radical conclusions about the real roots of exploitation and power in capitalist societies. Yet, contrary to common sense, these same scholars seek to explain the similarities and differences by focusing on the organizational strength of the two main sides or parties involved and on their strategies, thereby turning it into an issue of political science and organizational theory.

This only serves to shift attention from all the preceding and current attempts to alter the division of roles in labour relations, that is through the proposals for economic democracy advocated by workers' organizations during the 1970s and the growing exclusion of the former from the political negotiation process successfully pursued by entrepreneurs in the 1980s. The reasons for the present collapse of a broad range of economic and social experiments begun in the 1920s (the welfare states in the West and the planned economies in the East) call for inquiries that in range and depth go well beyond the institutional, juridical and organizational aspects.

FLEXIBLE SPECIALIZATION AS NEW PARADIGM

Those scholars seeking to develop the relatively new concepts of post-Fordism and flexible specialization have insisted on attempting to link entrepreneurial strategies and industrial relations to structural changes (Boyer, 1987; Sabel, 1982; Jessop, 1990). Conceptually, post-Fordism has created a lot of problems for a number of these theorists. The latter begin by depicting Fordism as a costly and inflexible caricature of a production system based on the waste of resources and manned by a passively integrated work force – a Fordism that in fact never historically existed. Post-Fordism is then defined as the opposite to the Fordism so depicted, that is the opposite of something that never existed.

The alternative is to address the critique to the economic system's inefficiency resulting from the lack of both real markets and capitalism's social efficiency, just as economists had done long ago. Yet this is the exact opposite of what post-Fordism represents and seeks to achieve. Let us take a more detailed look at the analytical bases of these differing forms of industrial organization.

Fordism can be summed up in general terms as

i) mass production and consumption;
ii) a high degree of standardization;
iii) the use of new technology in organizing the workplace, that is combining semi-skilled labour and the Taylor system with assembly-line technology; and
iv) Keynesian economic policies and market regulation.

Post-Fordism can be defined as

i) small firms with small-scale, high-quality output;
ii) product differentiation and flexibility of consumption forms;
iii) different combination of process innovation and product innovation, with the acceleration of the latter;
iv) labour organization based on flexible machines capable of combining microelectronics and communications technologies with flexible, multi-skilled workers; and
v) deregulation and targeting of wealthy markets.

The exponents of post-Fordism have expended a great deal of time and effort in portraying it as an alternative form of production. Yet, despite the spate of studies orchestrated and generously funded almost everywhere (from Italy to Africa and India), all the rhetoric has been unable to overcome the dearth of empirical demonstration. Post-Fordism turns out to be nothing other than the adaptation of Fordism to new technology and new market and political conditions.[2] The organizational changes of post-Fordism are not in fact very impressive. Of greater impact are the results attained by the new entrepreneurial strategies in destabilizing the welfare societies and the workers' movements in them. Yet the explanation for the success is to be found not in post-Fordism but

The Metamorphosis of the Firm 95

in the studies of the globalization of the economy and technology. The situation generated by new technology and growing international competition is destabilizing the old social contract that propped up the entire system of industrial relations. The new managerial criteria spawned by the demand for flexibility in production are absorbing the prior conflict between labour and capital in a common corporate strategy. The conflict culture is being replaced by the corporate culture, and the entire system of industrial relations is changing because of its growing immaturity.

The new business strategies seem to be successful in integrating the social parties at a higher level, thereby making the unions obsolete while keeping the power relationships unchanged. In this analysis the capitalist-entrepreneur's erstwhile dream of a classless society becomes the current one of the scientist (something we have already heard), and what is now the result of favourable conditions for capitalism and capitalists is portrayed as the realization of an age-old aspiration of humanity.

The enthusiasm of scholars like Benjamin Coriat for the Japanese model of flexibility (1991, p.185) does not seem to suffer in the least from the dissolving of the workers' movement and its total subordination to business strategies. Indeed, Coriat holds that transferring the Japanese approach to Europe would result in a broader-based democracy. These authors seem to be confusing reality with their own wishful thinking (or, better, the wishful thinking of capitalists)[3] as they are reducing the theory of society to that of organization and mistaking organizational forms for those of power.

Instead, the scientific question at issue here is

... devising an analysis capable of showing, despite the marked intervening structural changes, if and how a separation between those who hold the levers of power controlling the production process and those who do the actual work is being perpetuated and whether this still falls within the forms of capitalist relations between capital and social labour (with the ensuing reproduction in new forms of exploitation and alienation).
(Barcellona, 1990, p.14)

The forms of organization and of power, it seems to me, should be considered separately as their respective analyses lead to different results. Organization and division of labour make it possible to describe Taylorism, Fordism and flexible specialization as distinct production systems, whereas the theory of power provides an altogether different view of things in that such a distinction disappears. The objective of business strategies is to control labour. A Taylorist system achieves this by controlling the workers themselves – *the one best way* and a Fordist one by controlling both workers and technology (the assembly line). Flexible specialization appears able to accomplish this not only throughout production and distribution but even during leisure time by focusing solely on the control of technology and its full integration into the firm's organization. What distinguishes post-Fordism from these other systems is mainly its greater efficiency of labour control by means never seen before. Flexibility and decentralization in the form of organization are accompanied by a greater concentration of economic power in entrepreneurial strategies.

Standing behind all of this is the 'new relationship of science and capital'.

The key new fact in the current age is that capitalism needs to exert its control immediately not over the work force but over technological expertise. It is this new alliance between capital and know-how that has led, in appearance at least, to the removal of all external constraints to the production and reproduction capabilities of the capitalist model. Governing the production process is a matter no longer of managing the factory that turns out certain goods but, mainly, of managing the technical know-how that makes possible the 'linkings' of specifically determined technical applications to a given type of production (eg. automobiles, computer chips). In other words, the reflexiveness of technical know-how determines *capital's becoming autonomous from the immediate link to the individual means of production* – the given plant becomes 'relatively' indifferent for capital's enhancement. In short, capital becomes more abstract than it was even in industrial production because it is 'freer' from the territorial constraints of installation, the hiring of a given labour force and so forth.

(Barcellona, 1990, p.13)

INDUSTRIAL RELATIONS IN THE 1980s

There has been a vigorous resurgence over the last 15 years of studies on industrial relations. It should be acknowledged that a great deal of effort has been expended in this field of research to correlate the old school of thought dealing with labour relations and the labour marketplace to studies on the structural changes in the economy and policy, as well as to linking more closely theory building and empirical data.

Noteworthy in this connection for its methodological cogency and coverage of eleven Western European countries is the research project coordinated by Guido Baglioni and published in the early 1990s (Baglioni and Crouch, 1990). This study concludes that the weakening effectiveness of the collective bargaining process and of the trade unions themselves throughout the 1980s is to be seen as a return to the normalcy for industrial relations after the golden age from 1950–60 and the exceptional season between 1968 and 1975. While this is true if we look back upon the postwar period, it is too limited if we look ahead. Despite the interesting material presented and the highlighting of newly emerging phenomena, the study's theoretical framework remains grounded in crisis. The growing trends towards globalization, production decentralization and flexibility in the division of labour and employment between sectors and regions are all viewed from the theoretical underpinnings of crisis culture and national welfare systems. Thus, while Baglioni's analysis explains several major trends of the past, it is incapable of formulating forecasts that do not adumbrate those past experiences.

A similar line of inquiry, though focusing specifically on the institutions engaged in social dialogue and mediation, is found in the comparative studies of the state, the social parties and institutional seats of consultation in the European Communities (CNEL, 1991). The advent of the Domestic European Market in 1992 also stimulated inquiries into the Community's social dimension and its implications for entrepreneurial and union strategies (Amoroso, 1990). These studies of the nature of social representation in national and international institutions raised two key issues: the legitimacy of the current system and the legitimacy of the strategies employed by entrepreneurs and worker organizations.

The crisis of the current system of consultation and social mediation in all countries stems from two factors, an external and an internal one. The external is the formation of meso-institutions, that is marked concentrations of power, that are sweeping aside democratic institutions and the processes of consultation and social mediation. All the facets of social life that these institutions are supposed to regulate are increasingly coming under the control of lobbies and vested interest groups, which are making decisions that are then pushed through the democratic processes. The internal factor is the reaction of labour and management to these developments. Instead of reaffirming their legitimacy as historical organizations of social representation in which special and public interests converge, they increasingly identify themselves as interest groups, thereby bringing about the inevitable result of their own historical decline. Meanwhile, the demand for new historical class representation and social needs remains unresolved (Amoroso, 1992).

CORPORATE STRATEGIES IN THE 1990s: AN ALTERNATIVE OUTLOOK

Early in the decade I wrote that forecasting developments in entrepreneurial strategies for the 1990s should begin with an analysis of the major structural changes that had taken place in the industrialized economies throughout the 1980s. This rather tame observation tended to reduce the arbitrariness of the academic exercises with which many scholars continued to propound models of industrial relations and future scenarios as options to choose from freely on the basis of abstract criteria of efficiency and democracy. This while others kept advocating the need for unions and management to make decisions with an eye to a world that was either imaginary or, in any case, threatened by extinction.

The globalization of the economy and the development of new technologies have generated the structures of triadic capitalism – the transnational corporations in production and the Americanization of consumption and cultural patterns. The changes taking place in the system of industrial relations stem from the new corporate strategies that tend towards the destabilization of the existing situation rather than towards the regeneration of utopian pluralism and free-market conditions that have in fact never existed. Though the goal of these strategies is more limited and concrete than in the past, it is far more important as it aims to create a new form of capitalist market and new production systems.

The impact of business strategies can best be studied at the level of the firm since the national systems of industrial relations are in a state of collapse. All recent attempts to reformulate a European system of industrial relations are merely elements of the fallacy of extrapolation mentioned above. What makes the current situation different is the end of the relative autonomy of the system of industrial relations and its incorporation in the production system. Entrepreneurial strategy absorbs industrial relations in a new corporate culture by placing the firm at the centre of the economic, social and political system. It is evident that the success – undeniable at the moment – of this approach is bound to spell the loss of 50 years of constructive effort to create institutions capable of governing the European welfare state.

The general trend towards a global integration of industrial societies in the system of the transnational corporation travels different routes in different countries due to differing points of departure. We are experiencing situations marked by prolonged crises and pronounced destabilizations and others marked by transitions without conflict. This process is having a strong impact in the Scandinavian countries, affecting both the industrial system and the overall welfare system. This is the result of both the central position that labour organizations have occupied in some countries in the historical building process of the modern welfare state (Scandinavia) and the pronounced integration between production systems and welfare systems.

During the preceding phase which saw the rise of the national welfare states, the entrepreneurs had always viewed the system of industrial relations as a superstructure to be kept entirely separate from the production system. This view was reflected in the agreements between the unions and management which sanctioned the exclusive right of employers to direct and organise the production process. Economists attempted at the time to determine how industrial relations affected production by taking the two systems as relatively independent of one another.

Corporate strategies in the current stage are pursuing the merger of the two systems in a new production model. The core of this new system is supposed to be the company and the specific features of its nature are to be found in the concept of corporate culture. Here solidarity with other workers and citizens (the culture of the welfare state) is replaced by loyalty to and collaboration with the firm. New technology and flexibility are the key words for fully subordinating workers to employers. So radical a change in entrepreneurial strategy has implications for the entire system of industrial relations. To believe that one can become a part of this process while passively reciting the demands for economic democracy and industrial democracy the labour movement had rallied round and pressed for in the preceding stage and context means taking steps to legitimize these entrepreneurial strategies and, simultaneously, to obfuscate their eventual objectives.

The Changing Concept of Participation

A typical example of such obfuscating is the metamorphosis the concept participation has undergone. The term was originally conceived by labour as a tool that was supposed to limit the unconditional power entrepreneurs and capitalists wielded in making decisions about investment and labour organization. Participation has since become the integration of workers and their organizations into the chain of capitalist production and organization.

A strong labour movement and union participation in the postwar years had a considerable impact despite the second thoughts, criticism and dark clouds that could have gathered over the horizon. But to talk about participation in the bargaining context of the 1980s and 1990s – a period which has evinced the weakness of the labour movement – means mistaking the 'shadow of participation for real power' (Caffè, 1977), and entrusting to institutional mechanisms conceived for wholly different purposes and roles the safeguarding of that bond of solidarity which can only be ensured by the strength of union organisations and the labour movement.[4] Some of the major changes are discussed below.

The Corporate Union

Employers are pursuing the goal of establishing an in-house factory or corporate union, the result being that national trade unions and union federations are increasingly losing strength and legitimacy. The strength that derives from belonging to a co-ordinated and centralized structure disappears. Though taking every precaution dictated by the mass of empirical data gathered together in the volume cited *supra*, Guido Baglioni noted in the late 1980s:

> If there is no country in which an employer strategy of outright attack against labour unions prevails, it is also true at the same time that employers are attracted to methods of personnel management that represent, in terms of outlook or in terms of practices, a prospective alternative to the trade union method.
>
> (Baglioni and Crouch, 1990)

Furthermore,

> This powerful tendency entails changes in the behaviour of employers in the handling of industrial relations, compared with the past. The most important of these is the very widespread diminution of the role played by central organisations in favour of more restricted associations or individual company management.
> (Ibid., p.11)

Today this trend is unmistakable regardless of the situation in a given country.

Individual and Corporate Systems of Contract Negotiations

The empirical data in the study edited by Baglioni and Crouch cited above indicate that employers are pursuing a second level in destabilizing industrial relations. This is shown by the 'emerging dichotomy between protected and unprotected workers, between those with job security and the precarious'; by an unemployment that 'structurally weakens the labour force and objectively sharpens competition among working people when economic and wage policy must be made'; by the 'decline of the industrial work force and of blue-collar employment' that 'directly strikes at the historical 'heart' of the labour movement and the trade union outlook'; by 'the growth of employment outside industry' that 'normally generates types of workers further removed from the outlook and the values of the labour movement, fosters a more self-interested, instrumental attitude to unions, and by its composition creates a workforce market by strong divergence of interest'; by the 'segmentation, differentiation and the diversification of occupational statuses which complicate the formation and management of representative structures and make the goal of a generalised defence of the interests and the rights of working people harder to achieve'. (Baglioni and Crouch, 1990, p.9)

The Demand for Flexibility in Labour Organization, in Its Geographic Distribution and in Its Training System

The flexibility demanded by employers takes on a general and strategic significance in the new entrepreneurial strategies ('the employers' new frontier'). (Baglioni and Crouch, 1990, p.11)

Its introduction underscores that 'the economy is the engine of this transformation and all social forces are to be redirected towards this goal'. In a general trend of increasing concentration of power, other forms of organization, particularly among labour forces, will necessarily be disassembled and reshaped. The concept of flexible specialization has become the ideology of the new technocracy, which faces the difficult task of convincing others to abandon democracy and solidarity by creating the messianic expectation of a second industrial divide'. (Amoroso, 1990, pp.485-6)

Corporate Profit-Sharing Plans

The union response to the employer strategies of the 1970s was to challenge the latter's exclusive right to 'direct and organise production' and to demand the socialization of investments (a deliberate attempt to go beyond functional socialism). These demands formed the core of the economic democracy proposal introduced into the platform of the labour movement in countries like Denmark and Sweden (Amoroso, 1980).

The policy reasons behind these demands resided in the acknowledged difficulty the social-democratic governments of these countries had in dealing with the economic crisis and the power of the multinational corporations, without their being able to exert control over investment decision-making. While an orchestrated control of production involving workers and their organisations in management decision-making processes would have made it possible to cope with the changes to the system of industrial relations that the 1980s were to bring about, such an approach was incompatible with triadic capitalism's corporate strategies. Management successfully countered this purely political proposal by deflecting it onto the technical and economic terrain, that is making it an issue of fund managing through financial institutions (pension and other funds) and reducing everything to a formula of profit-sharing plans destitute of any decision-making power.

FROM FUNCTIONAL SOCIALISM TO FUNCTIONAL CAPITALISM

Depending on the country, these changes take on varying forms, which are linked to each one's historical traditions. The formula in

Italy is the famous leopard-spot solution, that is a re-arranging of spots that leaves everything in terms of power as it was before. The standard formula in the Scandinavian countries is the voiding of institutional tasks, that is the so-called salami tactic of cutting off one slice at a time. Functional socialism, the social-democratic strategy of the Scandinavian countries, is based on the idea of simply repeating with capitalism what they had done with their monarchies. In other words, the solution was to be sought not in the abolition of capitalism by forced expropriations but in altering its *modus operandi* by gradually stripping it of the prerogatives that the possession of capital conferred upon it. This optimistic vision of transition (worked out in the early 1970s) envisaged for the survival of capitalism in formal role in a play scripted and staged elsewhere, just as the monarchies had survived. It is my contention that corporations are implementing, in Scandinavia as elsewhere, the strategy of functional capitalism, whereby it is the labour unions that increasingly resemble the old monarchies – powerless figureheads – which are compelled to legitimize decisions and interests differing from those of their members.

NOTES

1. See, among others, the proceedings of the International Conference on 'Le organizzazioni di interesse nella democrazia: Prospettive in oriente e occidente', Cortona, Italy, organised by the Centro di Scienze Politiche, Fondazione Giacomo Feltrinelli, Milan, 29–31 May 1990; and Crouch, 1990.
2. Among the major exponents mention should be made of Sabel and Piore, 1984; Sabel and Zeitlin, 1982.
3. It is surprising that this approach seems to be gaining credibility among scholars with an in-depth knowledge of current development – a knowledge that should enable them to question it. Cf. A.J.M. Roobeek, 1991.
4. Two recent contributions that take an optimistic view of this issue are Baglioni, 1995, and Carrieri, 1995. Their 'master's voice' is expressed with the clarity and forcefulness of a realism that power alone can voice in a series of international reports: United Nations, 1994; World Bank, 1995; OECD, 1995.

6 Globalization and European Integration: Eurocentrism and Westernization

PREAMBLE

The effects of globalization on the process of European integration can be assayed in relation to both the limits it has placed on this process since 1989, exacerbating the existing regional and social disparities within the EU, and the ongoing attempts to force Europe's development into the Eurocentric strait-jacket, thereby turning it into a tame instrument of triadization of the world's economy. The effects on Europe are detailed in two surveys: one dealing only with the member-states of the European Union and the other with the overall picture of continental Europe and its outlying regions (to north, south and east).

The Members of the European Union

The first inquiry deals with the areas of the EU qualifying for the Union's regional assistance programmes since 1994. The backward regions (Objective 1) and those in industrial decline (Objective 2) include half of Italy, over two-thirds of Spain, all of Greece and vast peripheral areas in northern Europe (European Commission, 1994, p.18). The analysis strides the two post-war phenomena discussed *supra*, that is it highlights the legacy of *dualism* in Europe's geography and the advancing processes of *marginalization* in the old (backward) and new (industrial decline) areas. The welfare policies adopted for the backward areas by the member states and the regional EU subsidy measures have had little impact on both spurring endogenous development processes to overcome dualism and on facilitating the entry of the backward areas in the competition for rich markets to prevent marginalizaton.

Several studies in the 1980s announced the end of traditional disparities, such as the North–South divide in Italy, and envisaged their replacement by new forms of development (like the leopard-spot approach) and industrialization through flexible specialization, by networking territorial structures and by industrial districts planned as turn-key production systems which the regional economists then at the helm imagined they could build everywhere. It seemed, in short, that overcoming underdevelopment was merely a matter of information and freely choosing among tested models.

Similarly, dualism was to be extirpated by relying mainly on government measures (public-sector investments and income redistribution) and on the potential renaissance of entrepreneurial resources and local labour pools, while marginalization was to be obviated by relying on the spontaneous developments of the marketplace and large-scale public works projects in the hope that the surging growth of the rich markets would also ignite, thanks to new forms of decentralized production, local economies. Yet financing the growth of incomes in the rich markets and the investments in large-scale public works in actual fact drained the resources available to the consumer and investment sectors.

Italy is a good case in point. It witnessed in the space of a few months the end of the *Cassa per il Mezzogiorno* (the Development Fund for the South) and the public-sector companies (through privatization) and the beginning of a drastic policy of structural adjustment along the lines laid down by the International Monetary Fund – a recipe that has already led to the undoing of a number of Mediterranean countries like Algeria and Egypt. Leonardo Paggi's view cited *supra* about European development's being subordinated to the integration models of the *pax americana* foresaw the policies of globalization and destabilization of national states and welfare systems – policies whose main conduit is the Maastricht Treaty and the convergence standards and criteria adopted in it.

The study (see figure 6.1) which outlines the scenarios for European development stem from a series of surveys covering the broader territorial horizon of Greater Europe. The groundwork data, as well as the historical patterns, were taken from a French study dating to the late 1980s that combined more than 20 competition indicators. The findings show that European growth is being concentrated along an arc (the European banana) spanning London and Genoa via the tangents Amsterdam, Brussels, Cologne, Frankfurt, Strasbourg, Munich, Bern and Milan. The reinforcing of this integration process as set forth in the Maastricht Treaty, that is with a view to Europe's competing for the overall leadership within the Triad, comes

Figure 6.1 Traditional Heartlands and Growth Regions of the Community

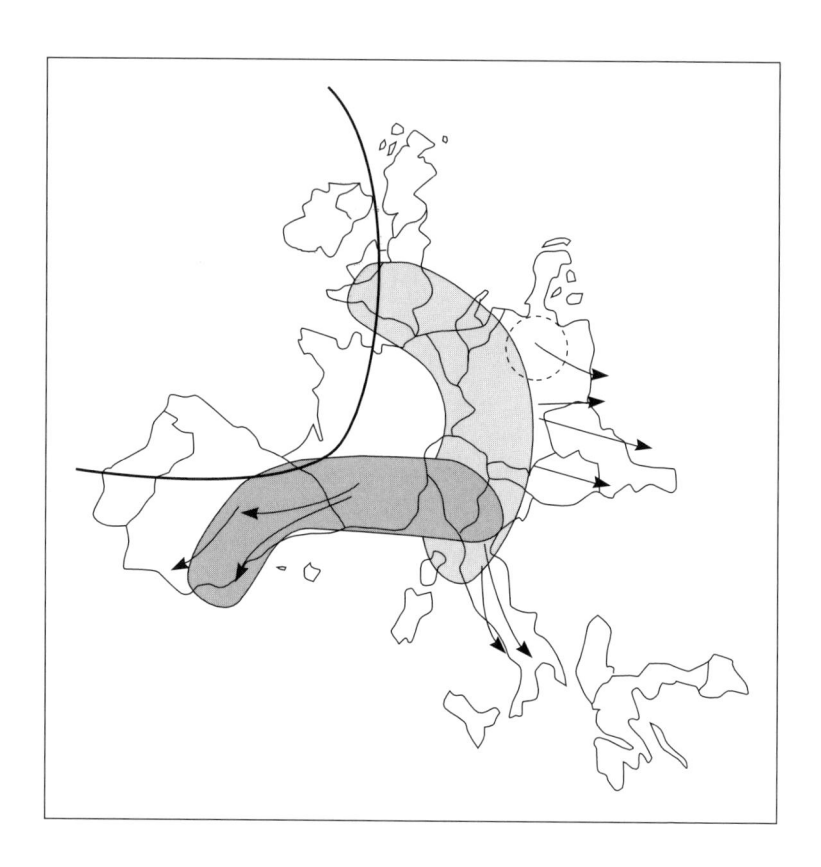

Source: CEC.

at a price – the growing marginalization of three-quarters of Europe's larger regions (the Baltic, Mediterranean, Danubian). (Datar, 1989; CENSIS, 1991; European Commission, 1994)

European Studies of the Triadic Approach

A number of studies by European scholars hold the 'triadic approach to be the least efficient way to use both the opportunities offered by science and technology and resources on a worldwide-scale' (Petrella, 1989, p.405). Riccardo Petrella points out that the triadic model does not benefit Europe because 'it compels industrialists, researchers, politicians and consumers to give priority' to technological options that 'will augment competition between firms, leading in many cases to a greater industrial concentration and oligopolies in Europe'. Nor is the triadic approach in the best interests of Europe because it might destroy 'the basis of Europe's social contract' (Petrella, 1989, p.406), although Petrella does acknowledge that it is the most widely shared approach. The support it enjoys from the United States, Japan and Western Europe is a sign of opportunistic and utilitarian short-sightedness. This view is supported by numerous studies documenting how the EU, through its policies in southern Europe and the Mediterranean Region, is moving in this direction at the urging of a large number of member states. This is also the backdrop to the numerous and frequent appeals spelling out the necessity to opt for Europe and the West, to remain in the global marketplace and so forth.

STUDIES OF MARGINALIZATION

A study of marginalization's impact as generated by globalization on Europe's large regions (the Baltic, Mediterranean, Danubian) corroborates the trends reported above. The quantitative factors were measured using economic and demographic indicators and the qualitative, which are more closely linked to the dynamics of the development process, concern science and technology.[1]

The Quantitative Factors of Marginalization

Demographic Growth
One key indicator in the analysis of migrations, the labour market, education and living standards is the *demographic curve*. Population growth in Europe's meso-regions exhibits a marked asymmetry between North and South. With respect to the balanced growth in the EU and the Baltic States, all the countries of the southern and southeastern Mediterranean Basin (except the Balkans) have a growth rate ranging from 2.3–3.6 per cent. The projections up to the year 2020 indicate a decline in the EU from 320 to 310 million inhabitants but a surge in the Mediterranean countries from 200 to 500 million people.

The difference in life expectancy between the North and Mediterranean South is about ten years, the rate of infant mortality in the latter is 40 per thousand and that of illiteracy is over 40 per cent. The Baltic Region is closer to the European Union, although its population is skewed by gender and age towards women and towards the young in its eastern part. The Balkans, excluding Albania, have a demographic curve similar to the Baltic Region and the EU, although demographically they are more homogeneous and economically split along an East-West divide. This is why the Baltic and Mediterranean seas are key boundary lines that are being placed under intense migratory pressure – the former because of differences in demographic potential and the latter because of a better standard of living.

An analysis of this kind is useful as it helps to define the type of economic intervention needed to devise production systems capable of creating employment and meeting the demands of the respective populations. An initial preliminary finding indicates that the rates of economic growth are higher than those recorded to date, despite the fact that we are dealing with situations exhibiting considerably exacerbated imbalances and the ensuing tensions they induce.

Distribution of GNP and the Employment Structure
Per-capita GNP and the employment structure affect the distribution of wealth. The distribution of per-capita GNP in the three meso-regions traces a new line of demarcation running south-west to north-east. It is an east-bulging convex arc exhibiting similar asymmetries between the northern and southern shores of the Mediterranean and the western and eastern ones of the Baltic Sea. With the exceptions of Libya and Israel, the annual per-capita income of the countries on the southern and south-eastern rim of the Mediterranean is about US$2500. This is in clear contrast with the higher figures for the EU and the Baltic Region. Although Poland and the Baltic Republics on the south-eastern shore of the Baltic Sea yearly earn about US$6000 less than the Nordic countries and Germany, no European country has a per-capita income of less than US$4900 except for the former Yugoslavia (US$2920) and Albania and Portugal ($US4250). While an improvement in these ratios among the various countries was recorded from 1960 to 1973, there have subsequently been no changes. A marked difference in the values of GNP as the indicator of living and consumption

standards, despite all the precautions taken in the use of the indexing parameters, is undeniable. The territorial imbalance between the concentration of wealth and population distribution which emerges from a comparison of the population and income data needs no further comment.

Examining the make-up of the production systems and the breakdown by share of GNP and employment indicates the importance of agriculture in all the peripheral areas with respect to the centre of the European Union. Just how important it is is shown by the fact that employment in the farm sector is over 20 per cent in most of the southern and eastern countries of Greater Europe, although it even evinces peaks of 25–50 per cent in such high demographic-density countries as Poland, Turkey, Egypt, Morocco and Tunisia (Gomez y Paloma, 1992).

These studies also highlight Europe's dependence on sources of energy and raw materials owned by Libya, Algeria, Morocco and Egypt on the Mediterranean's southern rim and by Norway and Denmark on the Baltic. Evident, too, is the unquestioned supremacy of the EU's centre (Germany) in output and export in the key manufacturing sectors, followed by Finland and Sweden; the only Mediterranean country with a positive profile in manufacturing is Turkey.

The Qualitative Factors of Marginalization

New features of structural dependence and marginalization that reinforce existing asymmetries can be derived from indicators reflecting the position of areas and countries *vis-à-vis* quality factors of development. The latter can be inferred from indicators tied to science and technology (educational and training systems, research facilities, licenses and patents, research and development outlays); to industrial inputs concerning the share of capital and technology in output, to the geographic range of the major multinational corporations and their foreign headquarters; to the extent of mechanization in agriculture and to the agro-food normalized balance.

Causes of Economic Marginalization
Often cited among the main causes of economic marginalization is the lagging ability of countries to innovate production systems and products so as better to meet internal demand and to play a bigger role in the processes of internationalization. It is a known fact that

in many economies technological innovation results from the cumulative effects of a large number of changes in technology rather than from radical discoveries. Several parameters concerning the ability to master technology indicate, in relation to higher education, that the level is high in the EU and the Baltic countries, excepting Finland, and that in Portugal and Poland it is about the same as that in the non-EU countries of the Mediterranean.

Measuring the distribution of technology output by the number of research facilities and patents shows a marked concentration of the former in the EU along the banana's arc. While the Baltic, Scandinavian countries and Poland exhibit the same capacities, the three Baltic Republics evince a lower science and technology (S&T) level. The Mediterranean Basin shows a strong asymmetry between North and South, there being but very few research facilities in the south and south-east except for Turkey, Israel and Egypt. The highest concentration of the number of patents is found in Great Britain, Germany, France, Italy and the Netherlands. A non-aggregate distribution within individual countries would indicate, for example, that the highest patent concentration in Italy is in the north, while Sweden alone in the Baltic Region has an S&T output comparable to the EU's centre.

The picture in the Mediterranean differs from that in the Baltic. While there is a marked capacity for technology output in France (followed by Italy), Spain, Portugal and Greece lag far behind. The countries on the southern and southeastern rim, with the sole exception of Israel, exhibit a very low level of technology output because of scarce technological infrastructures. Their position, however, suffers from an underestimate of the leeway for innovation and research that derives from the criteria used by the international survey organizations because these countries' efforts in the innovation of technologies appropriate to traditional production systems are not taken into account.

The Agro-Food Trade Balance
The agro-food balance of trade shows that the Baltic countries (excluding those of the former Soviet Union) enjoy a privileged position, that France and the Netherlands are the leaders in the European Union, and that the situation worsens as one goes further south. The Mediterranean region, excepting France and Turkey, is running a marked deficit, and throughout nearly the entire south and southeast of the Basin the normalized balance of food trade is

between −100 and −50. The data for farm industrialization (for example, tractor number, energy inputs) corroborate these asymmetries.

Research & Development and Education
The standing of Research & Development (R&D) and education indicate that while there is a high level of marginalization in Greater Europe's south and south-east, there is a marked concentration of both along the Rhine Valley. An exemplary case in the allocation of R&D outlays between North and South is Italy: only eight per cent of total government and a mere five per cent of private R&D expenditures are earmarked for the South.

The Main Asymmetries
The major asymmetries between countries, areas and regions, as well as the process concentrating economic power at the centre of the European Union, are confirmed by the data reported and discussed previously. Marginalization is particularly pronounced in the Mediterranean areas. Yet the differences between and within areas and regions do not always run along a North–South or East–West axis. This holds true both for the countries of southern Europe on the northern rim of the Mediterranean and those on its southern rim. The pronounced differentiation in the extent of marginalization being witnessed today in Italy and Spain is a result of the fact that several of the regions in each country which are most closely linked to the rich markets of the centre are becoming detached from the rest of the country while the other regions are undergoing a marked economic decline. The differences in marginalization among the countries on the Mediterranean's southern shore are due to the various ties that some have maintained with their former colonizers and with the EU's centre. These differences are important because they can reinforce or weaken both the ongoing processes of regional integration in these areas and their overall position within the world's economy.

MARGINALIZATION'S IMPACT ON PRODUCTION SYSTEMS

The impact of marginalization on the Triad's output has been thoroughly discussed, analyzed and frequently used to spin the myth of a new development model based on the three essential tenets of innovation, flexibility and competition. This mystification originated and evolved during the 1970s and 1980s, when what was being explained as decentralization and polycentric development was in fact an industrial spill-over of a few large corporations and a disorganized expansion of industrial activities. It is interesting to note how the leading exponents of industrial districts and local and regional models of industrialization so expertly mistook a process of increasing dependence and marginalization for a process of autonomy and endogenous development. Similarly, the marked concentration of the power represented by high technology was viewed as a golden opportunity for the furthering of democracy and enhancing participation.

Participation in International Trade

A study of the impact of globalization on the Triad's peripheral areas and of its ensuing distortion on output has instead been neglected. Specialization in Greater Europe by the late 1980s can be elucidated by looking at the participation of countries and areas in international trade. About 50 per cent of German and French and 40 per cent of British trade takes place within Greater Europe. Orbiting this core are Italy, Spain, the Netherlands and Denmark, which have an active balance of trade within this sphere but one that is based on a lower technology level. The trade flows within the EU indicate that these relations take place mainly among member countries (figure 6.2).

Trade relations with the peripheral regions are bilateral and limited to natural resources and low-technology products. Marked distortions have arisen within each of Europe's three meso-regions, and developments subsequent to 1989 have reinforced existing trends.

The Baltic Meso-Region

While the Baltic Region evinces a marked polarization towards Germany, its most important market, the trade links between the Nordic countries on the one hand and the Baltic States and Poland on the other remain weak. In addition, the end of the Cold War has seen the Baltic Republics and Finland distance themselves from the former Soviet market, thereby augmenting the economic precariousness of the latter. This new situation might turn out to be either the start of greater meso-regional cooperation in the Baltic,

Globalization and European Integration

Figure 6.2 Trade Among EU Countries

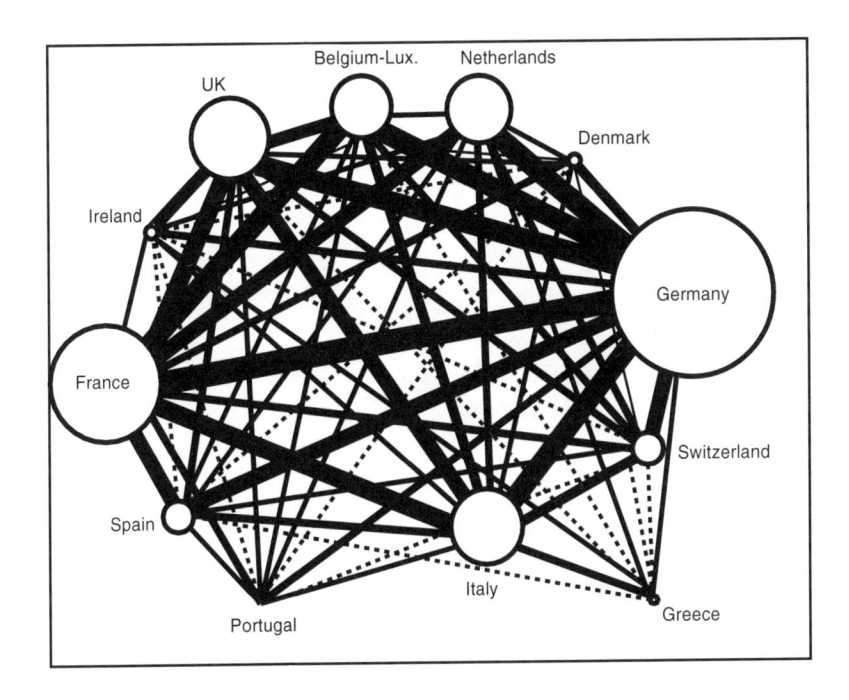

Source: B. Amoroso, S. Gomez y Paloma, D. Infante and N. Perrone, *Marginalisation, Specialisation and Cooperation in the Baltic and Mediterranean Regions, Synthesis Report*, Monitor-Fast (Brussels, 1993) p.36.

which would act as an East–West stabilizer in Greater Europe, or the harbinger of continued polarization towards the German market, which would lead to destabilizing effects both in the Baltic mesoregion and in the relations between the EU and Russia (figure 6.3).

The Mediterranean Meso-Region

The Mediterranean Region evinces even more marked forms of polarization (figure 6.4). The interregional trade spanning both sides and extending to the eastern end of the Basin is vertical in nature, although it is heavily influenced by the flows from France, Italy and, to a lesser extent, Spain. The trade between North Africa's Algeria, Egypt, Morocco and Libya and Europe's France and Italy

Figure 6.3 Trade Relations Among the Baltic Countries

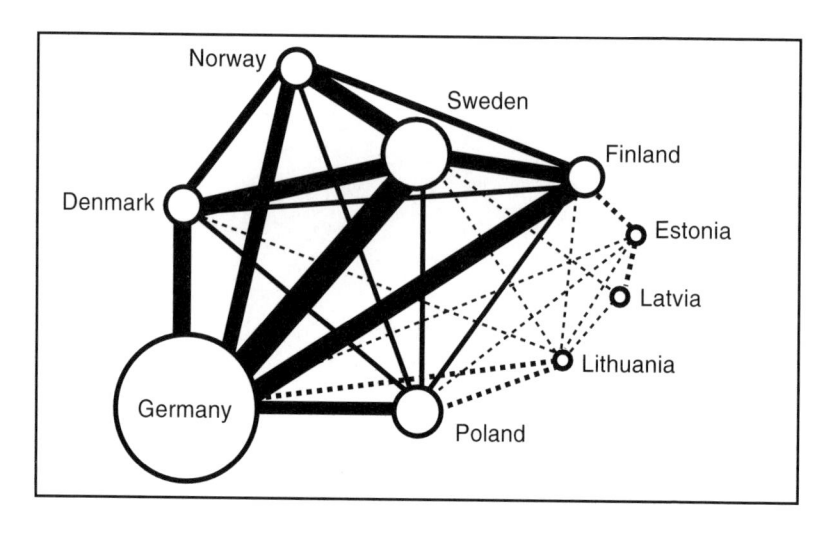

Source: B. Amoroso, S. Gomez y Paloma, D. Infante and N. Perrone, *Marginalisation, Specialisation and Cooperation in the Baltic and Mediterranean Regions, Synthesis Report*, Monitor-Fast (Brussels, 1993) p.34.

is still organized along colonial lines – natural resources, usually oil and natural gas, in exchange for manufactures, armaments or up-market items for the local *compradora* bourgeoisie. Generally speaking, all the countries of the southern and southeastern Mediterranean have been caught in the globalization trap, which on one shore generates growing expectations among consumers and on the other a flight of capital elsewhere.

All the demands placed upon these countries by the structural adjustment policies of the IMF and World Bank destroy the preliminary conditions for development, that is the growth of local and regional markets, and channel any existing capital to the Triad's rich markets, where it is useless to the country of origin.

Both the interregional trade in the Baltic and Mediterranean Regions and their dependence on the EU's centre bear marked similarities, the most significant being the polarization of trade. Each country in these two meso-regions trades with the area's leading market – Germany in the Baltic and France–Italy in the Mediterranean – without developing relations with the other countries there.

Globalization and European Integration

Figure 6.4 Trade Relations in the Mediterranean

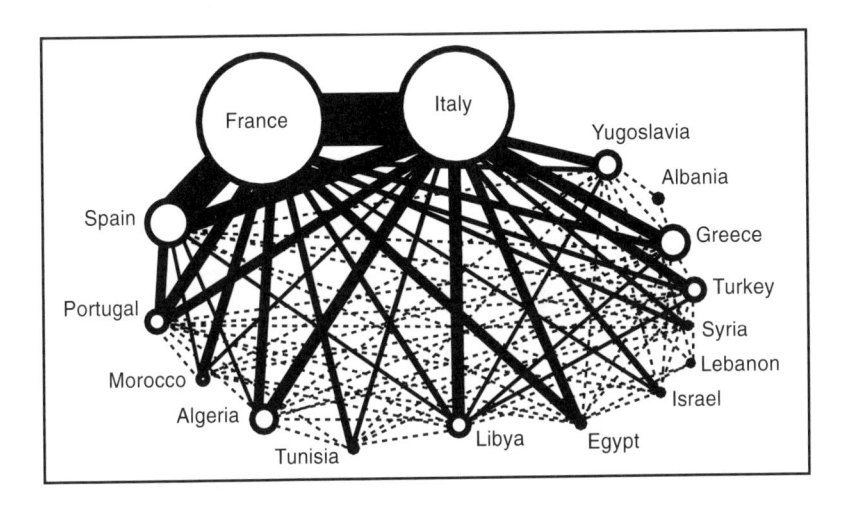

Source: B. Amoroso, S. Gomez y Paloma, D. Infante and N. Perrone, *Marginalisation, Specialisation and Cooperation in the Baltic and Mediterranean Regions, Synthesis Report*, Monitor-Fast (Brussels, 1993) p.35.

The model for relations between each country and the centre is a bilateral one, which thus tends to perpetuate the marginalization and destabilization of the meso-region as a whole.

While the model for specialization is found in trade relations, its roots are to be sought in output. The structural and economic changes of the last 15 years can readily be identified by looking at the specialization in exports of these countries. The comparative advantages in trade relations of specific goods like textiles, chemicals, fuel, machinery and equipment exhibit a dualistic specialization from 1970 to 1988. The EU's centre is specialized in high-technology products and enjoys an oligopolistic position in all the key technology sectors. Its main exports are technology-based goods like machinery, electromechanical components, chemicals and pharmaceuticals, and its market is increasingly becoming the rich one of the Triad's consumers. The other, marginalized, countries are specialized in the export of natural resources and specific technologies. For example, the countries of the Mediterranean's southern and southeastern rim are suppliers of natural resources and are specialized chiefly in manufactures of low technology input like foods, textiles and clothing. The lack of, or limited, development of their national markets in no way stimulates any kind of prospective growth.

NOTE

1. The findings of this study have been published in part in Amoroso, 1991, and Amoroso, 1992; the full study is in Amoroso, Infante, Gomez y Paloma and Perrone, 1993.

7 Social Class and Political Power: Authors, Actors and Institutions

SOCIAL CLASSES AND POLITICAL MOVEMENTS

Economic Power and Social Classes

The range and quality of the globalization process cannot but entail and induce deep-running changes even in the make-up of social classes, in the redeployment of centres of power and in the role of institutions.

As discussed *supra*, globalization's authors are the transnational corporations and the centres of industrial and financial capital, and its actors the institutions that manage for the former the working of the global village. This suggests redrawing the map of social classes, even within individual countries, and redefining both the national and international power groups so as to explain the ensuing new conflicts.

The Bourgeoisie

Several groups are subsumed today in this class.

i) *The global bourgeoisie*. It is linked to transnational industrial and financial groups. In Italy its high-profile exponents are industrialists like FIAT's Gianni Agnelli, Olivetti's Carlo De Benedetti and Benetton's Luciano Benetton, financiers like Mediobanca's Enrico Cuccia, and bankers like Carlo Azeglio Ciampi and Lamberto Dini. Behind them are the technocrats, bureaucrats, journalists and intellectuals who are linked to the running of international and EU institutions, the mass media and international lobbies.

ii) *The national bourgeoisies*. These are linked to business activities and professions having their own market and their own area of need (and demand) satisfaction in a given country. They arose during the development stage of the welfare state and, hence, are objectively linked to it, drawing support and legitimacy from the workings and protection of national systems. Included within this grouping are certain mid-to-large-scale national companies and the entire medium-small business sector engaged in producing goods and services, whether public or private.

iii) The *'compradora' bourgeoisie*. Product of the medium-to-small business, it grew up dependent for its production and its market on globalization and seeks to gain or preserve a share in globalization's rich markets. It exploits the comparative advantages provided by each country – cheap labour supply, government supports, entrepreneurial and specialization traditions – to produce low-cost goods and services for transnational corporations and consumers in the rich markets.

Globalization's social apartheid strategy, which results in the marginalization of large areas of the world and in the selective exploitation of their resources to the Triad's benefit, assigns to these bourgeoisies a role that is important in relation to both the economic profile they have and the part they play in the political destabilization of national systems.

What Working Class?

The destabilizing effects this new class make-up is having on national political systems are visible to everyone. Indeed, these same re-classifications also hold for the very composition of the social group once denominated as the working class or blue-collar workers.

The transitional nature of the current stage is particularly well delineated by the fact that this new mosaic of the social classes has no counterpart in the old system of political and social representation that had become so familiar in the post-war years. The confusion today between right and left, fascism and anti-fascism, progressives and conservatives arose here and will continue until the forms of representation and the various cultures they express fall into step with the structural changes that have taken place. This is especially true for political parties, trade unions and even business associations. The new divisions within their ranks are a sign of the divisionary processes now at work – processes that only radical changes can remedy.

Figure 7.1 Net Transfers to Developing Countries from Bretton Woods Institutions

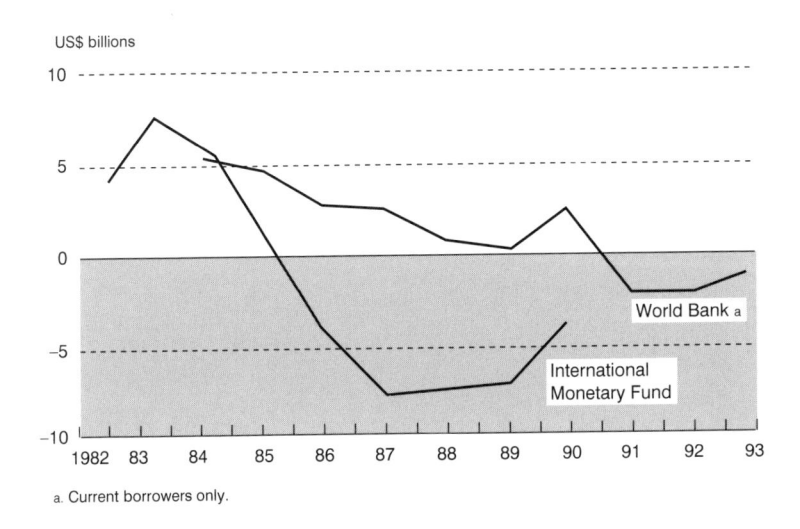

a. Current borrowers only.

Source: Human Development Report (1994) UNDP, 64.

THE INSTITUTIONS OF GLOBALIZATION

The Role of the Bretton Woods Institutions

In light of this discussion, it is right to wonder whether the Triad's strategies concern only the transnational corporations or whether they are part of a broader-based system of power involving all of capitalism's major institutions. Figure 7.1, which speaks for itself, shows that the role of the IMF and the World Bank, the major international financial institutions, has not been anti-cyclical, as one would expect, but the opposite, that is to drain the resources of Third World countries to further the trends of globalization. In the face of their serious state of dependency and their burden of foreign debt, many developing countries have agreed to severe restrictions on their national economic sovereignty by acquiescing, in writing, to the demands of the IMF in exchange for financial aid packages.

Policies of Structural Adjustment: The Causes of the Crisis

These measures, which have been imposed *de facto* on debtor nations, are called structural adjustment policies. Their fundamental message is that macroeconomic disequilibria are to be ascribed to

1) imbalances and distortions that are both internal (national budget), being caused by surplus global demand with respect to supply, and external (balance of payments), being caused by the failure of these economies to align themselves to international standards; and
2) problems of economic efficiency (productivity) caused by deficiencies in the use of resources, in the organization of markets and in the structure of businesses. Accordingly, what debtor nations supposedly need is not development policies and plans but the restructuring of a certain number of economic mechanisms, especially those concerning the system of resource allocation, so as to reactivate the spontaneous mechanisms of the market.

Policies of Structural Adjustment: Objectives

There are two objectives:

1) *stability* of price levels and exchange rates to return to long-to-medium-term macroeconomic equilibria and
2) *structural adjustment* to be implemented by overcoming the distortions causing the supply-demand disequilibrium.

These two conditions should enable over the short- and medium-term a return to long-term growth by resolving the disequilibria and introducing greater efficiency.

Monetary stability and equilibrium in the balance of payments are the two chief indicators of this approach. The economic policy measures adopted here concern polarity adjustment (currency devaluation), credit squeeze, reduction of the budget deficit, market liberalization and opening the economy to foreign markets. The reforms introduced regard cutting back the public sector, privatization and liberalization.[1]

The Origins of the Debt Problem

At the origin of this problem and its current exacerbation lies the cut-off of credit to the Third World in the early 1980s by the large commercial banks trying to collect the credit granted in preceding years, which in 1970 amounted to US$ 100 billion, in 1980, US$ 650 billion and in 1990 US$ 1.5 trillion. Yet the servicing of this debt (interest on the loans) amounts to far more than the loans themselves. Between 1983 and 1990 the developing countries paid US$ 150.5 billion to service the loans, a sum thus representing a net capital transfer to the wealthy countries. This amount (in real terms) is twice the cost of the Marshall Plan for the reconstruction of capitalist Europe in the aftermath of World War II.[2]

The task of breaking this credit deadlock with the developing countries and re-establishing economic cooperation and financial aid fell to the World Bank and the IMF. However, instead of reversing the flow of capital in pursuit of the spirit and philosophy informing the framework establishing them in the 1944 Bretton Woods accords, these two international institutions have pursued the line of the various regional development agencies and opened their tills only to start the interest collection on the debt owed to the creditors. Indeed, since 1985 the role of tax collector has intensified the transfer of funds from the poor to the rich nations as the IMF has been calling in not only the debts of international creditors but its own as well. Thus, between 1986 and 1990, transfers to the IMF alone have totalled US$ 31.5 billion, or about 22 per cent of all the capital funnelled back from the South and East to the North. This is the vicious circle in which debtor nations finance the loans extended to them but to secure them are compelled to underwrite conditions and implement structural adjustment policies that augment their economic and political dependence (ICPS, 1992, pp.3–4; George, 1996)

THE POLICIES OF GLOBALIZATION

The Stages of Structural Adjustment

The initial steps taken to implement these policies are always shock therapies, which involve a sharp currency devaluation and the end to subsidies and price controls. This in turn leads to the surge of domestic prices to international levels and a freezing of the population's purchasing power to dampen demand and curb inflation. The result of this deliberate pursuit is the dollarizing of domestic prices and stagflation.

The next phase encompasses the liberalization of foreign trade and an open-door economy. These measures accelerate the across-the-board alignment of internal prices to world market levels (dollarization of the economy) and, along with depressed purchasing power, cause important sectors of the economy to go under.

The third stage is the overhaul of public-sector finances, a goal expected to be achieved by sharply reducing wages and closing ailing, government-owned companies. The public enterprises running budget deficits are put under the care of a reorganization plan administered by the World Bank, a step that paves the way for the liquidation of public assets through privatization.

The last stage is the liberalization of the banking system, which effectively opens the door of the entire financial system to foreign banks and the privatization of public credit institutions. Moreover, the central banks are placed under quarterly auditing by the IMF, a step that removes any independent control over national monetary policy. The final step here is to abolish all the special credit lines for given sectors of the economy like agriculture and small businesses, a measure that further boosts imports.

The primary instrument used to control the national economy in a free market system, and set by the latter, is the interest rate. The ensuing results, the all too familiar currency speculations, are contributing factors to the unhinging of the weaker national economies. The re-introduction of formerly abolished (or semiconfidential) anonymous, secret bank accounts again opens the door to the export of capital and every sort of criminal economic practice.

The Effects of Structural Adjustment Policies

Even official sources have voiced doubts and criticisms about the real impact of these policies.

> It is impossible to say with any certainty whether these programs have worked or not.... On the basis of existing studies, it cannot be ascertained if the programs advocated by the IMF have improved performance in matters of inflation and economic growth. In fact, it is often found that the implementation of these programs

(of adjustment) is accompanied by a rise in inflation and a decline in the growth rate.[3]

Wherever these policies have been enacted, the lesson they teach is that the hoped-for, long-term stimulus effect on the growth and development of a country's economy has never materialized, whereas a process of dependent, passive integration with globalization's economic order has never failingly done so. In this sense, it would be wrong to accuse structural adjustment policies of failure. Rather, given the criteria governing the internal make-up and representativeness of the bodies charged with devising and applying these policies, the goal and natural direction of development are to be found in the integration and subordination of these economies to the worldwide market.

The Strangling of National Production Systems

The strict application of those liberalization measures aimed at opening markets and ending internal supports to a given nation's accumulation process has a double effect. It strangles the national productive structure, regarded as inefficient with respect to international standards, and channels skilled labour and risk (venture) capital towards the sound investments of world capitalism's centres.

The current state of the numerous countries in Eastern Europe and Africa, as well as Argentina and Brazil in Latin America, that have embraced the policies of the World Bank and the IMF helps empirically to check these analyses. The implementing of these policies has either stepped up or set in motion processes of de-industrialization and aggravated foreign debt, unemployment and political and social destabilization.

Their Effects in the Mediterranean

The implementing of these World Bank–IMF policies in both EU and Third countries in the Mediterranean Basin has resulted in social turmoil of such scope, and a rejection of the forms of modernization so widespread, as to encourage the rise of 'fundamentalist' movements on both shores and the escalation of authoritarian institutional responses to counter them. The economic measures resulting from these policies are public-spending cutbacks and ensuing loss of jobs as well as the institutional destabilization of all the income and rights safeguards necessary for the transformation of the centres and forms of power. Decision-making in a liberalized market about efficiency criteria, resource allocation and income redistribution is once again left to the pricing mechanism. Noteworthy is the cultural and institutional message of this approach. The authors of development are seen in the abstract as the firm and the consumer (civil society), whose capacity for action would be restricted by the intervention of the state and, generally, the public sector. Imposed from the outside and from the top down, these policies are paradoxically presented as democratic, decentralizing and from the bottom up.

The analysis conducted here indicates that while these structural adjustment policies are well focused on and effective in reducing the dimension and role of state intervention in the economy, they rely on the spontaneous effects of the new order to stimulate the national economic authors to action. Yet the application of these policies actually leads to overlooking the fact that eliminating the measures protecting national industry and incomes involves abandoning a large part of civil society's authors, the very ones whose condition is supposed to be improved. Civil society is thus restricted to small groups of entrepreneurs, predominantly *compradora* by nature, acting as middlemen or brokers for foreign capital, and consumers identified with the national political and technocratic elites (Amoroso, 1994, pp.82–3).

The State's New Political Role

This evolution brings to the fore important questions regarding consensus and legitimacy of a given society's government. The reason is that the declining role of the state in the economy increases its political stature through the strengthening of the role of the armed forces and the organs of state repression. A recent study published by Algeria's National Statistics Bureau very lucidly notes that

> ... the role of general entrepreneur of development that the State has performed up to now is being abandoned, or at least reduced to one of the many functions ensuring the coherent working of the planned mercantile mechanism. The State is thus increasingly taking on the role of Public Power directed not, as in the past, outwards but inwards.
>
> (Hamel, 1991)

The fragmenting impact these processes have on society are by now evident. Today's institutional systems depend on technocratic expertise to manage the economy, the role played by the IMF outside individual states, and on the instruments of political repression wielded by the national states from within. Examples abound. Purchasing power in the Czech Republic has fallen by over 60 per cent since the koruna's devaluation, and between 1989–91 industrial output declined by nine per cent in (then) Czechoslovakia, by 22.3 per cent in Bulgaria, by 34.5 per cent in Poland and by 38.9 per cent in Romania. The scope of these recessive phenomena is greater than that registered by the Depression of the 1930s in the West, and the attempt to hide the causes by invoking – inappropriately – Communism's bankrupt legacy, is increasingly less convincing.

The Fundamentalism of International Institutions

The countries of the Maghreb[4] today are a paradigmatic example of this social breakdown – an issue that seems unexplored by those Western views holding that the causes lie in the problematic nature of democracy in these countries and in their opposition movements. Any assessment of the forms and extent of the institutional conflict that omits the context discussed heretofore would not only lead to erroneous conclusions but would also reveal a thorough misunderstanding of the nature and bitterness of the conflicts in these countries (for example of southern Europe, Egypt and Algeria).

The imposing of international superstructures and their attendant regulations and consequences is paradoxically taken as the democratic-institutional order of these countries, and any resistance or attempt to reject this dictate is decried as anti-democratic. While the popular culture of these nations and their forms of resistance to such outside interference are seen as backward and conservative, the forms of deviant modernization forced upon them become a symbol of free and independent expression of their populace.

Economic Marginalization and Political Destabilization in the Maghreb

Estimates of the impact the policies of structural adjustment have had in Algeria and Morocco have proved more dramatic than the IMF has reported.[5] For example, the 1991 consumer price index (base 100 in 1980) was 309.6 in Algeria, 217.7 in Morocco and 236.5 in Tunisia, and the same index for food commodities was respectively 249.0, 217.3 and 244.6. While the average decline of family incomes in Morocco from 1982–86 was about 12 per cent; the drop was much sharper for families employed in the informal sector. It was the underlying cause of the 1981 Casablanca revolt, which left dozens dead and hundreds wounded, and the riots of 1984, which forced the government to withdraw the cutback in subsidies and the price increases for staples. Note that for Algeria, although the accords with the IMF were not signed until 1994, balancing the national and foreign debts was already a priority goal in 1979, as contained in the 1967–78 ten-year development budget, as was the 1986 commitment to eliminate the trade gap so as to re-establish internal and external equilibrium.

These examples are useful in drawing attention to two fundamental facts:

i) the need to achieve an economic performance that brings the main internal and external indicators into equilibrium is not at issue in these countries (as it is elsewhere) and
ii) the real problem involves determining the reasons, the need and the targets of structural adjustment – a debate in which differences of opinion appear to be greater.

THE PROBLEM AND POTENTIAL SOLUTIONS

The Subverting of Priorities in Economic Policy and the Role of the Public Sector

The need to deal with the worldwide crisis by restructuring national economies evinces inefffficiency factors in the public sector, especially the industrial segment, and the burden of external links. Raising these issues implicitly introduces a value judgment of the public sector that is grounded in a logic and based on criteria divorced from those governing its inception and development. It is thus not surprising that the conclusions drawn from the former are highly critical and anything but constructive.

Striving to find a balance between external and internal ties and their related objectives is polarized along the foreign one, resulting in the complete subversion of the relationship between independent and dependent variables. Employment and social needs are transferred from the former, independent variables, to the latter, the dependent ones, so that the external ties acquire a priority they had never before enjoyed.

Real Problems and Possible Solutions

Foreign debt ballooned to proportions in the 1980s that were far different from those it had in the 1960s and 1970s. The international debt crisis, the deterioration of exchange rates and fiercer international competition were the causes. There is thus no justification for the fatalistic assumption that nothing can be done about this phenomenon and that all other goals of economic policy are to be subordinated to it.

In this context a radical turn-around about how to view wages becomes the key element because of its effects on employment. The organizational and financial restructuring of firms, especially in the public sector, sees the concept of 'employment as the productive use of available resources' and turns it into 'employment as a simple cost factor (wages)', and as such a liability to the firm's financial performance.

As we have seen in the case of Algeria, the existence of and need to redress disequilibria in the economy have been recognized for some time – the problem is to identify the causes and how to remedy them. The causes are multiple, ranging from internal and international structural ones, those due to the marketplace or the lack of it (often, paradoxically, to both), to market forms, ownership and social systems, pricing, trade relations, interest rates and so on.

To balance a given national economy's accounts, the policy instrument of choice has naturally been spending cutbacks in relation to income. Yet this original idea, lifted from standard bookkeeping principles, fails to account for the fact that spending cuts are followed by reduced incomes. This sets in motion a vicious circle of stagnation and decline in the economy as the spending cuts drop incomes to a very low level. Pursuing the opposite policy to equilibrium, that is increasing output and incomes, is by no means easy, although the importance of the benefits to be reaped, even in terms of social stability and greater sense of community commitment in the citizenry, should be an incentive to this course of action.

Competitiveness and Output Efficiency

All efforts directed towards structural approaches and efficiency focus on competitiveness. Yet greater competitiveness does not automatically generate greater efficiency in that the need for the former signals the need for the latter but does not by itself lead to it. This is a result that can only be achieved if firms have access to the necessary resources and skills – something which requires a much broader range of action.

Some scholars have rightly pointed to the need for an approach to close the gap, affecting firms and production systems alike, between the need to adjust and the ability to adjust (Jacques De Bandt). Economic policies should concentrate their efforts in this direction instead of postulating such tautological axioms as the firms that have the ability will survive and those that have not will succumb. Such a statement is tantamount to a decree ordering many countries and production systems to cease existing, including those of the Maghreb. It also brings us full circle to the starting point of our discussion, which has highlighted exactly what is happening throughout the world *vis-à-vis* the policies of structural adjustment.

The Limits of Competitiveness

As pointed out to great effect in the 1994 report *Limits to Competition* by the Group of Lisbon, the basis for all these forms of intervention is an act of faith in internal competition and inter-nation competitiveness that is unacceptable, both ethically and in terms of economic efficiency. Ethically, it is an outgrowth of a Western fundamentalist credo that contrasts with the best that European culture has expressed on these topics, including the critical thought spanning a century of capitalist development. As to economic efficiency, it collides with all the most recent forms of social and economic development which see in the factors of cooperation (industrial and output synergies) the reason for the most significant advances in technology and industrial organization (Petrella, 1995).

Keynesian Policies: Limits and Possibilities

The gravity of these crisis situations has brought back to the scene the neo-Keynesian propositions focusing on price stability and purchasing power of the middle classes in relation to economic recovery.

The fruit of good intentions, these are attempts to draw greater attention to distribution issues and the state of national economies. Yet they cannot escape, because of both their content and the very intentions they declare, the trend of globalization and are thus unable to elude its effects.

The failure of these propositions, wherever they have been put into practice, is due to the difficulty of inducing higher rates of growth and investment while keeping to the scheduled foreign debt servicing payments. The common denominator of the neo-Keynesian propositions, now as in the 1960–70s, is the reliance on successful capitalist growth to achieve its aims. Yet, while the context during the 1960s and 1970s was one that embodied the growth of markets and jobs, today's is a context that is embracing the marginalization of the areas earmarked for intervention and an overall decline in employment.

A return to the Depression origins of Keynesian thought, so long as it prevented its reduction to technical contingencies of economic policy and bookkeeping, would likely help to rework the original instruments of intervention into forms consonant with the goals of full employment and the social orientation of production in the context of the new contradictions between capitalism and society.

NOTES

1. For a brief but cogent review of the issue, see the ICPS report, 1992. A review of recent papers on the subject can be found in Bello and Cunniman, 1994.
2. This part is largely based on the data contained in ICPS report, 1992.
3. Khan, 1990, cited in *Le Monde Diplomatique*, September 1992.
4. Arabic name for the region of North West Africa, including Algeria, Libya, Morocco and Tunisia.
5. For a critical analysis of the agreements signed with international financial organizations, see, among others, Benachenhou, 1993, and *Annales Marocaines d'economie*, no. 7, Winter 1993, with a dossier on structural adjustment and its impact on employment.

8 Alternative Policies to Globalization: a Polycentric View

> Everything I have mentioned today should add up to something entirely new; what's needed is a whole new approach to being... a new approach to tolerance, a new approach to becoming enlightened, a new approach to being progressive, a new approach to being free. It's a central problem of our lives.
>
> Pasolini, 1987, p.33

THE FOUR RINGS OF SOLIDARITY[1]

Rethinking Europe

The end of the Cold War is having a marked impact on Europe's process of economic and political integration, highlighting the inadequacy of its beginnings in 1952 and its grounding in the centrality of the European Union. It calls for a radical rethinking of the very concept of Europe and of European development. These thoughts are also supported by the recent *White Paper of the European Union* on 'Growth, Competitiveness and Employment'. The old liberalist fundamentalism of the preceding *Cecchini Report* on the internal market has been left behind without so much as a single self-critical reference (1988).[2]

The geo-economic and geo-political implications of the end of the Cold War are evoked with the return of the concept Greater Europe – from West to East and North to South – and with the planning of an integrated system based on clearly defined policy objectives. Despite the good intentions and declarations, much work remains to be done to move beyond the intellectual legacy of the Cold War, as is shown in part by both the White Paper's conceptual framework and its policy proposals.

The Cold War Legacy and Europe's Integration Process

Europe's history is marked by the diversity of its forms of industrialization and models of development in its major cultural and geographic areas – the North, West, Centre, East and the Mediterranean. The specific character of Scandinavia's or southern Europe's development forms has often been cited in connection to their economic and institutional performance.

The process of European integration in the modern version worked out in the closing days of World War II was predicated on a new political and economic system rooted in peace and cooperation among all the nations of Europe (Spinelli and Rossi, 1944). Yet what came to be the prevailing logic of the Cold War – already looming on the horizon a few months after the end of World War II – placed limits on this process. The advent of the Iron Curtain reduced European integration to a very limited area – Western Europe – and fostered the conceptual handicap that altered our perception of Europe, shrinking its original, accepted geographic boundaries from the Atlantic to the Urals to Western Europe and even to the West *tout court*.

Yet another effect was the physical handicap of reducing southern Europe to a buffer zone demarcating the eastern and southern boundaries of the European Union and the Western defences instead of exploiting one of its development poles. Similarly, because of the strategic position of the Scandinavian countries along the northern and north-eastern perimeter of the West's defences, the commitment to a genuine internationalization for a solidarity-based development of the welfare state, as advocated by Gunnar Myrdal with the words 'from the welfare state to the Welfare World', was thwarted (1960, p.176). Even the autonomous region of Central Europe disappeared once again, becoming the divide along which was concentrated the permanent tension between the two blocs.

Eurocentrism and Westernization

The Cold War added new constraints to the development of these regions and to the overall process of European integration. Its shrinking of Europe to the mere western appendage of the Continent's dimension reinforced the influence of the behavioural models of the older industrialized countries – France, Germany and the United Kingdom. The roots of the Eurocentric character of integration in the last 40 years are to be sought in the predominance of this model. Westernization and Eurocentrism have become the major distortions in Europe's integration process.

These events explain why southern Europe's diversity has been singled out chiefly for its negative impact on the EU's social and economic cohesion, and why it has always been seen in terms of disparity and backwardness. These are the same reasons why the Scandinavian model in northern Europe has been considered a deviation with respect to the market forms dominant in Western Europe.

Yet, despite the dramatic turn of events, the end of the Cold War offers the chance for a complete recovery of Europe's integration process by overcoming the Eurocentric and Western limits. With the amputation of the regional markets and the consequent severing of needs from output in this artificial form, development policies have inevitably taken on an extraordinary character – from the extraordinary measure for Italy's *Mezzogiorno* to that of the EU's regional policies and the welfare policies of the Nordic countries. These extraordinary measures were to all intents and purposes designed to compensate these areas for damages stemming from the Cold War and the spreading capitalist development model. Indeed, and surely not by chance, the 'return to the ordinary' of the 1990s, which was made possible on the one hand by the end of Communism's threat and on the other by the opportunity to begin to rethink Europe in its entirety, has led to today's dissension over the forms of extraordinary intervention wherever they have been fully implemented and, as in the case of Italy, to their abolition.

The Diversities of Southern Europe and Scandinavia: The Alternative Role

In this new context, the different regions of Southern Europe and Scandinavia might fall victim to economic marginalization and social and political destabilization should the 'ordinary' in Europe turn out to be the product of globalization. These two areas of the EU could instead be rehabilitated by transforming them into poles of polycentric development, which would also enable them to act as an interface between the European Union and the surrounding areas.

Reconfiguring the posture of the Scandinavian countries from EU boundary line and NATO's northern flank to the interface between the EU and the entire Baltic Region (Baltic Europe) could

Alternative Policies to Globalization 133

likewise turn Scandinavia's diversity into a factor of stabilization and development, with the added advantage of a strongly positive impact on central Europe. Similarly, remoulding Southern Europe's stance from EU periphery and NATO's Mediterranean arm to centre stage of Greater Europe's largest region (Mediterranean Europe) would turn its diversity into a force at the service of a real European development process, with the additional benefit of strongly positive effects on the Arab world and the Black Sea region.

From Eurocentrism to Polycentrism: Europe's Meso-Regions

Four important regions stand out in this new European geography – the European Union, Baltic Europe, Mediterranean Europe and Danubian Europe. Russia's natural ties to the Baltic Region, which had slackened during the Cold War, are today being strengthened and are extending Europe's reach into the area of the Confederation of Independent States (CIS); the Ukraine and the entire Black Sea Region meet Europe along the line of its south-eastern countries. Turkey, which has always been the convergence point and door of three continents, could become an important factor of stabilization and development in the relations between the Mediterranean and Black Sea Regions, should the influence the United States exerts to control and contain the Islamic world in this vast sphere wane.

The design of a new Europe mapped out by this hopeful hypothesis is heavily reliant on the diversities of its major regions and their cultures and, as such, it is naturally polycentric. In so broad a context, where there are marked asymmetries of development between countries, areas and regions, a goal of primary importance is overcoming the central role of the European Union, which is set in the old centre-periphery framework so congenial to it and upon which are based every economic policy since the 1960s.

The alternative to this type of development and these economic policies is to be sought in the direction of a polycentric European system grounded in cooperation and solidarity instead of competition and conflict. The soundness of and the need to pursue this alternative might bring about and manage co-development, and organize the cultural elements of a European development system featuring *four rings of solidarity* (figure 8.1).

Figure 8.1 Regional Scenarios of Europe

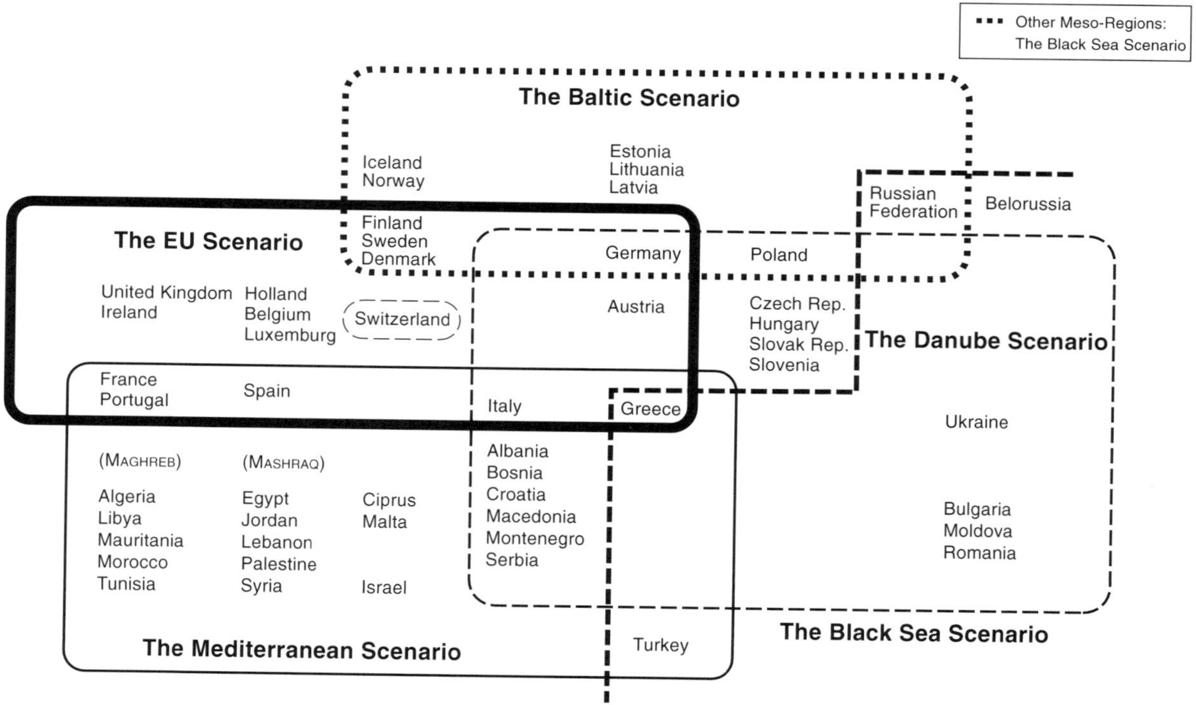

THE FIRST RING

Solidarity Among the EU Countries

The ring of solidarity should consist of the EU's member states. By re-activating all the productive potentialities that today stand idled, it should be able to move beyond both the current active transfer of capital, including the concentration of production facilities in the areas of the EU's core, and the passive transfer of incomes from the core to the periphery, as both transfers are the causes today of social and output disequilibria.

This can be accomplished by changing today's prevailing development model in which the various countries and regions are unequally weighted. The idea is to re-establish within the EU a sounder balance between markets and output so as to achieve development forms that are more respectful in their use of human and material resources. Given the concentration of capital and unused technological capabilities in both the EU's North and South, the efforts to integrate the southern European countries of the Mediterranean Region and the Scandinavian ones in the Baltic are to be encouraged. The role of these two areas of the EU must again become that of the core in their development process.

The posited solidarity between the European Union and current non-member states is based on a tradition of cooperation and mediation these countries have evinced with one another throughout the postwar period – a tradition that has also promoted since the early 1980s the various forms of the welfare state brought into being in each of these nations through the stipulation of social contracts by their leading social forces. The specific nature of the EU with respect to its triadic partners (Japan and the United States) resides in this very principle of solidarity, which permeates throughout its institutions and political movements.

Germany's Dominant and United Kingdom's Destabilizing Role

The roles of Germany and the United Kingdom seriously jeopardize, albeit for opposing reasons, the realization of a solidarity-based development model. These two nations represent two poles of globalization on the European Continent – Germany directly and the UK indirectly, as the proxy of the United States. While the collapse of the Wall has rekindled hopes for a polycentric integration grounded in Greater Europe, it has also led to the reunification of 'Greater Germany', the result of the same aspirations to hegemony and economic power once cultivated by past ideologies and today pursued by the tactics of triadic capitalism.

These tactics are driving European development towards forms that are no different from those generated by the Cold War in as much as they are based on broad processes of exclusion that we have defined above as marginalization. Yet this marginalization is more circumscribed than the exclusion process the Wall stood for. It leads to an increasingly pronounced concentration of wealth and power along the axis of the Rhine Valley against which the process of European integration risks being even more limited than that experienced by Western Europe during the Cold War.

The influence of Germany has become dominant, intrusive, *vis-à-vis* the prospects of autonomous development of both the EU and non-EU states. The deutschmark is increasingly acquiring the role of destabilization and political control that the dollar has played in its own sphere. It is worthwhile pondering in this connection the authoritative query posed by Augusto Graziani as to 'whether the European area, formerly dominated by the group of ECC countries, will still be shaped in some form of economic union, or whether it will take the simpler form of an area under the economic dominion of unified Germany' (1993, p.257).

The destabilizing role of the UK is the result of its acting as the representative of the political and economic interests of the United States. There can be little doubt that the clinging of these two important countries to their respective positions would make it impossible to forge the ring of solidarity and once more place Greater Germany on a collision course with Russia. This would also spell the end, yet again, to the design of a Greater Europe founded upon the multiplicity of its areas and cultures. The only alternative project to war is thus bringing the UK back into the European fold and encouraging Germany to take on a cultural and propelling role consonant to its specific traits – harmoniously incorporated in a framework of polycentrism and solidarity.

THE SECOND RING

Solidarity of the Baltic Region's Countries

The second ring of solidarity is to include the Nordic countries, currently engaged in a difficult process of restructuring, and the other nations of the Baltic Region. Solidarity among the former, more necessary today than ever before, if they are to deal effectively with the growing economic difficulties that many of them – especially Finland – are facing, should be extended to the entire Region. That these countries do not look only to Germany and turn their backs on Russia and the other eastern countries is in Europe's own interest, for it would prevent the forming of new suspicions and diffidence and promote development. The nature and extent of the issues confronting the countries of this Region, even despite the economic asymmetry recorded between the Baltic's eastern and western shores, are quite different from those affecting the Mediterranean – different as to the breadth of the demographic and migratory factors involved and different as to the extent of marginalization and social destabilization.

Russia and Germany

Both these European powers exert a very strong sway over the Baltic. The stability and security issues their relations involve in both the Baltic and along the Danube corridor endow any comparison of them *vis-à-vis* the equilibrium of Europe as a whole with dramatic connotations. A similar situation, with the tragic and devastating effects familiar to us all, is found in the Balkans of southern Europe. Yet the Balkanization of the Baltic and the escalation of tensions throughout the Danube corridor can be avoided only if the Nordic countries establish a bond of solidarity with the Baltic's eastern rim, thereby creating in the region an autonomous development pole that could even mediate relations between these two great powers fronting the Baltic Sea.

Leaning towards a convergence on Germany would not help to meet the needs nor resolve the unemployment problems now afflicting these countries, though it would increase the entire region's instability. The European Union can neither afford to prop-up prices (for example EU agricultural policies) nor transfer income (structural and like funds) for countries moving towards an impracticable and undesirable integration with the EU's core.

The European Union's efforts must instead focus on fully backing, through its member states in the region, the construction of an integrated economic system in the Baltic Region. For, within such a strong meso-regional framework, the marked output and technological potentialities of the Nordic countries, as well as their inexhaustible reservoir of institutional experience that is especially appropriate to the region's smaller states, could best be tapped. Nowhere is it more appropriate to speak of solidarity, which for over a century has been – and is still – the cultural ethos upon which rest the successes of the Scandinavian model (and the Nordic in general) (Amoroso, 1980).

THE THIRD RING

Solidarity of the Central European Countries

The third ring of solidarity is to be hammered out as a vast 'new area of innovation' in central Europe's Danube Region. This region can be transformed into an area of stability that is independent of both Russia and Germany and capable of making the most of its economic, institutional and cultural diversities. Every effort must therefore be made to support and promote cooperation and co-development among its countries, which includes the Czech Republic, Hungary, Poland and Slovakia in the *Visegrad* area; the regions of *Alpe-Adria*, which include Friuli-Venezia Giulia, Lombardy, Trentino-Alto Adige and Venetia in Italy, Croatia, Slovenia, Bavaria in Germany, Győr-Sopron, Vas, Somogy and Zala in Hungary, and Upper Austria, Burgenland, Carinthia, Styria and Salzburg in Austria. At the same time any tendency towards separatism as with the former Czechoslovakia, which inevitably leads to a divide like the Wall as well as providing fertile soil for ethnic and social conflicts and destroying any chance this Region has of aspiring to an autonomous role, is to be rejected and combatted.

The Supporting Role of Scandinavia and Southern Europe

The parallel contribution to this project of the Scandinavian countries to the north, which in the past have evinced a marked sensitivity

Alternative Policies to Globalization

and attention to this region of Mitteleurope, and those of Mediterranean Europe to the south, which are almost in symbiosis with it, should receive the EU's consideration and support. Linking this *third ring of solidarity* in Danubian Europe to the *second one* in the Baltic and to the *fourth* in the Mediterranean would contribute to bringing about the miracle of an independent region at the heart of Europe.

Divisions and Particularisms: the Hurdles to Solidarity

The historical and cultural identity of Central Europe and its past role as a bridge spanning East and West have been sharply blurred by its peoples' having lived for decades on and within the divide separating the twain, a fact which has driven a wedge of diffidence among them, and their choosing between one or the other European power having been forced upon them by their geographic position. These factors of crisis are to be found even today in the inclination towards the divisions and particularisms fomented by the hope in a rapid integration with the bloc of wealthy Western European countries, even at the cost of their own identity.

Coaxing to rise from the ashes of fragmentation the still burning members of an inter-country, regional solidarity – precondition for a European solidarity – must be the goal, rather than normative project, of a cultural reconstruction process. For perhaps it is in this very Region that development and security are coincident factors.

Placing innovation at the core of development's aims is not a cliché dictated by an intellectual fad. Rather, it is an attempt to respond positively to the need to rehabilitate an economic, social and institutional system that stems from deep-seated roots and traditions, thereby freeing it from the ageing processes caused by the passivity foisted upon it by the Cold War. This also means recognizing this Region's enormous potential for development, which has to be rekindled using the new opportunities for synergy and expansion the current situation offers.

The factors of the new solidarity are to be reconstructed by rediscovering the historical bonds with the past which had made the Danube an area of great cultural and political influence. This is what emerges from both a look at the social bonds and internal cohesiveness, attested in recent history by the area's resistance to the domination of the two great powers on its borders (Russia and Germany), and retracing the culture of solidarity proper to the labour movement over the last century, which even in the socialist systems had devised remarkably viable forms in practice. A critical yet non-destructive reading of these experiences, which adequately takes into account the undeniable knot of contradictions aggravated by the Cold War, can provide many leads in furthering and deepening this analysis.

THE FOURTH RING

Solidarity of the Mediterranean Countries

The fourth, and last, ring of solidarity involves the countries of Southern Europe and the Mediterranean, from the Maghreb to Turkey and the Balkans. Its outlines are set forth in the European Union's new Mediterranean policy (Economic and Social Committee of the European Union, 1993). The difficulties in achieving it are due to the goal's lack of appropriate content and to Germany's decisively throwing its weight behind the exploitation of eastern Europe's areas and markets. These difficulties are not surprising since the Mediterranean is the largest and richest region of Europe as to number of inhabitants and natural and human resources. Its rich and manifold cultural and religious traditions, as well as the pluralism of nationality and institutions, make it one of the world's most interesting laboratories for co-existence and solidarity.

The Arab world – one of the Mediterranean Basin's key components – has provided in the post-colonial age a prime example of the will to solidarity and union. The long list of the Arab world's failed attempts at union is a recurring theme studies cite as an example of the lack of its political homogeneity and symptom of scant solidarity. Yet the exact opposite reading is the more plausible and historically correct one in my opinion. For it is precisely the large number of thwarted bids for union undertaken over the few decades since the colonial era's end, attempts which have been confined within the successful destabilizations orchestrated time and again by interests alien to the process of unification itself and to the Mediterranean Region as a whole, that indicate the irresistible drive to solidarity.

History abounds in examples of how the support given by Western nations to the differing factions and nationalities making up the Arab world is intended not to promote their cooperation and solidarity but to divide and control them. This policy originated with the interference by the major European powers in the crisis of the Ottoman Empire, the aim then being to accelerate its collapse and to prevent at all costs the rise of a new, cohesive Arab force in the region. Those years of crisis, war and betrayal have left an invaluable legacy – the constantly pursued aspiration to the unity and solidarity of the Arab peoples, as in the case of the Palestinians.

The end of the West's hegemony in Europe and the revival of an authentic European *discourse* must be the starting point for a reassessment and support of Arab solidarity, one of the oldest and strongest segments of Mediterranean solidarity. This is all the more necessary as the new processes of the economy's globalization and the new world order politically administering them are introducing additional factors of division and conflict.

The marginalization of the Mediterranean south of the line stretching from the Po river and Madrid exhibits processes of further exclusion, which range from the pure and simple abandoning of men, markets and output to be isolated within a quarantine area (for example the Maghreb) to actively interventionist forms of a new colonization (including the Mashraq and Persian Gulf countries) to be placed under the firm hand of such emerging regional powers as Turkey and Israel. The inclusion of strategic points of the trans-European networks in the development plans of the Western countries makes explicit the oversight role assigned by the West to these two countries. The junctions for the flow of the two major commodities fuelling the economies of this area – oil and water – are to be found at Haifa in Israel for the former and in Turkey for the supply of the latter to the Middle East. The military control delegated previously to these two states is thus extended to the control of the most important economic infrastructure pipelines. (Khader, 1995)

SOUTHERN EUROPE: AN ALTERNATIVE ROLE?

The Mediterranean Interface

The paradox of the Southern European countries is to be seen in the stark contrast between the widespread failure to employ their production structures and technological capabilities – the result of their obsolescence in the EU framework with which they tried to integrate – and their urgent need to create regional and local markets in areas that are among the most populated in Greater Europe – the southern and south-eastern rim of the Mediterranean – and the most ignored. The role of Southern Europe in the post-Cold War era should be that of an *interface* to the rest of the Mediterranean.

Such a role would enable this area to become a strong and important nexus of interregional cooperation. For the growth of regional markets in some of the world's more populous areas would relieve the migratory pressures on the European Union, reduce the risks of political destabilization and military aggression and rekindle a balanced process of growth in Southern Europe.

The Costa del Sol South of the European Union

The advent of regional markets in the Mediterranean would entail a number of benefits. It would mean first and foremost the revival of Southern Europe's ports and cities, thereby promoting the growth and renovation of a regional Mediterranean network of infrastructures needed to provide new impetus and new horizons to such economic sectors as tourism, telecommunications and transport. The entire northern seaboard of the Mediterranean – from Italy to France and Spain – could become the EU's Costa del Sol, turning around in the process the decline of the area's main ports like Genoa, Marseilles and Venice by redirecting the century-old ties of orientation and specialization linking them to the cities of northern Italy's industrial triangle and to the EU's core.

A similar outlook also holds true for the other transport infrastructures. The EU's air traffic is being stifled by the congestion at the key airports of Paris, London, Frankfurt and Amsterdam. Flights today between Tunis and Cairo or from North to Central Africa are routed through these airports, causing enormous problems of energy waste, pollution, traffic safety and so forth. The decentralization of air traffic and communications with Africa, Asia and Latin America that could be achieved by upgrading the airports of southern Italy, Spain, Portugal and Greece would improve existing conditions in these areas and promote their development.

Towards a New, Decentralized System of Europe's Infrastructures

Similarly, Scandinavia in the EU's north could become part of an integrated decentralization plan of European infrastructures running to the eastern seaboard of the Baltic, with the potential for Stockholm and Copenhagen to regain their central role in such a system. Indeed, all these considerations clearly point to the primary necessity of developing polycentrically a broader system of land, sea and air transport links in these decentred areas rather than increasing traffic along the routes connecting them to Germany.

Yet, once these strategic long-distance connections that international organizations and large corporations are so strongly behind have been set out and implemented, the basic issue at stake which must not be forgotten is the creation of the secondary, though no less essential, networks of territorial links. For, if these networks are not developed, there is no way out of the triadic system's imperial designs.

The new European infrastructures would also generate positive affects:

i) the revaluation of scientific institutions, universities and research centres to sustain and raise the stature of the Mediterranean lifestyle (biotechnology, education and professional training);
ii) the revitalization of the Mediterranean's islands to promote the development of tourism and related integrated information systems; and
iii) the preservation and dissemination of the historical and cultural legacy, even via advertising.

New Technology and Meso-Regional Co-Development

Studying the conduct and industrial strategies of the transnational corporations in highlighting the negative features characterizing the current trend reveals the potentials advanced technology offers for alternative future scenarios. Such a study can contribute to the drafting of policy measures capable of reactivating at the international level regulatory mechanisms of the economy that are geared to the economic and social development of countries, areas and regions.

The new flexibility deriving from technology introduces horizontal specialization and cluster aggregation into production systems.

This innovative twist to industrial organization makes possible, through the relocation of certain parts or individual steps of the manufacturing process, new forms of decentralization between and within sectors to take advantage of benefits offered in various countries. Indeed, the issue today – evident even in the way the transnational corporations are organized to secure at all costs relative advantages – is no longer the transfer of entire sectors like textiles or foods from more developed to less developed areas but the creation of industrial complementariness so as to enable the gradual transfer of parts of the production process. Technological advances should thus make possible, in a context other than globalization, the growth of cooperation and co-development.[3]

What makes the current situation paradoxical is the fact that the technological flexibility underpinning these potential advantages is a double-edged sword. It encourages on the one hand cooperation within the transnational corporations or groups of them and continues on the other to fuel competition and rivalry between industrial systems and countries. Thus, if technological innovation is not accompanied by matching innovation in labour relations and ownership (an altogether different matter from neo-institutionalism's cries about negotiation, co-decisions, minimum incomes and so on), the increased cooperation within the corporate system promoted and produced by the new technologies will end up generating colonialism instead of co-development in relations between areas and countries.

The Maghreb's current economic and output profile is a pressing example of this private appropriation of the advantages offered by new technologies. Foreign investment in Morocco is a case that seemingly runs counter to the area's marginalization. Several French and Spanish companies in the agro-food industry decided to invest there, apparently in response to a strong incentive for development in this industry's local sector. Yet a closer analysis indicates that the real issue is output transfer aimed at exploiting, for the Triad's wealthy markets, cheap local resources (labour and raw materials) and the comparative advantages offered by the lack of legal protection of workers' rights and regulation of natural resources.

It should be noted that in similar decentralizing operations any plans to open and develop local markets and production systems in harmony with the local *habitat* are entirely lacking. Given their sole aim of improving a company's cost structure, such initiatives act as a brake on and a liability to the development of new markets and the broadening of the manufacturing and consumer base which, whether in Morocco or elsewhere, could have beneficial effects on employment throughout the Mediterranean.

While potential technical advances make it possible to expand the manufacturing and consumer base in Europe, they are dependent on the formation of enterprises and an entrepreneurship whose fortunes and ambitions are linked to those of new markets. Just as the process of Southern Europe's industrialization required at the outset combining a public system and a mixed economy to promote the needed symbiosis of public and private interests, so today it is necessary to encourage and promote area- and region-wide initiatives capable of reorganizing and broadening production systems. Only on such a basis will it be possible to engage the interest of Southern Europe's and the EU's large corporations in negotiating investments and production facilities in the region.

THE CRISIS IN SOUTHERN EUROPE (FORMER YUGOSLAVIA AND ALBANIA) AND THE IMPACT ON THE REGION'S DEVELOPMENT (GREECE AND ITALY)

Europe and the Balkan Crisis

The peril of new tensions and local wars between Russia and the regions of Carpathia and the Ukraine, in the Middle East and on the Mediterranean's southern rim is the major threat hanging over any process of political stabilization and economic development in Europe. Yet the current crisis in south-eastern Europe, which culminated in the Balkan-area war and the collapse of Albania's economy, has already had adverse effects on the European Union in general and the position of Italy and Greece in particular.

The war in the former Yugoslavia and the process of political destabilization that preceded and produced it – and that is still in progress – continues to exert a growing influence on the surrounding countries, especially those in the EU, where the matter is prevailingly seen in military terms. War strategies and armed forces are uppermost in Europe's thinking, which since the end of the Cold War has been preoccupied about establishing a continental security alliance inspired by the principles of economic and political cooperation among its nations. The war games inherited from old NATO strategies (as an unnatural extension of its role) are recycling armies and chiefs-of-staff that had appeared headed for retirement.

The support given to the nationalisms and local powers that be in the former Yugoslavia by certain segments of European and Western interests has helped to bring about the current war situation, which today threatens to have repercussions in Western Europe by reproducing the same destructive processes. Italy and Greece are especially exposed to these dangers.

Italy

The current crisis situation in Italy could be a prelude to the same sequence of events that brought about the collapse of Yugoslavia. The continuing armed conflict on its doorstep could lead to political links between factions and groups on both sides of the Adriatic Sea which have an interest in destabilization and, at the same time, reinforce the pressure of economic interests generated by the current situation.

Italy must simultaneously cope with the pressures brought to bear by three key phenomena – the war in Yugoslavia, immigration from there and Albania, and the crisis in the Middle East. If the peace initiatives should fail, Italy would be trapped between two major areas of conflict that would put its cohesion and internal stability under a great deal of strain.

Greece

The situation in Greece is also at risk. The pressures from the war on its northern borders, the conflict with Macedonia and the unresolved problem of its relations with Turkey, its powerful neighbour, place it in a particularly vulnerable position. The outcome could be tragic if the efforts being expended to bring stabilization to the Mediterranean countries by stimulating their development should fail and war prevail.

The economic initiatives recently enacted by the European Union to support development in the Occupied Territories of Palestine represent the beginning of a new attitude towards the problems in the Mediterranean. All the comments from Europe and the United States underscore that a positive outcome of the peace initiative depends on how quickly successful economic development is achieved there.

A financial commitment of three billion dollars over six years (against the ten billion requested by the Palestinians) can only represent initial good will, as it is not a significant investment when compared to the amount pledged to Eastern Europe. Note too that the aid earmarked for Palestine excludes any form of reparations for the occupation and is not a grant, which would have been logical to expect. Rather, it is a loan – a serious liability to the difficult process of Palestinian economic reconstruction. Estimates indicate that the Palestinian economy will have to set a galloping pace, at a 12 per cent yearly growth rate, to repay the loans. The situation being delineated is thus one that could give way to future conflicts and social tensions just like those that have occurred in other countries saddled with the burden of foreign debt.

GREATER EUROPE AND THE 'RIO GRANDE EFFECT' BETWEEN THE BALTIC AND MEDITERRANEAN SEAS

There is today a broad consensus of opinion, authoritative but not influential, that sees European economic integration as a table resting on four legs corresponding to Greater Europe's four meso-regions – the EU, Baltic Europe, Danubian Europe and Mediterranean Europe. Scandinavia's role in the reconstruction of Baltic Europe and Southern Europe's in that of Mediterranean Europe are of crucial importance to this process of integration.

The Mediterranean sea in many ways has already become Europe's Rio Grande because of the social, political and demographic problems focused along it that are placing enormous pressures on the countries of Southern Europe and, through them, on the EU in its entirety. The Baltic Sea and the whole area bordered by it, the Black and the Mediterranean seas will all be feeling similar pressures should the crisis in Russia and the other countries of the former Soviet Union worsen. The alternative to the reconstruction of a wall running from the Baltic through central Europe to the Mediterranean is to establish regional cooperation between the two shores so as to provide an effective response to the needs of the people and prevent the chaotic, illegal immigration to the West.

Production Systems, Population and Migrations in the Mediterranean

The Mediterranean region's development turns on the two key issues of rural development – whose importance can be seen in the fact that 40–60 per cent of its population lives in the countryside –

and increasing the number of small- and medium-scale enterprises that are so necessary to the growth of local markets. The process of industrial modernization in Europe during the last century led to the decline of the rural populace and fuelled the emigration of about 20 per cent of the population to Russia, the Americas and Australia. Should a similar modernization be dictated to the countries on the Mediterranean's southern rim, it would result over the next decade or two in an emigration of proportions so enormous and uncontrollable as to make plans of this ilk altogether unrealistic.

Current projections see the Mediterranean's population rising from the 360 million inhabitants of today to 450 million by the year 2000 and to 550 million by 2025. They also estimate that the population distribution of the 18 countries surveyed – now divided about evenly between the northern and southern shores – will change. Southern Europe's countries, from Spain to Greece, will account for slightly over a third and the countries from Morocco to Turkey on the southern and southeastern rim two-thirds of the total inhabitants. Population distribution by age group further indicates that by 2025 45 per cent of the population under the age of 15 will live on the southern and 24 per cent on the northern rim of the Mediterranean. In terms of labour market policy, this means that about 25 million jobs have to created before the end of the century and 60 million by 2025.

The Importance of the Rural World

These projections suggest that development in the Mediterranean must be based upon a concept of modernization which is grounded in a decentralized model of economic growth and which can regenerate the quality of life in rural areas and farm communities. The challenges to any development strategy are the creation of the premises for the survival and reinforcement of existing production systems (local industries and agriculture) and the introduction of new service and production activities necessary to the development of regional markets. The most pressing issues to be resolved are land reform, responsible and collective use of water resources, and the introduction of technologies to sustain agriculture and the Mediterranean food system.

The problems obviously differ from country to country, as do their solutions. Algeria and Morocco in the Maghreb have chosen two different paths to development and modernization. Neither has proven successful because too little attention was paid to the issues of endogenous development, and because of the conditions imposed by the IMF and the World Bank and the bilateral nature imparted to the relations between the EU and Arab states.

The Mediterranean and Development Models

Easing the demographic pressure on the Mediterranean's northern rim can only be achieved by matching the movement of persons from the South to the North with conspicuous transfers of capital from North to South so as to accelerate the development of internal markets in these areas. Yet that is not enough. Simply extending to the countries of the Basin's southern rim the Western production system and raising the consumption of a few elite groups within them to the bourgeois level cannot be pursued. For, at least in terms of intellectual coherence and scientific rigour, if we recognize the diversity represented by geographic areas, it only follows that we must recognize the diversity of production systems and their local forms of distribution and consumption, which are to be protected, strengthened and not destabilized in the name of abstract models of modernization.

The realization that a polycentric form of development is needed today in Europe is at last making headway, so that the solution to the problems of southern Europe may find strong support in the development of the Mediterranean Region as a whole. That is, southern Europe can play the role of interface with the rest of the Basin's countries, the Arab nations becoming the bridge to Africa, Turkey the door to the Middle and Far East and the centre of the infrastructure and communication links of the three continents.

Eleven countries – Bulgaria, Georgia, Romania, Russia, Turkey, Ukraine, Albania, Armenia, Azerbaijan, Greece and Moldavia – totalling 400 million inhabitants, established in June 1992 an area of economic cooperation in the Black Sea region. Of these countries, Turkey is already associated with the European Union and Bulgaria and Romania are about to sign a similar agreement. Successful cooperation among the Black Sea countries could dampen many tensions that today threaten the political stability and co-development in Europe and should thus be pursued with cogency.

Many signals indicate that the future development of world trade and economic cooperation, the negative impact of triadic globalization notwithstanding, will be based on the increasingly intensive relations within and between large economic regions. The current forms of unequal, bilateral exchange – raw materials for a handful of manufactured goods – will be transformed into a broader, more diversified system of cooperation running along better infrastructures and communications. In such a framework, Istanbul could become the key gateway of Europe's infrastructures to the 'hundred doors of the Middle East' and Asia, and, similarly, the Maghreb could transmit its positive effects to the far south of Africa.

NOTES

1. The text in this section was published, with several changes, in Amoroso, 1995, and excerpts from it appeared in the report by Treuner and Foucher, 1995.
2. For a critical discussion of the report, see Amoroso, 1990.
3. These issues are treated at length in Amoroso, 1992.

9 Toward Mediterranean Co-development

FOREWORDS

This chapter renews, as it deepens, the analysis of and reflection upon the issues and relations linking the European Union to the Mediterranean Region.

The moving forces behind this research initiative date to early 1990, when on the eve of Italy's semester at the helm of the EC the Economy and Labour National Council's International Relations Committee called upon the Italian government to spare no effort in focusing the Community's attention on the issues of the Mediterranean Region. The Committee had expressed in a number of documents its concern over a scenario depicting an increasingly developed and wealthy Europe ('EU+EFTA') flanked to the East and South by areas of intolerable social and political conflicts – a situation that might eventually transform Italy's role from a bridge spanning two continents to that of 'Fortress Europe's borderland.'

Subsequent events – the Gulf War and the civil war in former Yugoslavia – have confirmed the worst of these forecasts and halted efforts aimed at promoting relations of peaceful development and co-development in the Mediterranean Region. The weak peace initiatives that have ensued – the resumption of Israeli-Palestinian talks, joint EC-AMU cooperation accords – are taking place in a climate of heightened diffidence and hostility between Europe and the Arab world and of an escalating fierceness in the Yugoslav tragedy.

The events and developments that have marked 1992 are the focal points of this study. To them are to be added the all too familiar processes of political destabilization and economic marginalization in the South, not to mention the growth of political and economic instability even among the countries in the Mediterranean North and at the centre of the European Union itself. All of which brings with it the risk of the EU's withdrawing even further from issues external to it, or from new possibilities, because of its concentrating on building a Europe that is secure within its wealthiest areas and, hence, uninterested in the developments taking place in surrounding, less developed regions.

Two main lines of thought on development issues have taken up opposing positions in Europe today. On one side of the divide is the concept of co-development, a framework that would enable the southern EU countries to play a significant and progressive role as the linchpin of Euro-Mediterranean development. On the other is the Eurocentric view of development, visibly pointed eastwards, which would consign Italy and the other Mediterranean countries to a marginal position in the European order of affairs. If it proves possible to shape a development policy that encompasses both the East and the Mediterranean, it will perhaps be possible to achieve an equitable balance in Europe – a Europe that can not be restricted to the fifteen-member countries, much less to five or six countries, but one that must succeed in embracing the vast and complex geopolitical reality represented by the Mediterranean Region.

A Radical Change Toward the Mediterranean is Needed

It has recently, and authoritatively, been remarked:

> Though situated in and partaking of the life of the Mediterranean, and being both culturally and historically Mediterranean, our Mediterranean culture is in effect at a rather low level. For if we look at the cultural weight brought to bear on the issues of the Mediterranean and of Islam in France, or if we look at this same Mediterranean culture in Spain, our own Mediterranean culture is quite limited.
>
> (De Rita, 1992, p.3)

This study has from its very inception pursued two specific objectives. The first is to focus on economic development issues by highlighting their most salient social, institutional and labour-market factors. It is thus a matter of participating, together with the other research centres, in studies of the Mediterranean region by acting as a sounding board for the exigencies, interests and topics that are most germane to a body like the CNEL. The second is to bring these perspectives and ideas to the attention of a European-wide forum, the intention being not to export Italian views on these matters but to strengthen Italy's involvement in shaping a common European position on the Mediterranean.

'It is our impression that together with the Spaniards, the French and the Greeks we have something to contribute to the Mediterranean question' (De Rita 1992, p.4) by reason of history and religious, political and cultural affinities. The prevailing view of these issues within Europe is one of backward areas that, in the words of the Merloni Foundation, is still dominated by the 'textbook model of capitalist development' (Fondazione Merloni 1991), a model that has shown its limitations in the countries of these areas at least since the late 1960s. Unless there is a radical change in this attitude, the Mediterranean question will not only persist and intensify but will have, as is now occurring, marked repercussions on Italy and on Europe. These consequences, warnings of which for some time have been reported and recently reiterated, are 'in effect the expansionary movements of a system *qua* the European which, unless it is to become a Europe besieged in its fortress, can not but pass through the Mediterranean.' (De Rita 1992, p.3).

This chapter on the Mediterranean comprises five sections. *Part One* covers the cultural aspects of development and deals with the most salient recent trends shaping the cultural debate in the Arab world and the significance these factors may have for European-Arab dialogue.

Given the objective of co-development, policies of cooperation in the Mediterranean must be viable and applied in socio-economic contexts that are marked by a diversity or plurality of social ethics and entrepreneurial, consumer and institutional attitudes. An understanding of these varying backgrounds is a necessary premise to the establishment of durable collaborative ties. The issue is made all the more urgent by the fact that the Mediterranean is the divide or cross-roads of three important cultural and religious areas – Jewish, Christian and Arab-Muslim, each with its specific weight in the all-important sectors of social and economic organization. In comparison to the study main focus on cooperation and co-development policies, the emphasis on these subsequent topics is necessary because of their influence both on the diversity of conception and of organization with respect to the development of the two areas and on the concepts of society, modernization, institutions and rights of the citizenry (social, political and religious). The studies underpinning the indications contained in this chapter combine detailed treatments of the organizational forms of the economy and markets in the Islamic world in particular with a more general survey of the organization and role of science and technology in the Arab world, in Islam and in the Christian West as well as the theoretical principles of Islam's economic policies.

Part Two views the economic aspects of development from the standpoint of co-development. The importance that agriculture enjoys in the southern and south-eastern Mediterranean countries, both as to employment and share of GDP, explains the attention paid to what in these areas can justifiably be called the 'primary' sector of the economy. By developing further the analysis initiated in the *First Mediterranean Report* (Amoroso 1991) of modern and traditional agro-food systems and the conditions sustaining them, this section seeks to determine the areas of competition in the agrofood sector between the northern and southern rims of the Mediterranean. This is an issue often raised by grower and breeder associations in southern European countries because of the alleged competition to their commodities in the European marketplace from imported Afro-Asian Mediterranean products. Additional emphasis is placed on identifying specialized production fields that can enable the various Mediterranean areas to develop along the lines of exchange and technological cooperation. Attention is also devoted to the potential development of products earmarked to meet the demands of domestic markets, thereby reducing the agro-food deficit and redressing the severe food shortages afflicting local populations. This aspect is then linked to possibilities of developing Mediterranean commodities for export to European markets, an approach calling for cooperation on a Mediterranean-wide scale that would benefit the interests of all the region's inhabitants.

Part Three deals with the industrial sector and examines potential development strategies geared to replacing the model of a north-south Mediterranean trade based on the exchange of manufactured goods for raw materials. The emphasis here is on the need to pinpoint regional strengths capable of generating an industrial development via competitive structures and economies of scale. In an attempt to circumvent the dead-end alternative between the export-led and self-sufficient market, possibilities of how these two development models can be integrated in the individual areas are examined by positing the formation of a domestic market, sufficiently developed, that acts as a decision-making basis for specialized exports to world markets. North–South synergies are possible in both sectors.

The creation of products and consumer demand primarily aimed at the domestic market, the development of appropriate technologies and aid in the form of training programmes can play important roles in accelerating development. This is also an occasion for the northern countries both to extend their market reach and to expand hitherto under-utilized production capacity. The current technology and industrial organization of the northern countries, which are increasingly oriented to production systems in horizontally integrated networks, constitute an important opportunity to participate in this specialization and development. The condition necessary to accomplish this task is the creation of infrastructures and training programmes, and the business enterprises of the northern Mediterranean can in this connection play a positive role in terms of both their economic and social interests.

Part Four concerns the social aspects of Mediterranean development. It highlights the increasingly dramatic phenomenon of migration, its implications for the country of origin and of destination, the features making up immigration and the kind of responses evinced in both individual and social behaviour.

Part Five examines the policies and institutional aspects of Mediterranean development. Foreign debt and investment, area and regional policies, the labour market, research, education and financial cooperation are the key issues under review. The complementary character of economic development issues and the goal of co-development can be addressed properly only if the social bodies capable of discerning objectives, formulating proposals and laying the ground work for the creation of institutions to implement the necessary measures are found. As a first step in this direction, a proposal is advanced to convene a 'Mediterranean Forum' under the auspices of the trade unions and business organizations engaged in development and to draw up a 'Framework Programme' for development and economic cooperation in the Mediterranean.

CULTURE AND RELIGION IN MEDITERRANEAN DEVELOPMENT

Preamble

The consensus opinion among most experts is that some of the most lasting negative fallout from the Gulf War is the harm done to the image that both shores of the Mediterranean formed of one another. The exigencies of military propaganda, crude and oversimplifying, set back decades the tentative approaches towards a reciprocal understanding that in the last ten years had slowly begun to make headway. It is thus necessary to pick up the strands where they had been left, firmly reject received images of countries, peoples and religions insidiously painted to serve ends other than understanding and co-development, and set about reconstructing the detailed *tableau vivant* that stirs behind every colour print. (ILO, 1980, 1984; Bassetto and Bastenier, 1988; Luyckx, 1991; CNEL 1992).

Culture and Mediterranean Identity

Our point of departure is the tumultuous nature of the historical process marking events in the Arab world today. It is a process that provides ample food for critical, and self-critical, reflection on our own history and development, which in turn should give us cause to ponder our own cultural evolution over the last century. Contemplation of the most salient features, which are noted below, draws an interesting parallel that it has to the disquiet currently permeating European culture and Christianity. They are, once again, beset by doubts about their existential values and the direction of modernization. It is from this parallel – in each side's critical re-reading of its own history and in the need to rediscover one's identity and the values on which to base a renewal – that the outlines of greater hope can be identified, a hope that goes beyond simply resuming a dialogue limited to the repetition of hackneyed commonplaces all to familiar to both parties.

Yet, if it is not capable of progressing in substantially new forms, the ethos of dialogue and cooperation will prove in the long run a patient but sterile intellectual exercise, an incessant talking 'from opposite sides of the divide,' a round-table discussion protracted 'until the cows come home.' This ethos must be receptive, capable of advancing towards intellectual acceptance and of 'opening the door to intelligence.' A truly constructive dialogue, though based on the rediscovery of diversity, must move to promote convergent historical and cultural factors. For, in the end, were these latter to prove non-existent, the very theme of a unitary Mediterranean identity, from which our discussion originated by taking its inspiration from well-known approaches (Braudel), would collapse.

There is no doubt that in the current, highly conflictual situation the tendency on both sides of the debate is to place the accent on diversity as the element dividing the two cultures. Yet, this feeling of diversity underlying the discussion, must not serve as a political excuse to justify disengagement. These two cultural worlds, far from being antithetical one to the other, have in fact repeatedly crossed paths, and swords, throughout history, thereby enriching through reciprocal relations their heritage of knowledge and experience. In alternating phases the apogee of one has coincided with the nadir of the other, stimulating throughout this extended contact the processes of reawakening and renewal.

The Arab World and Modernization

How do the Arabs define their culture today and how do they meet, while maintaining this cultural cohesion, the challenge of modernization? It is widely felt that many important questions have gone unanswered, interweaving with the variegated political developments in various countries, over a historical period covering no less than a century. The reasons for the weakness of the Arab world have been sought, by turns, in its recourse to religious reformism and Islamic fundamentalism, in the search for its identity and origins, in its lack of civil liberties and social rights as decried by Arab socialism, in the attempts at Arab unity against the national and social boundaries artificially set up by foreign powers, in the drive to economic development and modernization. Yet none of these efforts has succeeded in going beyond the slogan stage and translating into a concrete model capable of constructing new interpretative paradigms.

Each of these explanations has at one time or other, and in one country or other, been the prevailing thought pattern. Today it is Islam, with a rapid feedback throughout the Mediterranean Arab countries, that again appears to be the reply of record. The extensive presence of Islamic movements leads to reflection not only on their socio-economic and political causes but also on their roots. While these movements are of various type, two factors seem common to all of them: the deep-seated crisis in various sectors of public life in the face of modernity's pressing demands as a cause and the reform of Arab-Islamic society as an end.

The former of these two main tendencies can be traced back to the modernization of Islam through a process of adaptation to the pressures of the contemporary world and the latter to the need to 'Islamicize' this modernity by cleansing it of its essentially Western-rooted innovations. A number of other, diversified positions, ascribable to the weight assigned to each facet of the problem and to the choice of method needed to bring about the desired transformation, can be found within these two overarching issues. The picture that emerges from the debates appearing in the press and from the numerous meetings and conferences being held in the Arab countries is a richly textured one.

Islam Today: The Historical Background

No brief survey of the positions that such a multi-faceted debate expresses is possible without over-simplification. Yet, once identified, the main lines seem to lead back to an attraction, often in reaction to a sense of frustration, that an increasingly expansive and aggressive European civilization – its technological and scientific as well as military arms being in the forefront – seems to have elicited from the Arabs in the later nineteenth century. Whence the drive to possess these techniques as well as the technological and scientific knowledge and the patterns of consumerism that go with them, although at the cost of neglecting speculative thought. This gave rise in turn to a far-reaching movement intent on producing and translating literary and educational texts through which numerous European technical and scientific terms entered Arabic. The will to grasp what Western culture had to offer was very strong indeed.

Why did these efforts fail and why did the dialogue break off? The explanation can be found by looking at the history of European-Arab relations from the late nineteenth century to the First World War. Europe, the exporter of ideas of 'progress', 'modernity', 'freedom', 'democracy', as well as of colonialism, a very painful era for the entire Arab world, gradually led itself and its culture down the road to dictatorship and racism. The struggle for survival forced upon the Arab countries in those years and, with the gaining of independence, their ensuing efforts to establish nation-states founded upon Islam led to their placing great emphasis on building institutions and organizations to ensure the defence and continuance of the state.

The hopes, all the expectations for a more closely knit, better informed, freer 'global village' that up to the late 1980s had been nurtured by the advances in high technology were again disappointed. For once again Western technology had become an instrument of domination and death, especially in the Islamic world. The globalization of the economy and of the new technologies loomed no longer as the short cut to a more efficient, more righteous world order but as the surest way back to colonialism.

The Debate in Arab Culture

What, then, in their own debate is the Arabs' response to the stasis that has affected the culture of these countries for at least the last century? While there is obviously no one, unanimous response, there are several that recur more often than others. The first is the very marked emphasis put on the need to accelerate scientific learning in all its aspects and its dissemination throughout society. There is too the rediscovery that scientific progress is not an exclusive bailiwick of the West. Here the example of Japan, with its capacity to adopt and employ Western technology and science to its own ends without violating its own traditions, is naturally of interest.

These and other variations on the theme are all part of the internal debate in the Arab countries today, quite apart from the cultural bludgeoning that Western-coined slogans on Islamic and fundamentalist movements seek to spread. One further perspective can be drawn from the historical events alluded to thus far: so long as the West and Europe continue to send troops to Arab countries, the Islamic response will necessarily take on the semblance of revolt and fundamentalism. Yet the need for dialogue and cultural understanding is not for this very reason less pronounced, and it must be decided whether the vested interests of war and oil are to continue to dominate those of peace and cooperation among the peoples of the two shores.

Two further considerations are here in order. Arab learning and culture have been far more active in studying Europe than Europe's of the Arab countries. This is evident above all in the fact that most Arabs know at least one European language and use it freely to advantage in their dealings, thereby facilitating them, with foreigners. The other is that Arab culture is multi-faceted, a result of the great social, cultural and national differences within these countries. This augers well, offering enormous possibilities, in promoting dialogue. But it most move forward on many fronts: from popular to academic culture, from the institutional and political to the informal levels of society.

Needless to say, a more widespread understanding in Europe, at least in southern Europe, of Arab history and language would be very useful. The study of the history and civilization of these peoples from elementary to secondary schools, greater efforts in the teaching of Arabic, which is as important as classical Greek and German, would help us to avoid some of the surprises and confusion that recent events in the Arab world have elicited because of our ignorance. Understanding what really occurs on the southern shore of the Mediterranean would greatly enrich us as persons and just as greatly add to the European debate on these same topics and in our own society. It would also enable us to see that an important breach is opening in the dialogue within these societies, to which we owe our solidarity and support so that they may grow and develop.

MEDITERRANEAN AGRO-FOOD SYSTEMS: SPECIALIZATION AND MARGINALIZATION

Introduction

A brief review of the salient features of the Mediterranean's agro-food system and of the individual areas is an essential prerequisite for the analysis of the proposals hinging on innovative specializations, cooperation and co-development.

(i) *Agriculture continues to be the key economic sector in the Mediterranean Basin.* With the exceptions of France and Italy, farming still contributes significantly to employment and GDP in a great many areas of the region, the former ranging from 20–40 per cent and the latter form 10–38 per cent. The employment data in particular reflect the much broader socio-economic role played by rural market towns and their populations, which in large measure are dependent upon traditional farming enclaves than at first glance the figures might seem to indicate. In the Maghreb and Mashraq, for example, an estimated eight million small farm holdings (less than 5 ha), which are family-run, low-yield operations, occupy slightly more than 10 per cent of the total area. To this production structure, which is often at the edge of sustainable viability, gravitates either directly or indirectly a population estimated as ranging from 30 to 60 million persons (depending on calculation method), or 20–35 per cent of the total populace. This represents the largest potential reservoir of migration over the next few years.

(ii) *A food deficit measured as the balance of import-export trade is common to all Mediterranean countries.* The exceptions in this case include France in Europe, Morocco in the Maghreb, Turkey in the Mashraq and the Balkan countries (excluding the former Yugoslavia). A look at the patterns over the last two decades shows that only France and the former Yugoslavia registered advances in the agro-food trade balance, whereas the overall downturn was more marked in the countries of the non-EU regions – the Balkans, Mashraq and Maghreb – than in the Union countries. The performance of the agricultural as opposed to the other economic sectors in the individual countries worsened everywhere, except in the Balkans, the non-EU areas being the hardest hit. In these latter, only fruit and vegetable output kept pace with population growth.

(iii) *The marked reliance of the Mediterranean, as opposed to the EU and other regions of the 'Triad,' on the agro-food industry, its distribution and research.* The 1990 rankings of the world's leading agro-food companies include only 8 French and 3 Italian as compared to 37 American, 19 British, 17 Japanese, Dutch, 3 Swiss, 2 Swedish and 4 Australian firms. In addition, an analysis of the strategies of the two largest Mediterranean groups, the Italian Feruzzi and the French Groupe BSN, confirms the marginalization of the non-EU Basin countries in favour of marketing and production policies aimed at Central Europe and, in isolated cases, at EU-Basin countries offering the best business opportunities (e.g. Spain). The data on research (especially in biotechnology) and industrial manufactured goods (i.e. tractors, fertilizers, etc.) provide further confirmation. One example of this 'integration-subordination' of Mediterranean farm commodities to the distribution network of north-central Europe is canned tomato: Great Britain is the largest importer of Italian tomatoes and 70 per cent of Italy's output is controlled by three supermarket chains, Sainsbury, Tesco and Safeway.

There is too an evident asymmetry in the distribution of the main offices of multi-national enterprises in Basin countries: their concentration is visibly high in the EU, 204 groups, and notably sparse in non-EU states, only 36 overall. This bias in turn translates as marginalization when looking at the expansion of these groups in terms of branch offices in individual countries: the few multi-national agro-food firms operating in the non-EU Basin register an average of only 1.2 branches per country as opposed to the 5.6 of the multi-nationals in Union countries.

(iv) *Policy and market shortcomings* vis-à-vis *the needs of the agricultural systems*. The inadequacy of the farm policies pursued hitherto, whether by national governments or the EU, can be seen in the general tendency to reduce commodity prices and investment rates in agriculture, especially in the southern and south-eastern Mediterranean. This is a result of the enactment in key agro-food products of measures designed progressively to encourage the import of Union commodities into the southern Basin countries at prices below those of their domestic markets. The basis of this policy is the joint EU–US effort to reduce grain, dairy and meat surpluses as well as the downward trend in the international prices of these commodities. The effects include a further weakening of Mediterranean agricultural systems and their increased reliance on 'Triadic' agro-business, even where they had established forms of cooperation. Tunisia is an emblematic case in point, though not the only one. Special trade measures were adopted to encourage imports of cheap milk from the EU to meet growing urban demand, a strategy requiring the building of plants to process the imported powdered milk. The overall effects of this operation have been to complete the destruction of the local dairy industry and an increase in unemployment, the trade deficit and dependence on foreign technology.

In Morocco, too, forms of cooperation and the development of new commodities have been implemented without taking into account the compatibility of production systems, with adverse effects on the country's overall agro-food system. Intensive cultivation for the European market of citrus fruits, early horticultural produce and greenhouse crops in the Agadir Region have caused overexploitation of the water tables of the Souss Valley, leaving droughtruined both the land and the small farmers in the surrounding areas and increasing unemployment in the cities. Paradoxically, the effects on local agricultural systems of these ill-planned development schemes are all the more devastating the more developed are the infrastructures and transport systems in these countries. For it is via these systems that the liberalization of farm-commodity imports is able to spread rapidly to the farthest reaches of the country, thereby involving even the traditional farm systems far removed from the entry ports.

The international community over the last two decades has begun to reassess the nature and roots of the North–South issue. The UN has established the International Fund for Agricultural Development (IFAD), charging it with specific tasks for the poorest areas and production sectors. The Non-Government Organizations (NGO) were founded at the same time to enact, via a strategy designed fully to involve local counterpart groups, development projects whose economic goals are closely linked to social issues, especially employment. Yet, despite these changes, the many and important institutions with briefs for the Mediterranean seem unable to deal decisively with the link between the decline of the peasant communities in the southern Mediterranean and the customs levies enacted by individual countries. Although the EU is about to allow limited fruit and vegetable imports from the Maghreb, such a measure by itself is not sufficient to fuel the economic growth of these countries and must be reinforced by a gradual regulation of EU exports to the southern Mediterranean. For a gradual levy mechanism of this kind is imperative in these countries: on the one hand to prevent sudden price increases overwhelming the urban populace and on the other to regulate targeted commodity price increases, the only means that peasant-farming communities threatened with extinction have to pursue via innovation the economic strength to resist.

It should be noted that the mention of innovation in this context refers not to the application of northern technology, which is largely designed for other ecosystems and adaptable only at high cost in those of the southern Mediterranean, where in any case they would be useless to existing peasant production systems. Nor, certainly, is the introduction of Dutch livestock breeds the answer to what the rural Maghreb, and southern, labour force needs to upgrade production performance. The conditions determining whether these farms will remain in the marketplace are to be found instead in the revaluation of local genetic resources and crop-management techniques – solutions that in the short term will surely prove less profitable for EU exports. Thus, to pricing policy must be added credit measures consonant with the area's type of agriculture and the introduction of innovations based upon the implements and crop practices currently in use by these farmers.

Environmental Imbalances

The most pronounced dichotomy in Mediterranean agricultural systems is the same one that has accompanied the history of Italian farming throughout the second post-war period: that between the modern and traditional systems. The production-oriented rule of thumb that in the 1960s and 1970s guided Italy's agricultural policies in the nation's efforts to modernize the system took its inspiration from what has been called the *bone* and *meat* classification: the former, obviously, to be thrown away and the second to be 'cured' and developed. From this interpretative framework, revealing as it may be, were fashioned concepts of economic and agricultural policy that on the one hand entrusted to the government and local community authorities the defence and development of modern systems (the meat) and on the other abandoned to their own devices the protection of traditional sectors (the bone) (Rossi-Doria 1958).

The experience of the subsequent decades has shown that the unpaid social costs, which stemmed from the crisis of the traditional sector, are transformed into overhead costs (or at any event in a 'due notice' to be paid by the state), and that the result in the best of cases is a 'tax transfer.' Indeed, once the bone was thrown away, the meat left had little taste. For, once the Mediterranean's agricultural system lost the traits linking the modern and traditional, the peculiarities of which should have been promoted, its produce today appears as a less than useful commodity both on Mediterranean markets and on the international market as a raw material 'for blending.'

This pattern has been repeatedly documented in the Mediterranean record. The effects over the last twenty years of the resulting imbalances can be seen in the concentration of Mediterranean farm production in the limited irrigation-fed belts, especially in the southern part of the Basin. The extent of arable land in many countries has today diminished overall, a fact that has reinforced both migratory tendencies and the degradation of the ecosystem. The encroaching desert in arid regions and the increasing salinization of the soil in the irrigated ones are the most evident aspects. Local governments are being supported by international funding in their efforts to control desertification. Tunisia's Sahel is an example: the desert is advancing at a rate that reduces the arable land by 0.16 per cent yearly. With the aid of funds provided in part by the

United Nations, the government has implemented a project to reconvert current crop systems over vast tracts of land by alternating yearly grass crops with tree plantations: the latter, because they are mid-to-long-term crops, are better able to check soil erosion.

A more enduring stewardship of the Mediterranean's Afro-Asian arid areas, however, requires the renewal of *traditional* agricultural systems as well as targeted reforestation projects. For these systems – a mix of crop and livestock farming – the maintenance and renewal of soil fertility are primary concerns. The management practices employed for these purposes, *qua* crop rotations involving consecutive years of fallowing, make possible the re-adjustment over the medium-long term of the chemical-physical structure of the soil that is necessary to stem the encroachment of the desert. Desertification is in effect the last stage of a prolonged erosion, which in the Mediterranean's Afro-Asian zones is largely due to crop techniques imported but a few decades ago – techniques based on extensive mechanization and monoculture plantings of vast tracts of acreage in grass-cereal or industrial crop rotations that consume large amounts of soil resources. Examples of resolving such problems by resorting to practices of traditional farming systems can be found today in the Middle East, especially in Syria where the only effective remedy to the decline of the arid areas was a return to techniques used in pasture management.

The migration of population from internal and highland areas in EU countries of the Basin has been a topic of economic and political concern for nearly thirty years. For example, these countries have enacted legislation and economic policy measures aimed at protecting the environmental decline of highland areas in the wake of a thinning local populace. The concept of the social importance attaching to farmers in the EU's mountain zones, in recognition of the interdependence of the environmental status of these lands and the areas lying below them as well as of the stewardship of the ecosystem as embodied in the management practices typical of traditional farming systems, was introduced long ago. Any policy of Mediterranean cooperation should thus recognize not only the production but also the social role played by traditional farming systems in light of the environmental stewardship that the crop techniques developed by them imply.

Towards Cooperation and Co-Development

It is imperative that these lessons be learned today so as not to repeat the same mistakes on a far greater scale and to re-establish a role for agriculture in this context. These are the reasons why this report places so much emphasis on the modern and traditional systems of Mediterranean agriculture. The point of departure, then, is the premise that Mediterranean policy must walk, in this as in other production sectors, on two legs towards two primary goals.

The two legs represent the modern and traditional farming systems and the two primary goals the development of a modern agro-food system capable of competing in a wealthier global marketplace and of meeting the essential demands of its own domestic market within a given region and area. The provisions of such a strategy require both planning and a concerted production that transcends the limits of that planning. Several indications in which to ground this work can be found in existing material. The directions to be pursued and elaborated in creating a modern Mediterranean agro-food system oriented to exports for world markets are surveyed in the following pages.

(i) *A Mediterranean consensus for commodity specialization and trade.* Such a concert of effort is to be made even within the crop and livestock production systems themselves, and hence oriented not so much to inter-industrial as to intra-industrial compatibility. Worthy of note in this connection is the fact that, in so far as ecological-crop calendar discordances and the ensuing intra-Mediterranean potentialities are concerned, the climatic conditions in North Africa are conducive to growing such vegetables as tomato in January and February. Concerted planning in staggering supply so as to put Mediterranean produce in European markets throughout the year can not but be charged to a regional, all-Mediterranean body. Intra-Basin agreements between grower associations and trade unions can be negotiated under the auspices of *Regional Mediterranean Consortia,* which can be established to transform what today appears an insurmountable obstacle of nature, which by itself turns men into enemies or at least into competitors, into an economic growth factor of the Mediterranean areas as whole.

(ii) *Promotion of Mediterranean produce by its 'trademark' production structure – modern and traditional – as a guarantee of genuineness and health*. By exploiting the experiences acquired in given areas (for example the Emilia-Romagna) and in given lines (fruit and vegetables), produce can be marketed with characteristics that are the result of a mix of private and public capital investment programmes enacted on a long-term basis and of low-chemical input, that is biological and integrated pest and disease control methods.

(iii) *Detailed information and updates on market competition factors for planning price policy and import duties*. This would likely highlight the inadequacy of simple import barriers to protect EU growers *vis-à-vis* the adjustments necessary in the face of changes in the overall context. The demands and policies pursued in EU-'Third' country trade relations have been based on the assumption that any opening of borders to the southern Basin nations results in a short-term loss of share to EU growers in their traditional northern European markets. Quite the contrary. The competition to the EU's Mediterranean produce in European markets comes, and is already a powerful presence, from agro-food systems *qua* the Californian and South African that are as modern as those in the EU. The former have learned the valuable lesson of the importance of promoting regional qualities and of organizing trade networks for world-market access.

In turning attention back to the reduction of economic and social imbalances besetting the Mediterranean region today, serious misgivings are to be advanced about whether the simple possibility of exporting fruit and vegetables to European tables effectively constitutes a real development factor for Maghreb and Middle-Eastern agriculture. Currently available data would seem to support the assumption that a reversal of the depressed conditions of the southern Basin's traditional farming sector can not come about save through a much more complex series of measures than this free-trade option.

The options that need to be promoted and pursued in defending and developing the traditional Mediterranean agro-food system oriented to the domestic market and to the stewardship of the environment are as follows.

(i) *An agricultural policy strategy aimed at co-development in the Basin's southern regions and targeted to traditional farming systems*. Such a package of measures would entail shifting from the short to the long term expectations of returns on investment – a rescheduling that in turn implies a leading role for the public sector and specific policy decisions to define the framework within which are to be plotted the agricultural policy provisions.

(ii) *Specific intervention to benefit traditional production systems.* These policy measures must be based on (a) import levies designed to protect local growers from the international price system and (b) the designation of free-trade zones between countries of similar labour productivity. It should be noted that, at least on paper, the EU has for some time appeared favourably disposed to solutions of this kind for non-industrialized countries. One evident example is the cooperation in the sector of exports from developing nations that was implemented in the mid-1970s with various Latin American bodies for regional integration (Central American Common Market).

(iii) *Labour and land policies tailored to the sector's requisites.* This implies the drawing up *in loco* and the enactment of economic projects of high labour coefficient employing scant local resources with 'no-waste' methods.

(iv) *Structural policies.* The growth of a nation-wide agro-industry with scaled-down facilities that exploit processing and marketing techniques rooted in the economy and local culture.

(v) *A capillary system of services specifically oriented to farm enterprises.* In addition to offering such services as crop transport and distribution, this system should disseminate extension-service information, both managerial and technical, to support decision-making processes and the crop and livestock requisites of growers.

(vi) *Research and development of specific technology.* The emphasis is to be placed on safeguarding the techniques, often among the oldest of such practices and in danger of disappearing, proper to these farming systems. It is in fact because of their survival and the layers of knowledge acquired through the ages that they are held among the most valuable assets of man's common heritage.

(vii) *Protection of Mediterranean germplasm and livestock breeds.* Appositely established institutions are to monitor throughout the Mediterranean transactions of genetic material to private concerns, whether multi-national or national, and international organizations. The Mediterranean is in fact one of the world's main reservoirs of genetic variability, especially in its Near

Eastern end which is one of the areas where for several plant species it is still possible to find a high degree of genetic difference as well as species that have disappeared everywhere else. This germplasm constitutes the raw material needed to add new or replenish traits in the most commonly cultivated species. It should be noted in this connection that in the last fifty years the genetic variability of the twenty most widely grown crop species has diminished by 75 per cent because of standardized breeding programmes. This increasing genetic uniformity is today the cause of genuinely disastrous outbreaks, and their transmission speed, of plant pests.

The most important stewards of local ecotypes today are the peasant farmers in those geographic and crop-producing areas least affected by modernization. The reservoir of genetic variability in the Mediterranean Basin is thus mainly concentrated in traditional agricultural systems, and hence the crisis and the progressive disappearance to which these same systems seem fatally condemned today raise serious doubts about the neutrality with which these phenomena are viewed. A provisional look indicates that one of the heavier weights on the scales of this crisis is the transfer of genetic value from the rural populations of the Basin's traditional agrarian societies to the firms controlling the gene banks. In order to grasp the economic import of these transactions, suffice it to say that the search for and the storage and marketing of rare plants can translate into yearly sales for a company of nearly 200 million US dollars, and that the seed sales of wheat cultivars crossed with differing *trait-donor* varieties amounted to about 1.8 billion US dollars annually over the last few years.

Other examples worthy of note involve the livestock breeds belonging to traditional farming systems. The result of breeding carried out over millennia in the ecosystems where they are found today, the local sheep, goat, cattle and camel species are the only ones that can survive the rigours of the arid climate prevailing in a large part of the Basin's non-irrigated lands. The species of native ruminants are thus the only vector through which man can harness the energy contained in the thinly covered hill and mountain pasturage scattered over those barren lands, not to mention the pre-desert steppes. The key term, it bears reiterating, is scattered, for these resources *per se* are not scarce. The repeated attempts to replace this indigenous livestock capital – for capital it is in a very real sense – with stock bred almost entirely over the last few decades in the rainy ecosystems of northern Europe and the United States can not but result, as the record already shows, in failure. Northern-bred bovine stock are indeed highly productive yet, and quite apart from the problems of climatic adaptation, they are both anatomically ill-suited to wild grazing, especially in rough terrain, and are wholly dependent for their considerable output on high resource inputs *qua* meadow-grown green forage and hay – resources that are indeed scarce in the Mediterranean ecosystem.

Natural and Structural Potentialities

Despite the continuing decline in competitiveness of traditional production structures, they have not, as might be expected, disappeared. Only the emigration of the entire family would spell the end to all farming activity. This is a rather remote possibility in that the older members of a farm family, apart from the elderly, of course, would be hard-pressed to find employment outside the farm, and the cost of subsistence is far less on the farm, if for no other reason than the minimum amount of produce that can be raised for self-consumption. This is why migration from the farm in the southern Mediterranean tends to be a partial phenomenon, often involving only one member of the family, and why it does not result in the depopulation of entire rural areas.

There is a positive note implicit in this situation: the survival in these rural communities of a know-how persisting throughout the techniques and systems of traditional agriculture. In other words, despite signs of disgregation, a social fabric still exists that is capable of transforming local natural resources into the basic staples of subsistence. This is no mean achievement when it is considered that the loss of this expertise is one of the most pressing problems arising from the changes currently affecting agriculture in vast areas of such regions as the former Soviet Union and Latin America.

In addition to the features of its production structure, the agro-food system evinces in the three non-EU Basin areas notable technical and scientific potentialities. Apart from the expertise in techniques developed for arid climes by the Israelis and Syrians, this can be gauged by the number of institutions of higher learning with curricula in agro-food disciplines. A glance at the geographical distribution of the university faculties that are to varying extent within the sphere of the primary sector clearly shows that their

Figure 9.1 Mediterranean Scenario: Agro-Food Education Institutions (1992)

○ Faculties of Agricultural Sciences, Veterinary, Forestry, Fishery, Food Technology
● Higher Education Institutes on Mediterranean Agriculture

Source: S. Gomez y Paloma, (ed.) *Agro-Food and Biotechnology in the Baltic and Mediterranean Regions*, p.39, FOP 347. Brussels: MONITOR-FAST, 1992.

levels of concentration in the Balkans and the Near East are comparable to those in the Basin's EC countries. This indicator also provides a measure of the capital investments in the form of technical-scientific knowledge that, potentially at least, 'Third' countries in the Mediterranean have made. It would not be groundless to assume, in the light of this gauge, that the lack of results this technical-scientific potentiality has thus far shown in the field of production can be traceable to a development model that is partially inadequate to the characteristics, both socio-economic and of the ecosystem, of these areas – characteristics that are more import-oriented (in this case securing technical and learning advances from northern Europe as opposed to the United States) than focused on developing the peculiarities of the region through intra-regional cooperation (figure 9.1).

Biotechnology is another potentiality of the Mediterranean,

especially in North Africa and the Middle East. Genetic engineering, as applied to the reservoir of germplasm in the areas of the 'Fertile Crescent', can be employed to offset, at least in part, the climatic handicaps by breeding high-yield cultivars resistant to abiotic stress (especially drought). Noteworthy in this connection are the various joint agreements and scientific contacts among international organizations, universities and Mediterranean research centres. Biotechnology can also help in recovering local empirical practices by acting as a bridge between scientific and empirical learning and by promoting diversity, genetic above all but even technical and social, as a mechanism of stability in farm ecosystems. Biotechnology thus becomes both an element of collaboration and a potential field of endeavour aimed at enabling the Mediterranean to re-acquire its long-held role of cross-roads and meeting ground for economies, societies and cultures.

The Mediterranean: Basin of Marine Resources

Although the Mediterranean yields far less fish than demand requires, its catch commands high market value, its limited piscine resources being renowned for their quality. Suffice it to note that Mediterranean fish commodities account for only 1.2 per cent by weight but 5 per cent in value of the world's total. Nonetheless, it is currently estimated that the Basin's entire output is barely enough to cover 25 per cent of its population's demand for fish products. Countries like Portugal are net importers of fish.

Despite the relative dearth of fish in the Mediterranean as compared to the oceans, initiatives focusing on this important natural resource are not lacking. Tunisia, for example, has unveiled plans to build twenty new fishing ports, in addition to its having signed joint international ventures in this sector with Algeria, Mauritania and Italy. These latter projects are worthy of mention in another sense too, for they constitute the first visible signs in the rebuilding of a single Mediterranean Region. To these endeavours must be added the more or less recent opening of new fishing harbours in Libya (1983) and the ongoing renovation of others in Algeria.

To these considerations must be added another: a joint regulatory agency, with a trans-national and intra-Mediterranean management involving nations, individual regional administrations of the fishing grounds, trade unions and industry associations, would seem to be both opportune and advisable in this sector. Mention should be made in this connection of the General Council for Fishing in the Mediterranean, one of the first concrete examples of international cooperation in the region. A supra-national, intra-Basin body charged with planning and regulating the fish industry would also be the best way to transform the frequent disputes among the seaboard countries into a common source of action for the common benefit. Such an institution could even become the centre of a framework within which finally to press beyond the all too consolidated tendency towards the stop-gap or short-term measure *qua* the practice whereby the weaker side grants fishing rights in its territorial waters to stronger competitors under the guise of a licensing fee. The example of the 1988 pact negotiated through EU mediation by Spain and Morocco is a good case in point.

The high potentiality of the Mediterranean as a pool of marine resources is on the other hand implicit in the integration options open to today's production system, especially along the lines of introducing in the work cycle a stand-down period for resource reproduction and renewal. In other words, moving along lines that benefit the fishing industry. The Mediterranean's favourable climatic conditions and numerous inlets and lagoons make it possible to estimate in about one million hectares the coastline areas suitable for aquaculture, 80 per cent of which are situated in Greece, Italy and Egypt. To this must be added the expertise already acquired and its continuing development at various research centres in this field.

Yet there is a cautionary proviso to the effect that any changes in current fishing practices aimed at a more intensive exploitation of the volume of water through the techniques of aquaculture as opposed to deep-sea fishing, though they may undoubtedly engender considerable profits, should be subject to the solving of the problem, or at least that it be taken into consideration, of the Mediterranean's marine pollution, already at record levels. It needs no further reminder than to register the fact that about 20 per cent of the world's oil-tanker traffic passes through the Sea, which accounts for barely 0.7 per cent of the earth's marine area. The importance accorded to the pollution issue is shown too by the several clean-up programmes, which are strongly supported by all the coastal nations, established some time ago and funded by leading international organizations.

SPECIALIZATION AND COMPATIBILITY OF MEDITERRANEAN INDUSTRIAL SYSTEMS

Markets and Production Structures

This book has already recalled several facts: the asymmetries between the countries on the Basin's northern and southern rims, the approach to trade relations still dominated by the old resources-for-manufactures paradigm and the absence of horizontal markets within and between the region's various areas. The brief of this part is to determine the regional strengths that can engender a development capable of meeting domestic demands and of successfully competing in the international marketplace.

The specialization of regional development is, in certain respects, a premise for the subsequent development of an inter-regional trade. The question here is one of identifying market niches, technological potentialities and human resources which can combine synergistically in a specialized output that both meets regional demand and produces a surplus for export to European and international markets. This type of analysis is purposed to identify both the areas of possible conflict and competition with and the compatibility or complementary nature of counterpart industries in the northern Mediterranean countries so as to determine common industrial policies that are better suited to some rather than other manufacturing companies and to a closer cooperation in the industries that produce capital goods and develop new technology. In the latter case, it is not a matter of simply identifying common ground between producers and consumers of new technology but of planning training programmes in a joint effort aimed at promoting development and the production of new technology in the southern countries.

This effort can only proceed via dialogue with industrialists, trade unions and community representatives to decide upon the right, as well as the possible, objectives. The task of research and researcher alike is to focus attention on the constraints of the market and of the structures of production and technology upon which action and interaction must be based to keep objectives and expectations from becoming no more than wishful thinking. Research can also act as a technical support in identifying the framework of the complementary factors necessary to any nascent development programme.

Foreign and Transnational Investment

Among the market constraints that are crucial to a meso-regional analysis like the present one are the 'triadic' development processes discussed in Chapters 2 and 3. Other facets of TNC operations and strategies are noteworthy in order to determine the potentiality that the technology they control offers in the perspective of future development scenarios and of alternatives and to identify possible strategies of policy intervention aimed at reinstating supra-national regulatory measures in economic and development matters pursuant to social goals of benefit to countries, areas and regions.

Three of these aspects are of particular importance. New modes of flexibility accruing to TNCs by new technology constitute the first. They enable a horizontal specialization of output and organization via production-system clusters. These are forms of industrial organization designed to exploit, as they employ, the relative advantages found in various countries by decentralizing entire lines or individual stages of production. This undoubtedly opens up new prospects for a Mediterranean cooperation geared to co-development if the attention of the large industrial groups of southern Europe in particular and the EU in general can be refocused to converge on the Mediterranean. The second concerns the growing importance of internal stability, infrastructures and professional training in the decision-making processes of large companies, including the TNCs themselves, in matters of investment allocation. This view is confirmed by the eastward shift in resources, and it is in these sectors that the Mediterranean must, and realistically can, rapidly regain lost ground. The third confirms the meso-regional approach to development taken by this study from its inception. The creation of a European market capable of holding significant shares in world markets depends on its capacity to achieve a size that only a Europe stretching from the Baltic to the Mediterranean can afford. The survival of southern Europe's industrialized nations – France, Italy and Spain in particular – is bound up in their ability to extend their industrial base to the entire Mediterranean 'region' by integrating it in processes of co-development.

Co-Development and New Technologies

Technological innovations have engendered new forms of decentralized production and decision-making, both between and within sectors, that provide new impetus to industrial co-development. The TNCs have pioneered exemplary models of industrial organization in this respect. Industrial development in Asia has made extensive use of these organizational forms, an example from which much can be learned. Advances in technology thus make it possible to overcome the old dichotomy, and source of conflict between the countries of the Basin's northern and southern rim, inherent to resource allocation among various economic sectors.

Today the issue is no longer, nor necessarily, the relocation of industrial sectors (e.g. textiles, foods) but industrial compatibility or complementariness, a factor that enables gradual and partial transfers of production capacity within which the comparative advantages of each single company, area and region can be exploited. Then, too, global competition demands that Europe expand a consumer and industrial base that is much narrower than that of Japan and the United States.

These new systems of business growth are called industrial 'clusters', the most successful of which are found in South-East Asia where they have been applied by Japanese corporations to exploit the comparative advantages offered by the region.

The large industrial groups of the EU are following this lead too, although they are doing so by by-passing the Mediterranean in favour of Central and Eastern Europe. According to 1991 UN data, Community members accounted for 31 per cent of the 602 total joint ventures in Czechoslovakia, 36 per cent of the 556 in Hungary, 63 per cent of the 869 in Poland and 42 per cent of the 1531 in the former Soviet Union. Unlike the investments of the Japanese in Asia and of the US in Mexico, these figures reflect the fact that, as the UN has pointed out, many investments in Central and Eastern Europe have been made with an eye to future potential than to immediate earnings. (EU industrial expansion in these areas of Europe also includes Italy, Fiat in particular.) It is, however, a picture from which the Mediterranean is notably absent.

These statistics show on the one hand the potential for integration and co-development offered by the new technologies and industrial strategies in the Mediterranean in general and with the EC in particular, and on the other the need to lay the ground work necessary for implementing this development.

Specialization and Industrial Cooperation

Chapter 6 documents the structural features of Mediterranean specialization dominated by the relative advantages of position enjoyed by Italy and France which in turn are dependent on and threatened by the industrial hierarchy in both the European (Germany) and world-wide (the US and Japan) marketplaces. This is clearly reflected in the overall picture of Mediterranean trade relations, which evince the absence of area markets throughout the southeastern Basin. An analysis of the substance of this exchange – raw materials of the Arab countries for northern manufacturers – does nothing to enhance this profile. A summary breakdown of industry specialization in the Mediterranean countries brings to light the following features.

(i) Algeria, Libya, Syria and, to lesser extent, Egypt evince specialization in industries that are either energy-intensive (refining, basic chemicals, fertilizers, basic steel, concrete) or raw-material oriented and based on continuous-cycle, large-scale and mainly state-owned plants.
(ii) Morocco, Egypt, Jordan, Turkey and Greece are heavily specialized in traditional labour-intensive sectors, for example food, textiles, clothing, shoes, that transform local raw materials in largely small-scale plants both publicly and privately owned.
(iii) The former Yugoslavia, Albania, Turkey, Greece and Egypt exhibit relatively specialized, small- and mid-scale machine industries of public and private ownership for the manufacture of semi-finished and finished goods.
(iv) France, Italy and Spain have highly specialized industries for mass-market consumer durables and capital goods, the former dominated by large public- and private-sector companies and the latter by small- and mid-scale private firms.

The Objectives of Cooperation

One of the eventual levers to be employed in developing joint ventures among Basin countries is the exploiting of existing, and complementary, compatibilities between industrial structures. The marked presence of a traditional manufacturing sector in most of the southern and south-eastern nations on the one hand and of specialized producers in machine tools and equipment for such a sector in the northern-rim nations on the other can be seen as a step in the right direction towards the creation of a joint network that amalgamates both suppliers and buyers. For it is through cooperation that businesses can develop new, more advanced technologies than would otherwise be the case in a simple buyer-seller market. It is an option that provides manufacturers and purchasers with a range of highly compatible, and complementary, resources.

This kind of cooperation could achieve several key objectives: (i) increase output by introducing both new technology and training of personnel; (ii) promote specialization and diversification to increment local and regional market share and at the same time to raise incomes and consumer demand; and (iii) create an independent capability of innovation. The sectors most directly interested in enhanced production methods and, as a result, in technology transfer are the food, textile, clothing, shoe, iron and steel, petrochemical (especially basic chemicals) and electric and non-electric machinery (and measuring and monitoring instruments) industries. An enhanced position of non-EU Basin countries in these sectors would result in the promoting of demand for technology in EU members and in expanding supply in local and foreign markets for higher quality products.

The new methods technology offers to cluster organization in industry can be put to good use in several of the above-mentioned sectors, thereby enabling both parties to be active players in promoting and controlling the development of new ventures. The main advantage of these horizontal modes of industrial organization is their inclusion in the production cycle of businesses that, despite their relative disadvantages in certain sectors, can contribute productively where they enjoy relative advantages, thus becoming part of a complex production structure from and through which they can learn and exploit in order to enhance their own specialization. A detailed knowledge of the requisites of each country's industries and sectors is, of course, the basic premise on which realistically to build industrial cooperation in joint-venture agreements. Several key elements in this connection have been brought to light by the ongoing efforts of this study's research group and are discussed below.

The Food Industry
Enhanced productivity can be achieved by modernizing the technology employed in storage and by the development of new products and production processes. Climatic conditions and export requisites demand full compliance with health standards and with

storage techniques (drying, freezing, pasteurizing, canning, bottling and so on) designed to prevent the growth of micro-organisms and commodity deterioration. Such innovations also tend to promote the development of new products having higher quality ratings. Production techniques in the food industry are among some of those most affected by the micro-electronics revolution, with displacement effects occurring throughout the southern European countries (Italy and Spain in particular). Machinery that incorporates micro-processors are currently employed in food, beverage and tobacco plants to control sterilization, drying, freezing and ingredient quality. A technology transfer in these sectors, apart from increasing output and quality, would also mean enhanced development of Europe's food-machinery industry.

The Textile Industry
Production systems and organization need to be upgraded. Manufacturing innovations, which can easily be secured in the machine-tool market, mainly concern the so-called 'open-end' spinners, which could replace the 'ring' models in the coarser products, thereby increasing yarn output two- or more-fold over traditional spinners and relegating the latter to the finer and more prized production. Shuttleless looms, which double production by markedly reducing the number of steps required by shuttle models, and electronic sewing machines, which programme tasks, would cut pre-sewing time and increase both flexibility in changing patterns and the quality of the finished product. Such technological changes in the more important stages of manufacture like spinning and weaving would directly result in substantial hourly gains in labour productivity and in cost-cutting. For their part, the EC countries, already faced with increasing competition from textiles of non-EC Basin countries, would reap benefits in terms of production and research in the machine-tool sector. Italian industry is on the other hand already familiar with the advantages deriving from producer-user cooperation in the textile industry.

The Clothing Industry
This is another sector that has been radically altered by the micro-electronics revolution. The major technological advances include computer-aided sales, procurement, graphics and CAD-DAM systems in design and quality control of both product and cut, and programmable sewing machines in *stand-alone* and sequential

configurations. These innovations have drastically changed not only production schedules and methods but also, and mainly, product quality and life span. The advances in design, especially, have made the ready-to-wear clothing industry highly innovative in styling, colours and patterns, although the cost-benefit ratio of all these advances varies widely depending on the machine and how it is employed. The introduction of these technologies in the clothing industry of Mediterranean countries requires capital investments relatively higher than traditional machines, a more skilled labour force and an upgraded division of labour. Yet the greater output spurred by these innovations leads also to marked labour savings in both manufacturing and organization. The spread of computerized machinery has often resulted in a limited creation of new jobs and problems of personnel training and relations with the rest of the service structure for the industry.

The Shoe Industry

This is one of the most labour-intensive sectors in that the manufacturing process is largely one of assembly and can require up to a hundred separate steps. The overall process is divided into five stages: design, cut, sewing, assembly and finishing. The technological innovations that have been introduced into each (CAD, laser cutters, automatic sewing machines, etc.) have markedly raised output and quality. For the Mediterranean countries that have already acquired a relative specialization in this industry the introduction of these new techniques has brought numerous advantages. For example, they make it possible for the industry as a whole gradually to update its methods without having to transform itself completely. This would still leave the shoe industry labour-intensive yet well-positioned to offset adverse effects on employment through the service industries linked to it. These innovations would also mean cuts in production costs and the resulting benefits for a market whose size is basically determined by the given number of inhabitants. Then, too, the marked flexibility of these new production techniques would enable local manufacturers to follow more readily changes in both domestic and export demand. Given that these latter are advantages that only mass-production facilities of the largest firms are capable of offsetting, it would be a signal achievement to reach these goals in the southern Mediterranean, where the industry is largely made up of small manufacturing plants mostly independent of one another.

The Steel Industry
Steel-producing technology is relatively easy to procure in today's marketplace, the decision about which process to adopt being mainly based on raw material supply, energy costs and production scale. There are essentially two steel-producing techniques: the basic oxygen process (BOP) and the electric-arc furnace (EAF). The former employs ferrous metals, is highly integrated and currently employed by countries enjoying an abundant supply of raw materials. The latter relies mainly on scrap iron, is commonly found in traditional, high steel-consuming countries with scrap recycling problems and is increasingly employed in the production of special steels.

The steel industry has often been synonymously associated with industrialization. Even in industrializing southern Basin countries (for example Algeria, Egypt, Turkey) it has been pursued in order to meet domestic and export demand. Yet this strategy has been enacted in a market depressed by a drop in world steel demand, and today there is a surplus production capacity of standard steels in the Mediterranean's north (Italy and France) and south (Algeria, Egypt, Turkey). By contrast, there is a growing demand for manufacturers with detailed knowledge of customer needs who produce special steels at low energy inputs with resistance to stress and corrosion. In such a situation the southern Basin countries can only address these problems, and prevent further loss of market share, by being encouraged to convert their plants in line with new demand to DR-EAF technology for special steel production, which should be limited further to those steels that are readily adaptable to purchaser needs. Development accords in this sense could be negotiated even with manufacturers who want to enter the local market for consumer durables (for example appliances, automobiles), machinery or equipment, while their subsequent success will depend to a great extent on the reliability and quality of supplies and on a thorough knowledge of the markets themselves.

The Petrochemical Industry
The Mediterranean is a region of both producers and importers of oil and its by-products. The current pattern is for each country to build its own refining industry to meet local and, in many cases, export demand. The reasons behind this strategy are to be found for producers in the fact that sales of crude oil (extraction revenues) bring higher profits and for importers in the necessity to differentiate in origin crude oil imports because of market fluctuations. The result

in both cases is surplus refining capacity and a pollution well beyond the strictly necessary because none of the national industries wants to pay the clean-up costs.

Yet these costs could be avoided by negotiating accords between producers and importers to carry out the entire production process in the producer country. The resulting advantages even for importers are obvious given that the overhead outlays for a local refinery are double those built for a large-scale operation. Then, too, the construction of large, safer and more advanced and flexible plants designed to refine a mix of products (heavy oil, fuel oil, petrol, kerosene, etc.) in response to market demand could also promote research and development projects for new petrol-based fuels with the oil companies of the European Union. Other advantages might include the marine transport sector as finished products are less polluting and the tankers carrying them could be smaller.

Accords could also be negotiated to develop the basic chemical industry in the oil-producing countries, for this is an industry that is closely linked to oil in by-products such as ethylene, propylene, methanol, benzene, xelene, toluene, etc., that are needed by a wide range of industries (plastics, paint, synthetic fibres, etc.).

The Mediterranean could become a good example of integration of the oil-chemical industry 'pipeline.' Such an innovative approach would make it possible to deal in a different way with both the issues of restructuring-reconversion facing the European chemical industry and of research in environmental protection (for example low-emission and low-energy chemical processes, more sophisticated synthetic fibres, advanced materials). This is the terrain on which to build new relations in technology exchange between the EU petrochemical industries seeking new partners to share venture risks in the R&D of new products and processes and Mediterranean oil producers seeking new markets and advanced technology.

The Machine-Tool Industry
The capacity of a country to maintain and develop over time its industrial capability depends on its ability to adapt or produce new tools for the manufacture of goods. All industrial output depends on the production of machine tools or on machines and equipment made by them. The world's six most industrially advanced countries – France, Germany, Italy, Japan, the UK and the US – are also the leading exporters and importers of machine tools. This is a strategic sector, in which a part of the 'triadic' competition

takes place, that exerts its influence not only over such important industries as automobiles, aeronautics, chemicals, oil and pharmaceuticals but also over traditional industries like the textile, food and shoe. It is also a sector that, being by definition one that manufactures 'machines to produce machines,' has itself been markedly affected by new computer technology and that continually tests its own products in its own output processes. Accordingly, its development significantly influences all other industrial development given that it is the main engine driving the processes of innovation and higher productivity in most manufacturing sectors.

The most signal innovations introduced in this sector – automated systems of process control, numerical control systems, machine systems and automation systems – were dictated and made possible by advances in computer technology. The wide-spread use of electronics also changed the face of personnel skills and training in the industry. The ability to promote development in such an industry today depends in large measure on the capacity of its enterprises to build direct links to the electronics and computer industries.

The capacity to produce and adapt to new technological advances depends in turn on such a sector. France, Italy and, to a lesser extent, Spain are the Basin countries with a highly developed machine-tool industry consisting of medium- and small-sized companies that often contract out the production of parts and components. The Mediterranean could become an arena within which to initiate technology transfer in the machine-tool sector, beginning from the need of the above countries to upgrade facilities, to develop advances and to produce spare parts. The creation of a regional association of machine-tool producers could be the first step in developing a local industry in this sector. The establishment of joint ventures between EU and southern Basin countries could be another way of promoting production of components and parts for local and European markets. There is in this connection a tradition of spare parts output in the former Yugoslavia, Albania, Egypt, Turkey and Algeria that could be retooled via local and international investments.

Technology Transfer

The key role played by technological advances in industrial development also calls attention to the transfer issue. The pivotal question here is eliminating the conditions of uncertainty that concern both the supplier and the purchaser. Specific accords, usually denoted as passive and active, can be useful in resolving these issues.

Passive accords are aimed at indirectly creating a climate of certainty for those who invest in or transfer technology. They can be employed to promote targeted investment in areas or countries in which, for reasons of security or lack of products, the supply of capital and technology is very high. The issue of investment 'security', for example, is an important factor for both the supply and demand of technology. Companies that transfer technology must be certain that in the event of disputes, war, nationalization or strikes their investments are nonetheless protected. The same assurance also holds for those who purchase technology in regard to servicing, the supply of spare parts and assistance in upgrading the technology. Another important point to include in such accords is the problem of double taxation on profits (home and transfer country) that regards direct investments: a single levy, preferably in the transfer country, would be advisable.

There is also the issue concerning the size of local markets as a barrier to the entry of businesses. Multi-lateral agreements between the EU and other Basin countries could promote the creation or targeting of investments in a local market that extends beyond single national markets. And, in so far as regional cooperation organizations are concerned, such as the AMU, agreements sanctioning exports throughout the area or among all the signatories of such pacts could be worked out.

Active accords for cooperation stipulate the obligations and benefits of the contracting parties and the resources earmarked for investment, such as capital and technology. Several forms of these agreements are possible yet all are aimed at providing: (i) technical consultancy; (ii) assistance in given tasks; (iii) management advice; (iv) training and updating personnel; and (v) supply of facilities and machinery. Agreements of this kind are widely employed among TNCs and large corporations when operating in developing countries.

An example of an active accord, which could be extended to those Basin countries with a relative specialization in traditional industries (textiles, clothing, shoes) is SPRINT, a project sponsored by ENEA in collaboration with the large- and small-scale textile businesses centred around Prato, in Italy. It was employed to transfer technological advances to small companies via: (i) monitoring of automation and control systems, product design, new production technology; (ii) upgraded organization of information input and communication between firms in advances in management techniques; and (iii) consultancy in the choice of materials and energy use. The project placed special emphasis on the use of CAD techniques and computer links to data banks for both large and small businesses.

The adoption of a similar project in countries like Egypt, Morocco, Syria and Turkey could lay the foundations for technological upgrading of businesses and for the creation of a computer network linking local companies to technology producers and prospective markets. This kind of a network, by virtue of the low cost of information, would have the additional advantage of keeping local industries, which would otherwise gravitate to large urban centres, decentralized. Such a project could also be adopted by the shoe industry to bring together the region's producers by developing an intra-industry trade based on specialization (sole and vamp producers, assemblers and marketers).

Technology is usually transferred through a series of intermediaries or stages (TNCs and multinational companies, small and medium enterprises, patents, licenses, copying) that influence to varying extents the process of technological upgrading depending on the sector and geographical area. Private enterprise and individual initiatives, however, will continue to play key roles in technology transfer, especially in regard to multilateral accords aimed at creating a certain industrial framework. Nor can TNCs and multinational conglomerates be ignored in discussions of industrialization and development. To the weight they bring to bear on the world's economy must be added the fact that they account for nearly 80 per cent of the technology transfers throughout the world. They enjoy several advantages in this connection: (i) global operations and the capacity to monitor the input and output of their techniques; (ii) the capacity to organize these techniques via worldwide affiliates; and (iii) the capacity to respond to any variation in costs and world markets.

In the event of the creation of regional markets, the multinational corporations, with their capabilities, can be attracted to them and take an active role in the industrial modernization of the non-EU Mediterranean nations. Entering a single market governed by uniform rules both increases the potential for profit and lessens investment risks. The question at issue then becomes preventing investment decisions being made by these companies alone and that the benefits of such a regional market accrue only to foreign enterprises.

One way to prevent this happening could be the creation of new international enterprises, formed by the countries making up the local market and the TNCs interested in access to it, and invested with the decisional power to 'target' a given geographical area and to 'distribute' by sector the foreign investment. Another possible approach is to set up joint ventures enabling greater control over worker training, business management and the establishment *in situ* of R&D laboratories to upgrade existing technology and to develop advances. The participating countries for their part would ensure the protection of the regional market, the quality of local supplies and the transfer abroad of the TNC's share of the profits.

While the TNCs and multi-national conglomerates could play an important role in technology transfer in the so-called resource-intensive and scale-intensive sectors, the small- and medium-scale foreign companies could lead the way in the labour-intensive sectors and in the production of capital goods. Italy, France and Spain are among the EU countries with particular expertise in developing innovative small businesses in the so-called traditional sectors, expertise that could be transferred to other Mediterranean countries via multilateral agreements ensuring investment protection against political instability and strikes and the possibility to transfer profits abroad.

Political stability based on the certainty of law is fundamental for the development of an efficient and competitive small- and medium-sized industry and for the growth of an intra-industry trade based on production specialization. The large multinational companies and TNCs enjoy greater possibilities of risk compensation and of influencing governments and EU agencies through their lobbies. By contrast, the small and mid-sized enterprises that invest abroad do so at greater risk and, hence, need more than a positive political and juridical situation to safeguard their investments and profits.

MIGRATIONS AND THE LABOUR MARKET

The Migration Issue

The migration issue continues to unfold in all its telling detail according to an all too familiar scenario. Migratory pressure increases in a series of dramatic sequences that call to mind the frequently encountered images of the Vietnamese 'boat-people' and Mexican 'wetbacks.' Its ever more forceful effects erupt upon the communities exposed to them, accompanied by backlashes of racism and intolerance that are as foreseeable as they are reprehensible. The reactions of governments are ever more embodied in measures of defence and police control and ever less in remedies of the causes. The weakness of 'Fortress Europe' is measured in the comments of the establishment press, not by its inability to enact concrete initiatives of development to halt the drain of youth and workers from their areas, but by the lax control of its borders that are increasingly seen as walls to be fortified and defended.

Migration: Dynamics and Causes

The dearth of effective problem-solving policy responses is often blamed on a poor understanding of the phenomenon. Yet much, or at least enough, about it is known to disqualify this argument as an explanation for the inertia shown in confronting the problem. Migration has been the topic of a number of conferences and studies. (Roque, 1989; CNEL-Regione Emilia Romagna, 1992; Foudazione Bzodolini-Ministero degli Esteri, 1992). Taken together, these efforts represent a forum that, if nothing else, has shed sufficient light on the dynamics of migration, on its causes and effects, on the numbers involved, on its geography and its other aspects.

The most notable indication to emerge from this debate is that the impetus and implacable drive displayed by the migratory phenomena in their path from South to North in the Mediterranean arise from dynamic forces at work in the countries of origin, forces that in turn have been loosed more by conditions inimical to the sustenance of life than by any demand for labour in other countries. Migration is, then, the result of the uprooting of a work force from countryside and city by growing poverty and unemployment as well as the widening of the gap between North and South in the conditions of life – forces that have their own dynamics and are independent of those at work in the labour market of host countries.

If there is a magnet attracting migration northwards, it is surely not the demand for labour but the myths of well-being and consumerism so widely advertised by Western 'culture.' There is no doubt that a reduction in the amount of information of the type that is being broadcast today on Western countries by our mass media would be a first step in the right direction. Yet the difficulties in accomplishing such a task are no less formidable than those needed to accomplish co-development, for both cases call for a re-examination of our way of implementing and perceiving development. The organization of the labour market in the various countries involved thus explains not the migratory currents running northwards from the south but their distribution over the countries against whose shores they wash. The first is the 'efficiency' of the control systems deployed by a given country. It is beyond the scope of this study to undertake an analysis of or advance value judgements about this policy area. Suffice it to remark that the effectiveness of police border controls, the inflexibility of legislation concerning visas and political asylum, the hostile attitude of citizens towards foreigners and hence the popular support for such legislation are all factors making it more difficult for immigrants to gain entry to and survive in countries abroad. The second is the extent of organization of both the labour market and the social control that it can exert over businesses. Wherever there is a 'submerged' or 'hidden' sector of the economy and unauthorized labour exploitation is widespread and tolerated, they will encourage the entry and more stable settlements of groups of immigrant workers. The third factor could be called the attitude or ethic of acceptance of the host society and hence the positive, active support for these groups by volunteer and government organizations. Yet, even when this cultural ethos exists, it is not extensive enough to exert a significant influence over migration's distribution.

Migration: Profile and Impetus

Current data make it possible to sketch in, from the varying perspectives offered by the varying statistical sources, the composite features of migration and draw from them a distinctive profile of it in Italy. The portrait that emerges from these several viewpoints should provide a fairly good likeness of the phenomenon. Let us take a look at the resulting painting.

A first set of data indicates the provenance areas of immigration and subsequent regions of settlement. Table 9.1 shows the distribution of immigration by country of destination and area of origin. A comparison to the other major EU countries indicates in general the small number of legal immigrants in Italy, although the question of illegal immigration remains an open one, and in particular

Toward Mediterranean Co-development

Table 9.1 Where they come from

Country Population in thous. (31.12.90)	Total legal immigrants	Legal immigrants as a % of total popul.	Eastern Europe and former USSR	North Africa and Turkey	Other (incl. other European countries)
Germany* 77 555	5241.8	7	1036.7	1775.1	2430
France 56 184	3607.6	6	N.A.	1613.6	N.A.
Netherlands 14 864	692.4	5	17.5	363.7	311.2
Belgium 9895	904.5	9	5.8	243.5	655.2
Italy 57 657	781.1	1	99.3	127.9	553.9
Britain 57 121	1875.0	3	237.0**	N.A.	1638.0**
Switzerland 6628	1100.3	17	156.0	71.1**	873.2
Austria 7595	413.4	5	150.8	N.A.	262.6

* *Data for Germany as of 30.9.90; last available figures for USSR and Czechoslovakian emigrants from 31.12.89.* ** 1989

Source: *Perspectives for Metalworkers in the Mediterranean Basin*, presented at the IMF Conference for the Mediterranean region 7–9 Oct. 1992, Sardinia, Italy.

the share of immigration to Italy from the Maghreb countries.

A second series of data indicates the reasons for granting the resident permits, distinguishing those issued for work from those for simple immigration. Tables 9.2 and 9.3, based on several statistical sources, note the reasons for issuing the residence permits and those for expatriation. Immigration exhibits a rather even spread throughout Italy, the greater concentrations found in some regions being due perhaps to employment opportunities in the manufacturing, agriculture or service industries. Table 9.4 provides an estimate of immigrant employment by region of settlement and by economic sector.

While a more detailed analysis of the relationships linking these migratory currents to local labour markets must be left to the many available studies of this question, several general remarks are in order. Pockets of black-market or of under-paid labour, as well as local industry demand for labour because of area shortages in it, are to be found in the Provinces of Foggia, Caserta and Campania,

Table 9.2 Resident permits issued in Italy as of 31 December 1990 by region and reason for issuance (per cent breakdown)

Region	Study	Work	Tourism	Family	other or not indicated	Total
Piedmont	7.5	59.1	3.8	13.4	16.2	100
Valle d'Aosta	0.7	53.5	10.3	15.6	19.9	100
Lombardy	5.2	60.5	8.4	13.2	12.7	100
Trent-Alto Adige	2	46.3	5.7	14.1	31.9	100
Venetia	8.6	53.9	4.4	21	12.1	100
Friuli-V.Giulia	8.8	41.8	3.6	23.3	22.5	100
Liguria	3	51.3	4.6	13.7	27.4	100
Emilia-Romagna	6.3	62.1	6.2	11.6	13.8	100
Tuscany	14.8	43.6	9	13.8	18.8	100
Umbria	52.5	3.8	39.3	1.5	2.9	100
Marche	15.5	37.6	13	15.5	18.4	100
Lazio	5.6	5.1	7.2	8.5	27.7	100
Abruzzi	9.2	43.6	11.9	18.6	16.7	100
Molise	2	23.1	14.8	28.6	31.5	100
Campania	8.6	39.6	7.9	22.2	21.7	100
Apulia	9.1	38.3	3.8	25.3	23.5	100
Baslicata	1.6	59.1	6.1	18.1	15.1	100
Calabria	2.2	36.2	5.8	20.2	33.6	100
Sicily	3.4	36.8	4.7	13.3	21.8	100
Sardinia	3.1	43.5	1.7	16.8	34.9	100
ITALY	9.7	48.7	8.8	13	19.8	100
Centre & North	10.7	49.3	9.5	11.6	18.9	100
South	5.8	46.6	6.1	18.4	23.1	100

where the labour market is generally under the control of the *Camorra*, an organized crime group, in the Marche Region and for fishing in Sicily, for fruit workers in Trentino-Alto Adige, and for Alpine crops in the Val d'Aosta. Immigrant labour is also in demand in such other labour markets as urban domestic help in particular and in service industries and agriculture in general. Small-scale businesses in the central and northern Regions of Latium, the Emilia-Romagna and Lombardy also recruit immigrant labour.

Charter of Extra-EC Immigration

A 'Charter of Extra-EC Immigration,' which was drawn up in 1992 and approved at the Bologna Conference on migration, pointedly notes the need for 'a combined and flexible strategy to control the flow of entry as well as of development in the countries of origin.'

Table 9.3 Reasons for expatriation, 1990 (per cent)

	Censis Survey		Residence Permit
* Work	..		49.3
Lack of work	49	employee	22.7
Seeking higher income	49.2	self-employed	2.6
		Iob placement list	18.4
* Study	20.3		9.7
Professional skill	16		
* Family	12.7		12.5
* Political asylum	..		0.6
* Political motives	24.5		..
* Religious motives	3.9		5
* Avoid military draft	5.8		..
* War	9.1		..
* Elective residence	..		5.6
* Poor social services	16		..
* Tourism	..		8.8
* Experience other culture	17		..
* Health	..		0.3
* Judical motives	..		0.1
* Adoption list	..		0.5

Source: Censis and ministry of Home Affairs

It also reiterates that:

> Regulating the influx of immigrants can not be accomplished only by means of police control and humanitarian assistance, as is still being attempted today under the umbrella of an emergency policy. Rather it must be effected according to criteria of long-term planning that take into account actual possibilities for immigrants to enter the labour market and establish themselves in the social system. Nor will such a strategy *per se* be sufficient if it is not accompanied by constant efforts designed to promote economic development and social progress in the homelands of these immigrants.[2]

POLICIES AND INSTITUTIONS OF COOPERATION AND CO-DEVELOPMENT

Co-development, as repeatedly pointed out, calls for the planning of specific development policies and the creation of institutions

Table 9.4 Estimate of immigrants employed in Italy as of 31 December 1990 by region of residence and economic sector (per cent)

Region	Farming	Industry	Other	Total
Piedmont	8.3	40.6	51.5	100
Valle d'Aosta	19.6	31.7	48.7	100
Lombardy	5	42.6	52.4	100
Trent-Alto Adige	15.7	25.4	58.9	100
Venetia	10.5	39.8	49.7	100
Friuli-V.Giulia	4.6	40.2	55.2	100
Liguria	2.8	28.7	68.5	100
Emilia-Romagna	11.8	39.7	48.5	100
Tuscany	5	29.1	65.9	100
Umbria	11.1	22.3	66.6	100
Marche	8	33	59	100
Lazio	4	15.3	80.7	100
Abruzzi	14.1	30.9	55	100
Molise	9.7	25.7	64.6	100
Campania	9.1	19.9	71	100
Apulia	20.7	27.8	51.5	100
Baslicata	25.2	26	48.8	100
Calabria	21.8	17.7	60.5	100
Sicily	13.6	24.5	61.9	100
Sardinia	8.5	24.9	66.6	100
ITALY	8.5	28.5	63	100
Centre and North	6.6	30.5	62.9	100
South	13.4	23.6	63	100

capable of implementing them. The specific policy areas in which compatibility or complementariness needs to be achieved are economic, development and investment.

Compatibility in Development Policies

These policies can be grouped around strategic development sectors.
Foreign Debt. The level of debt besetting many Basin countries is such that, if no solution consonant with development objectives is found, no programme will be seen as much more than wishful thinking. The plans for debt restructuring requested by the IMF and the World Bank run in directions that differ from this premise, and destabilizing effects in individual areas and regions can ensue from them. The proposals advanced by the EU's Economic and Social Committee, which call for foreign debt management linked

to the financing of the economic restructuring of these countries, represent a constructive alternative to them.

There are several mechanisms of debt reconversion that can be employed on a case-by-case basis depending on the type of debt and policy to be pursued: debt-to-local money swap, debt-to-export swap and debt-equity swap. The common thread running through these options is the linking of foreign debt amortisation to the growth of domestic output and consumption. One of the impediments to foreign investment in Mediterranean countries is a limited domestic market and industrial base, even for a relaunching of exports. Yet without such a recovery the chances of paying off even the current foreign debt are just about nil.

The error in the restructuring policies recommended by the international financial bodies is their basic assumption that debt repayment and hence economic recovery must start by restraining the domestic market and consumption. Such a premise would lead to a situation opposed to that needed to attract new investment and hence would promote a balanced financial statement at zero-sum economic growth.

The debt-equity swap, for example, requires that an amount of local currency equivalent to the debt be reinvested in the debtor country's industrial enterprises, that is foreign investors and the government swap at a favourable rate of exchange a share of foreign debt for domestic resources (businesses, various assets) controlled by the latter. This transaction results in an internal conversion of the foreign loan, negotiable in the debtor's currency, that promotes domestic investment and, hence, increases the chances of growth in production. The EU could draw up reconversion plans of this kind, with the Community itself as guarantor, which provide for the debt reconversion of the Basin's countries in the acquisition of shares in local state and private businesses. Area or regional accords would enable these agreements to include provisions for the transfer of profits and capital and access to the markets of the Basin's countries. Several forms of debt reconversion of this type have been implemented with some success in Latin America and Southeast Asia and have found limited application in Yugoslavia and Morocco.

Private Foreign Investment

Private foreign investment in the Mediterranean by large companies and TNCs depends on the conditions these countries are prepared to offer. The typical package offered thus far by individual countries has included low-cost labour, tax benefits and other fiscal inducements for plant establishment. The results, despite some successes in the Maghreb, have largely been a failure, nor have there been any signs that a turnabout in the growing trend of foreign companies to pull out of the Mediterranean is imminent. Thus the success of any alternative development strategy will mainly depend on two factors: the actual and potential size of the domestic market and the services offered by the region in the form of infrastructures and training. Economic growth in both cases coincides with the development of the domestic market and the conditions of life of the populace: this is what is here meant by co-development.

A series of initiatives can be implemented in this field:

(i) *Industry consortia and venture-capital funds.* The creation of enterprises capable of financing ventures and sustaining new businesses within the framework of innovative industrial projects with limited financial resources must be encouraged. Local governments could unite in common cause to promote share holdings by foreign financial firms in these joint ventures by the creation of venture-capital companies through tax incentives (no tax on profits) and the participation of state banks.

(ii) *Listing of companies on the major European stock exchanges.* The objective of such an initiative is to encourage the leading firms in the Mediterranean to compete in Europe's capital markets. This would help to increase the confidence in the industrial investments of southern Basin countries both of prospective investors in the developed countries and of immigrants willing to invest their savings in industries in their homelands.

(iii) *Industrial leasing.* This is an approach to the solving of investment problems in small- and medium-scale businesses: a firm can acquire capital goods by paying a regular rental fee, with the lessee having the option at the end of the contract either to gain title to the property for a nominal charge or rendering it. This mechanism has several evident advantages. Once a framework of confidence and reciprocal guarantees is established, leasing agreements are relatively easy to contract, requiring no deposits or down payments by the lessee. It is thus up to individual governments to introduce legislation that regulates leasing transactions, enables international leasing companies (merchant banks and financial houses) to establish joint ventures with local capital and creates programmes to train

personnel in auditing the financial state of these enterprises.
(iv) *BOT accords.* The build-operate-transfer model is a type of franchise financing for privately owned and financed projects in which the fixed assets and right to the profits of the business are transferred to the state at the end of the contract (for example 30 years). In this case too provisions are to be made to allow profit transfer and access to and from local markets.

Area and Regional Policies

These policies must be geared to creating 'domestic markets' and regional development based on the EU model, that is through agricultural and industrial measures designed to protect both traditional sectors and nascent industries especially in the start-up stages. Mention has already been made of the industrial problems besetting the Basin and of the instruments needed to begin addressing them. An attempt was made to respond to the question of how to develop the relationships between the Mediterranean's northern and southern countries by taking as a point of departure the compatibilities or complementariness between the two zones and pursuing the path of regional markets, technological innovation and cooperation for co-development.

The fostering of inter- and intra-industry trade relations between EC and non-EU Basin countries and, internally, among the latter via the creation of regional markets is designed to construct an economic web (like the EU network) able to increase synergies and each country ability in satisfying internal needs.

Labour Market Policies

These policies can employ the region's differentials in demographic make-up positively to regulate the flow of labour and migration or to create in co-ordination with economic policies concrete options enabling citizens to choose either to remain in their countries or emigrate.

Educational and Research Policies

The creation of added value depends on the skills of labour and on the R&D of new technology. Advances compatible with environmental conditions, with local resource use and with waste reduction must be in step with development in order to ensure a successful take-off of the economy. Too many 'economic miracles' burn out in the span of decade, leaving conditions worse off at the end than they were at the beginning.

Policies of Financial Cooperation

The organization of financial cooperation in support and co-ordination of the development process has been the subject of many proposals and studies. It is the focal point of such demands as the foreign debt management cited *supra*, an increase in the EU contribution to co-development from the current 0.17 to 0.5 per cent of Community GNP, and the abandoning of the bilateral approach to development in EC-Mediterranean relations.

CO-DEVELOPMENT INSTITUTIONS

Compatibility of production systems is geared to establishing interdependence between sectors for a uniform and integrated development in a given area. The surveys conducted on successful (for example via industrial and high-tech parks) and failed ('cathedrals in the desert,' abandoned projects) development projects in the backward areas of France, Italy and Spain underscore the need for a detailed study of compatibility and complementariness for each investment proposal. For such compatibility is not always discernible by the individual entrepreneur (and not only because of externalities related to infrastructures or labour but also because of industrial and commercial inter-dependence) in that it presupposes a study and detailed knowledge of the local characteristics of production, what is called in technical jargon the 'industrial environment.'

The task of studying these complementary factors must be assigned to specific bodies charged with co-ordinating development by sector and area via the following steps: survey and research (experts), setting of objectives (politicians), creating consensus and the participation in the planning of framework programmes for areas and sectors (experts, business and labour), drafting the overall framework, approving (politicians) and implementing the plan (planning groups, public administration, business and labour), and the establishment of institutions for cooperation and co-development.

Proposals for the establishment of cooperation and co-development institutions have been drafted by a number of research centres and advanced by political bodies, both national and EU. Well-known are the Union proposals for a 'Conference on Mediterranean Cooperation,' a 'Forum on the Mediterranean' and for a 'Mediterranean Council of Cooperation,' and those for a 'Mediterranean Development Bank,' for an 'Agency for Cooperation and Economic Development in the Mediterranean' and for various institutions for financial, commercial and industrial cooperation, which have been adopted by the EU's Economic and Social Committee in recent documents and date back more than a decade (ICEPS 1990/1, Linguaglossa 1991). The main obstacles to the task reside in the fact that foreign policy and security considerations always take precedence over economic cooperation, thereby blunting its impact, and at the same time the political problems within the region's individual countries, which further complicate the matter.

Given this overall picture, the factors involved and the need to pursue both the dialogue and the process of establishing Mediterranean institutions for cooperation and economic development, this study remarks that the trade unions and industry associations in particular and the social organizations engaged in co-development in general are the most appropriate agencies to initiate and manage this process. The following group of proposals are formulated in an effort to identify an agenda of objectives.

1. The task of the Italian Council of Economics and Labour (Consiglio Nazionale dell'Economia e del Lavoro), having discussed the matter with its French and Portuguese counterparts, is to convene a Forum, with the participation of the trade unions, business associations and non-state organizations engaged in Mediterranean development, to debate and draft indications for the region's development. This Forum should determine the evolutionary lines of economic cooperation and set the priorities for future work. Among the topics for study are the forms of cooperation, the areas and sectors slated for development, Mediterranean projects for joint development, the establishment of networks in transport, communications, energy supply, and in education and research to integrate the Basin as a region.
2. The documents approved by the Forum will form the basis for the establishment of research groups, including trade unions, business associations, non-governmental organizations (NGOs) and experts, to draw up development programmes by sector for the individual areas and the Basin as a whole. These groups

shall be charged with determining needs and production capacities. Their reports are to be presented at area conferences (Maghreb, Mashraq, Balkans, Southern Europe) for further debate and analysis. The groups can later become socio-economic observers per area and sector.
3. These reports shall be employed under the co-ordination of experts to draft a 'Mediterranean Framework Programme,' divided by area and sector, which is to include overall priorities, objectives and investment and development projects.
4. This Programme is to be discussed at a second Mediterranean Forum and, once approved by it with the necessary revisions and addenda, is to be implemented through an 'Agency for Economic Development and Cooperation in the Mediterranean.' The tasks of this Agency will be:
  (i) to serve as the terminal for existing financial channels (EC, international projects, management of state debt and private and public investment.);
  (ii) to ensure that each project is enacted according to the criteria of complementary compatibility of the necessary investments; and
  (iii) draw up proposals for the Forum.

Figure 9.2 Start-up Proposal Outline for Economic and Social Cooperation in the Mediterranean

START-UP PROPOSAL OUTLINE FOR ECONOMIC AND SOCIAL COOPERATION IN THE MEDITERRANEAN
FORUM FOR ECONOMIC COOPERATION AND DEVELOPMENT *Ratification of Policies and Priorities for Mediterranean Cooperation *Establishment of Research Groups for the Drafting of Sector Programmes
AREA CONFERENCES FOR THE DRAFTING OF SECTOR PROGRAMMES
PUBLICATION OF THE MEDITERRANEAN FRAMEWORK PROGRAMME
FORUM FOR ECONOMIC COOPERATION AND DEVELOPMENT *Ratification of Framework Programme *Institution of the Agency for Economic Development and Cooperation in the Mediterranean *Institution of Social-Economic Area Observers

NOTES

1. This chapter reproduces the content of the Second Mediterranean Report, published in Italy by the CNEL in 1995. I thanks friends and colleagues for their contributions in the elaboration of this Report by their advice and by their studies: Andrea Balletto, Antonella Caruso and Nico Perrone for the historical part; Sergio Gomez y Paloma for the agro-food systems; Riccardo Cappellin and Davide Infante for the industrial systems and regional policies; Michele Bruni and Renzo Turatto for labour market and migration; Andrea Amato and Bichara Khader for Co-development policies and EU policies.
2. 'Carta dell'immigrazione extracomunitaria,' Bologna, 28–29 May, 1992.

Bibliography

Adorno, T.W. *Minima moralia. Reflexionen aus dem beschädigten leben*. Suhrkamp Verlag, Berlin und Frankfurt am Main.
Alvi, G. *Le seduzioni economiche di Faust* (Milano: Adelphi, 1989).
Allievi S. and Dassetto F. *Il ritorno dell'Islam. I mussulmani in Italia* (Roma: Edizioni lavoro-ISCOS, 1993).
Amato, A. 'From Eurocentrim to Regional Cooperation. EC's Regional Policy in the Mediterranean', MONITOR-FAST, EC Brussels: FOP 344, July 1993.
Amin, S. *Delinking. Towards a Polycentric World* (London: Zed Books Ltd., 1965).
Amin, S. *I mandarini del capitale globale* (Roma: Datanews, 1994).
Amoroso, B. *Rapporto dalla Scandinavia* (Roma-Bari: Laterza, 1980).
Amoroso, B. 'A Danish Perspective: The Impact of the Internal Market on the Labour Unions and the Welfare State', *Comparative Labor Law Journal*, vol. 11, Philadelphia (1990) 483–97.
Amoroso, B. 'Gli effetti del mercato interno sul mercato del lavoro e delle istituzioni sociali della Comunità Europea', *Saggi di politica economica in onore di Federico Caffè* (eds Acocella, N. Rey, M. G. and Tiberi, M.), vol. I, Milano: F. Angeli (1990) 267–85.
Amoroso, B. *Primo Rapporto sul Mediterranneo* (Roma: CNEL, 1991).
Amoroso, B. 'Industrial relations in Europe in the 1990s: new business strategies and the challenge to organised labour', *The International Journal of Human Resource Management*, vol. 3 (1992) 331–45.
Amoroso, B., Infante, D., Gomez y Paloma, S. and Perrone, N. (eds), *Marginalization, Specialization and Cooperation in the Baltic and Mediterranean Regions: Synthesis Report*, FOP 343, Brussels: MONITOR-FAST, DG XII, EC (1993).
Amoroso, B. 'Industrial restructuring at a Regional Level', *Welfare State in Transition* (eds Amoroso, B. and Jespersen, J.) Annals 1994/95 (Roskilde: Department of Social Sciences, Roskilde University, 1994).
Amoroso, B. *Secondo Rapporto sul Mediterraneo, Nuove prospettive di cooperazione economica, tecnologica e istituzionale* (Roma: CNEL, 1995).
Amoroso, B. *Scandinavian Perspectives on European Integration* (Roskilde: Federico Caffè Centre, Roskilde University, 1995a).
Amoroso, B. *Terzo Rapporto sul Mediterraneo, Ripensare l'Europa, ripensare il Mediterraneo* (Roskilde: Centro Federico Caffè, Università di Roskilde, 1995b).
Annales Marocaines d'economie, no. 7 (1993).
Archibugi, F. *Insights into European Cohesion* (Brussels: EC Commission, DG XXII, 1993).
Baglioni, G. (ed.), *Le relazioni industriali in Italia e in Europa negli anni '80* (Roma: edizioni lavoro, 1989).
Baglioni G. and Crouch C. (eds), *European Industrial Relations. The Challenge of Flexibility* (London: SAGE, 1990).

Bibliography

Baglioni, G. *Democrazia impossibile?* (Bologna: Il Mulino, 1995).
Baran, Paul A. and Sweezy, Paul M. *Monopoly Capital. An Essay on the American Economic and Social Order* (London: Penguin Books, 1966).
Baran, Paul A., *The Political Economy of Growth* (London: Penguin Books, 1973).
Barcellona, P. *Il capitale come puro spirito. Un fantasma si aggira per il mondo* (Roma: Editori Riuniti, 1990a).
Barcellona, P. *Il ritorno del legame sociale* (Torino: Bollati Boringhieri, 1990b).
Barcellona, P. *Democrazia: quale via di scampo* (Molfetta: La meridiana, 1995).
Bassetto F. and Bastenier, A. *Europa: nuova frontiera dell'Islam* (Roma: Edizioni Lavoro, ISCOS, 1988).
Bello, Walden and Cunnima, Shea, 'De l'adjustement structurel en ses implacables desseins' *Le monde diplomatique*, September 1994.
Benachenhou, M. *Inflation, évaluation, marginalisation* (Alger: Dar Ech'rifa, 1993).
Berger, S. and Piore, Michael J., *Dualism and Continuity in Industrial Society* (Cambridge: Cambridge University Press, 1980).
Blair, J.M. *Economic Concentration. Structure, Behaviour and Public Policy* (New York: Harcourt, Brace, Jovanovich, 1972).
Bobbio, N. 'Il profitto e il potere', *La Stampa*, Torino, 6 1989, 1.
Bobbio, N. 'The Upturned Utopia', *New Left Review*, no. 179, (1989a).
Bonanno di Linguaglossa, Un'agenzia per la cooperazione e lo sviluppo economico del Mediterraneo, Ministero Affari Esteri, Roma.
Botta, F. (ed.), *Sul capitale monopolistico* (Bari: De Donato Editore, 1971).
Boyer, R. *The Search for Alternatives to Fordism: A Very Tentative Assessment* (Paris: CEPREMAC, 1987).
Braudel, F. *Afterthoughts on Material Civilization and Capitalism* (Baltimore and London: The Johns Hopkins University Press, 1977).
Braudel, F. *The Structures of Everyday Life. The Limits of Possible Civilization and Capitalism, 15th-18th Century* (New York: Harper & Row, 1981).
Braudel, F. *Une leçon d'histoire* (Paris: Les Editions Arthaud, 1986).
Caffè, F. (ed.) *Autocritica dell'economista* (Roma-Bari: Laterza, 1975).
Caffè, F. *Economia senza profeti* (Roma: Nuova Universale Studium, 1977).
Caffè, F. 'Un cammino difficile', *Economia senza profeti* (Roma: Nuova Universale Studium, 1977a).
Caffè, F. *Lezioni di Politica economica* (Torino: Boringhieri, 1981).
Caffè, F. 'In difesa del "welfare state"', *Saggi di politica economica* (Torino: Rosenberg and Seller, 1986).
Caffè, F. 'Sono bastati cinquant'anni', *La solitudine del riformista* (Torino: Bollati Boringhieri, 1990).
Cantaro, A. *La modernizzazione neoliberista. Le istituzioni e le regole del nuovo ordine* (Milano: F. Angeli, 1990).
Carrieri, M. *L'incerta rappresentanza* (Bologna: Il Mulino, 1995).
Cecchini report, 'The Economics of 1992: an assessment of the potential effects of completing the Internal Market of the European Community', *European Economy*, N. 35, Brussels: CEC, DG II (1988).
CENSIS, *Social Europe. In search of a Common Culture* (Milano: F. Angeli, 1991).

Bibliography

CNEL, *The Economic and Social Councils in Europe. Role and Perspectives* (Napoli: Edizioni Scientifiche Italiane, 1991).
Coriat, B. *Ripensare l'organizzazione del lavoro. Concetti e prassi nel modello giapponese* (Bari: Dedalo, 1991).
CNEL *Costruire la società multirazziale* (Marietti: CNEL, 1992).
CNEL *Lo spazio Mediterraneo* (Marietti: CNEL, 1992).
CNEL-Regione Emilia-Romagna, *Il governo dei movimenti migratori in Europa: Cooperazione o conflitto*, Bologna, 28–9 May 1992.
Collotti Pischel, E. 'Prefazione', *Le Thanh Khoi 1979*.
Crouch, C. *The origin of the relations between states and organized interests in Western Europe* (London: Prentice Hall, 1990).
Crouch C. *Industrial Relations and European State Traditions* (Oxford: Clarendon Press, 1993).
Daneo, C. *Agricoltura e sviluppo capitalistico in Italia nel decennio 1951–1960* (Milano: Edizioni Avanti, 1964).
DATAR, *Les villes européennes* (Paris: La Documentation Francaise, 1989).
De Rita, G. 'Lo spazio mediterraneo' (CNEL, 3 January 1992), p.3.
Economic and Social Committee of the European Comunities, *The Mediterranean Policy of the European Community* (Brussels, 1993).
European Commission, *Europa 2000+, Cooperazione per lo sviluppo del territorio europeo* (Brussels, 1994).
Fanon, F. *I dannati della terra* (Torino: Einaudi, 1962).
Fondazione Aristide Merloni, *Dalla frontiera allo spazio comune. Ipotesi progettuale di una via transadriatica allo sviluppo* (Roma 1991).
Fondazione Brodolini-Ministero degli Esteri, *Rapporto sulle migrazioni nel Mediterraneo* (Roma: 1992).
Fromm, E., *To Have or to Be?* New York: Harper & Row Publishers, 1976.
Fuà, G. 'Lagged Development and Economic Dualism', *Quartely Review*, June, Banca Nazionale del Lavoro, Rome, (1978).
Fuà, G. *Problems of Lagged Development in OECD Europe* (Paris: OECD, 1981).
George, S. *Il debito estero dei paesi del bacino mediterraneo*, CNEL Ufficio Studi Internationali, Rome, 1996.
Giarini, O. and Loubergé, H. *La delusione tecnologica. I rendimenti decrescenti della tecnologia e la crisi della crescita economica* (Milano: Mondadori, 1978).
Glotz, P. *La socialdemocrazia tedesca a una svolta* (Roma: Editori Riuniti, 1985).
Gomez y Paloma, S. *Agro-food and Biotechnology in the Baltic and Mediterranean Regions*, FOP 347 (Brussels: MONITOR-FAST, 1992).
Gomez y Paloma, S. *Dévelopment économique et systèmes agraires: une region de la plain du Po* (Rome: FAO, 1995).
Graziani, A. *L'economia italiana: 1945–1970* (Bologna: Il Mulino, 1972).
Graziani, A. *Crisi e ristrutturazione dell'economia italiana* (Torino: Einaudi, 1975).
Graziani, A. 'Domestic and International Economic Changes. Embarassing Correspondences', in *International Review of Applied Economics*, vol. 7, no. 3, (1993) p.253–66.
Hamel, B. (ed.) 'La Question de l'Emploi et du chomage en Algerie 1970–1990', *Collections Statistiques*, no. 48, Alger: Office National des Statistiques (1991).

Bibliography

Hirshmann, A.O. 'The Welfare State in Trouble: Systemic Crisis or Growing Pains?', May, *American Economic Review*, (1980).

Hirshman, A.O. *Essays in Trespassing. Economics to Politics and Beyond* (London: Cambridge University Press, 1981).

Holland, S. *The Global Economy: from Meso to Macroeconomics* (London: Weidenfeld and Nicholson, 1987).

Holland, S. *The Market Economy: from Micro to Mesoeconomics* (London: Weidenfeld & Nicolson, 1987a).

ICEPS *Progetto di proposta per la creazione di una istituzione finanziaria internazionele per il Mediterraneo* (Rome, 1991).

ICPS report *La malfaisance du FMI et de la Banque Mondiale*, Union International des Syndicats des Industries Chimiques, du Petrole et Similaires (Montreuil: CEDEX, 1992).

ILO *'Islam and the New International Economic Order'*, The Social Dimension, Geneve (1980).

ILO *Lavoro, culture e religioni*, Geneva, November 1982 (Roma: Edizioni Lavoro, 1984).

Infante, D. *Produttività, progresso tecnico e squilibri regionali* (Bologna: CLUEB, 1992).

Istituto Gramsci *Tendenze del capitalismo italiano*, vol. 1 (Roma: Editori Riuniti, 1962).

Jessop, B. *Fordism and Post-Fordism* (Copenhagen: C.O.S., 1990).

Kapp, K.W. *The Social Costs of Private Enterprise* (Cambridge MA: Harvard University Press, 1950).

Keynes, J.M. *Essays in Persuation, The Collected Writings of John Maynard Keynes*, vol. IX (London: Macmillan, 1972).

Keynes, J. M. 'National Self-sufficiency', (1933), *The Collected Writings of John Maynard Keynes*, vol. XXI, *Activities 1931–1939* (London: Macmillan, 1982), pp.233–46.

Keynes, J.M. *The General Theory of Employment, Interest and Money* (London: Macmillan, 1946).

Khader, B. 'Il dividendo della pace. L'economia palestinese e regionale'. Bruno Amoroso (ed.), *Terzo Rapporto sul Mediterraneo, Ripensare l'Europa, ripensare il Mediterraneo* (Roskilde: Centro Federico Caffè, Università di Roskilde, 1995).

Khan, M. 'The Macroeconomic effects of fund supported adjustment programs', *IMF Staff Papers*, vol. 37, no. 2 (New York, 1990).

Klinderberger, C.P. *Europe's Post-War Growth. The Role of Labour Supply* (Cambridge MA: Harvard University Press, 1967).

Kregel, J.A. 'Budget Deficits, Stabilisation Policy and Liquidity Preferences: Keynes's Post-War Policy Proposals', in Vicarelli F. (ed.), *Keynes's Relevance Today* (London: Macmillan, 1983), pp.28–50.

Latouche, S. *The Westernization of the World: The Significance, Scope and Limits of the Drive toward Global Uniformity* (Cambridge: Polity Press, 1996).

Le Thanh K. *Storia del Vietnam. Dalle origini alla occupazione francese* (Torino: Einaudi, 1979).

Lehmbruch, G. 'Concluding Remarks: Problems for Future Research on Corporatist Intermediation and Policy-Making', Schmitter P.C. (1979).

Lewis, W.A. 'Development with Unlimited Supply of Labour', Manchester:

The *Manchester School of Economic and Social Studies*, May 1954.
Lindbeck, A. *Can Pluralism Survive?* (University of Michigan: Ann Arbor, 1977).
Lunghini, G. *L'età dello spreco. Disoccupazione e bisogni sociali* (Torino: Bollati Boringhieri, 1995).
Lutz, V. 'The Growth Process in a Dual Economic System', *Quartely Review* (1958).
Luyckx. *Les religions face à la science et la technologie*, EC-MONITOR-FAST Brussels (1991).
Marshall, A. *Industry and Trade* (London: Macmillan, 1919).
Marx, K. and Engels, F. *The Communist Manifesto* (London: Penguin Books, [1848] 1968).
Melotti, U. *Marx and the Third World* (London: Macmillan, 1977).
Myrdal, G. *The Political Element in the Development of Economic Theory* (London: Routledge and Keegan Paul, 1953).
Myrdal, G. *Economic Theory and Underdeveloped Nations* (London: Gerald Duckworth & Co., 1957).
Myrdal, G. *Beyond the Welfare State* (Connecticut: Greenwood Press, Publishers Wesport, 1960).
Myrdal, G. *The Challenge of World Poverty. A World Anti-Poverty Programme in Outline* (London: Penguin Books, 1968).
Myrdal, G. *Asian Drama: An Inquiry into the Poverty of Nations*, 3 vols. (London: Penguin Books, 1968, pp.1834–5).
Myrdal, G. *Objectivity in the Social Research* (New York: Pantheon Books, 1969).
Myrdal, G. '"Growth" and "Development"' in *Against the Stream. Critical Essays on Economics* (London: Macmillan, 1973, pp.182–96).
Myrdal, G. *Value and Social Theory* (New York: Harper & Row, 1958).
Noble, D.F. *America by Design. Science, Technology, and the Rise of Corporate Capitalism* (New York: Alfred A. Knopf, 1977).
Noble, D.F. *Forces of Productions* (New York: Oxford University Press, 1986).
Nunnenkamp, P., Gundelach E. and Agarwal E. P. J. *Globalisation of Production and Markets* (Germany: J.C.B. Mohr (Paul Siebeck) Tübingen 1994).
OECD *Science, Technology, Industry*, STI Review, N. 15 (1995).
Offe, C. and Wiesenthal, H. 'Two Logics of Collective Action: Theoretical Notes on Social Class and Organisational Form', *Political Power and Social Theory* (Greenwich Conn.: AI Press, 1980) vol. I, pp.67–115.
Ohmae, K. *The Triadic Power*, 1977
Orati, V. *Scandinavian Lectures. The End of Political Economy and the End of Economic Policy* (Roskilde: Federico Caffè Centre, Roskilde University, 1996).
Paci, M. 'Crisi, ristrutturazione e piccola impresa', *Inchiesta*, n. 20, Bari: Dedalo, (1975).
Paci, M. 'Reddito minimo garantito, il fascino di un obiettivo limite', *Politica ed Economia*, Dicembre, Roma (1988).
Paggi, L. *Americanismo e riformismo. La socialdemocrazia europea nell'economia mondiale aperta* (Torino: Einaudi, 1989).
Parboni, R. 'I cinquantamila della borghesia mondiale', *Politica ed Economia*, 7–8 luglio Agosto (1988) pp.3–4.

Bibliography

Pasolini, P. P. 'Il "discorso" dei capelli', *Scritti corsari* (Milano: Garzanti, [1973] 1975).
Pasolini, P.P. 'L'articolo delle lucciole', in *Scritti corsari* (Milano: Garzanti, [1973] 1975a).
Pasolini, P.P. *Volgar' eloquio* (Roma: Editori Riuniti, 1987).
Perna, T. *Lo sviluppo insostenibile. La crisi del capitalismo nelle aree periferiche* (Napoli: Liguori Editore, 1995).
Perrone, N. *Il dissesto programmato. Le partecipazioni statali nel sistema di consenso democristiano* (Bari: Dedalo, 1991).
Petrella, R. *Four Analyses of the Globalisation of Technology and Economy*, Brussels: EC-MONITOR-FAST (1991).
Petrella, R. and Saussay, P. *Living together. Reshaping science and technology priorities to serve the basic needs and aspirations of 8 billion people*, Brussels: EC-MONITOR-FAST (1993).
Petrella, R. 'Europe in a global context', *Samfundsøkonomen*, København, April (1993).
Petrella, R. (ed.), *Limits to Competition*, The Group of Lisbon (Cambridge, MA and London: The MIT Press, 1995).
Polanyi, K. *Primitive, Archaic and Modern Economies* (New York: Doubleday & Company, 1968).
Polanyi, K. *The Great Transformation. The Political and Economic Origins of Our Time* (Boston: Beacon Press, [1944] 1971).
Polanyi, K. *The Livelihood of Man* (New York: Academic Press Inc., 1977).
Porter, M.E., *The Competitive Advantage of Nations*. London: Macmillan Press, 1990.
Querini, G. (ed.), *Cee, Mezzogiorno, Mediterraneo nuove prospettive di cooperazione economica* (Napoli: Edizioni Scientifiche Italiane, 1982).
Roque, M.A. (ed.) *I movimenti umani nel Mediterraneo Occidentale* (Institut Català d'Estudis Mediterranis, Barcelona, 1989).
Rolland, R. *Vita di Tolstoi* (Milano: Casa Editrice R. Caddeo e C., [1913] 1921).
Romeo, R. *Risorgimento e capitalismo* (Bari: Laterza, 1959).
Rossi-Doria, M. *10 anni di politica agraria nel Mezzogiorno* (Bari-Roma: Edizioni Laterza, 1958).
Sabel C. and Zeitlin, J. 'Historical Alternatives to Mass Production', *Past and Present*, no. 108 (1982) pp.133–76.
Sabel, Charles, *Works and Politics: The Division of Labour in Industry* (New York, Cambridge University Press, 1982).
Sabel, C. and Piore J. M. *The Second Industrial Divide: Possibilities for Prosperity* (New York: 1984).
Sachs, W. (ed.) *The Development Dictionary. A Guide to Knowledge as Power* (London: Zed Books Ltd, 1995).
Salvati, M. 'Sviluppo capitalistico e proletariato marginale nel libro di Massimo Paci', *Quaderni Piacentini*, n. 52 (1974).
Schmitter, P.C., 'Still the century of Corporatism?', in Schmitter, P.C. and Lehmbruch G. (eds.), *Trends Towards Corporatist Intermediation* (London: Sage, 1979) pp.7–52.
Schmitter, P.C. and Streeck, W. *The Organisation of Business Interests: A Research Design to Study the Associative Action of Business in the Advanced Industrial Societies of Western Europe*, Discussion Paper, IIM/LMP (1981) pp.81–113.

Sereni, E. *Vecchio e nuovo nelle campagne italiane* (Roma: Editori Riuniti, 1956).
Sereni, E. *Due linee di politica agraria* (Roma: Editori Riuniti, 1961).
Sereni, E. 'Il nodo della politica granaria', 1959, reissued in Sereni E. *Capitalismo e mercato nazionale* (Roma: Editori Riuniti, 1966).
Sereni, E. 'Da Marx a Lenin: La categoria formazione economico-sociale' *Critica Marxista*, n. 4, (1970) pp.29–79.
Silva, M. 'Contribution à la definition d'un style Méditerranèen de dévelopment', *Etudios de Economia*, vol. 4, n. 1 (1983).
Sofri, G. *Il modo di produzione asiatico – Storia di una controversia marxista* (Torino: Einaudi, 1979).
Spinelli, A. and Rossi E. *Problemi della Federazione Europea* (Roma: Ed. Movimento Italiano per la Federazione Europea, 1944).
Thurow, L. 'Socialismo e capitalismo. Ma la storia non finisce', *Il Corriere della sera*, Milano (1990) 1.
Tobin, J. 'The Monetarist Counter-Revolution Today – An Appraisal', *Economic Journal*, marts (1982).
Treuner, P. and Foucher, M. (eds,) *Towards a New a European Space* (Hanover: ARL-DATAR, 1995).
UNDP *Human Development Report* (New York and Oxford: Oxford University Press, 1993).
UNDP *Human Development Report* (New York and Oxford: Oxford University Press, 1994).
UNDP *Human Development Report* (New York and Oxford: Oxford University Press, 1995).
United Nations Centre on Transnational Corporations *Transnational Corporations in World Development* (New York: United Nations, 1988).
United Nations Centre on Transnational Corporations *World Investment Report. The Triad in Foreign Direct Investment* (New York: United Nations, 1991).
Transnational Corporations and Management Division, *World Investment Report. Transnational Corporations as Engine of Growth* (New York: United Nations, 1992).
United Nations Conference on Trade and Development *World Investment Report. Transnational Corporations, Employment and the Workplace* (New York: United Nations, 1994).
Vianello, F. 'I meccanismi di recupero del profitto', Graziani, A. *Crisi e ristrutturazione dell'economia italiana* (Torino: Einaudi, 1975).
Vicarelli, F. (ed.), *Keynes's Relevance Today* (London: Macmillan, 1985).
World Bank, *World Development Report. Workers in an Integrating World* (Oxford: Oxford University Press, 1995).

Index

Note: 'n.' after a page reference indicates the number of a note on that page.

accumulation process and dualism, theories, 37
  Fuà, 40–2
  Graziani, 39
  Klinderberger, 38
  Lewis, 37–8
  Lutz, 38
  production structure, 39–40
active accords, 184–5
actors, 51
  globalization, 53
  internationalization, 54
  meso-regional cooperation, 54
  universalization, 52
adaptability of capitalism, 17
Adorno, Theodor, 5
Africa, 8, 57
Agency for Economic Development and Cooperation in the Mediterranean, 198
Agnelli, Gianni, 117
agriculture and agro-food systems
  capitalism's revision of history, 8
  marginalization, 109
  market model, 80
  Mediterranean countries, 154, 160–3: cooperation and co-development, 166–70; environmental imbalances, 164–5; marine resources, 172–3; modernization, 25; natural and structural potentialities, 170–2
  trade balance, 110–11, 161
air traffic, 142
Albania, 108, 145–6, 177
Algeria
  agricultural sector, 172
  industrial sector, 177
  investment in, 67–8
  Italy compared with, 5
  modernization, 148–9
  state's new political role, 124
  structural adjustment policy, 105, 125–6, 127
Amato, Andrea, 32n.13
Amazon River Basin, 15
Americanism, 80–3, 91–2
Americas, 8, 57, 58
Amin, Samir, 46
Amoroso, B., 81, 102
anthropology, 9
apartheid, worldwide, 48, 79, 118
aquaculture, 173
Arab world
  Mediterranean co-development, 153–4: culture, 156–7, 159–60; modernization, 157–8; religion, 158–9
  Mediterranean regional solidarity, 140–1
archaeology, 9
area development policies, 195
Argentina, 57
arms trade, 5
Asia, 57, 58
authors, 51
  globalization, 53
  internationalization, 54
  meso-regional cooperation, 53–4
  universalization, 52
automobile industry, organization, 63, 64
  General Motors, 66
  Toyota, 66, 68

Baglioni, Guido, 97, 100–1
Balkans, 108, 137, 145–6

207

208   *Index*

Baltic countries
  agro-food trade balance, 110
  demographic growth, 107, 108
  Greater Europe, 147
  gross national product, 108
  marginalization's impact on production systems, 112–13, 114
  polycentrism, 133
  regional scenario, 134, 137–8
  technology, 110
Bandt, Jacques De, 128
banking system
  structural adjustment policies, 122
  transnational banks, 55
Baran, Paul, 23
Barcellona, P., 95, 96
basic oxygen process, steel production, 181
Belgium, 36
Benedetti, Carlo de, 117
Benetton, Luciano, 117
biotechnology, 171–2
black market, 41, 42
Black Sea regional scenario, 134
Blair, J.M., 40
Bobbio, Norberto, 72–3, 75
booms, and foreign direct investment, 58
bourgeoisie, 117–18
  'compradora', 118
  global, 117
  national, 117–18
Boyer, Robert, 93
Braudel, Fernand, 9
  capitalism, 15, 177–18: market, 16–17; material life, 15–16, rise to prominence, 10
Brazil, 57
Bretton Woods institutions, 119
  see also International Monetary Fund; World Bank
Bruni, Michele, 199n.1
buffer enterprises, 40
build-operate-transfer (BOT) accords, 195
Bulgaria, 125, 149

Caffè, Federico, 6, 76, 81
Cambodia, 67
capital accumulation, 70
  Americanism and reformism, 80–3
  end of history, 70–4
  globalization and new technologies, 74–80
Casablanca revolt (1981), 126
Cecchini Report, 130
Central American Common Market, 168
central banks, 122
Charter of Extra-EC Immigration, 190–1
China, 9, 58
Ciampi, Carlo Azeglio, 117
city-states, Middle Ages, 10
class, social, 91
  bourgeoisie, 117–18
  Braudel's analysis, 17
  economic power, 117
  working class, 118
classical economy, 35
clothing industry, 179–80
Club of Rome, 77
co-determination, 28–31
co-development, 27–31
  Mediterranean, 151–5:
    agro-food systems, 160–73;
    culture and religion, 155–60; industrial systems, 174–86; migrations and labour market, 186–91;
    policies and institutions, 191–8
cog enterprises, 40
Cold War legacy, 130, 131, 132
  Danube region, 139, 140
collective bargaining, 93
Collotti Pischel, Enrica, 9
colonialism
  Arab world, 158, 159
  industrialization, 134: and economic growth, 27
  and modern trade relations, 114
  new, 80
  partitioning of human societies' interactions, 9

Index

socio-economic formations, 13, 14
communism, 4, 70
Communist Manifesto, 4
companies, *see* firms
competition, 52–3, 167
competitive advantage, 52–3
competitiveness, 128
'compradora' bourgeoisie, 118
computer industry, 183
Confederation of Independent States (CIS), 133
construction industry, 80
consumer price index, 125–6
consumption dualism, 39
contract negotiations, 101
cooperation, 27
  meso-regional, 53–4
  objectives, 177–83
Coriat, Benjamin, 95
corporate profit-sharing plans, 102
corporate strategies (1990s), 98–102
corporate unions, 100–1
corporatism, history, 90–2
crime, 5
Crouch, C., 100–1
Cuccia, Enrico, 117
cultural genocide, 9, 15
culture
  Mediterranean, 152, 156–7: Arab countries, 156–7, 159–60
  and partitioning of human societies' interactions, 10
  underdeveloped countries, 20
  Western, 187
Czechoslovakia, 125, 138, 176
Czech Republic, 125

Daneo, Camillo, 25
Danube regional scenario, 134, 138–40
Darwinism, 26
debt, foreign, 192–3
  origins of crisis, 121
debt-equity swap, 193
demand dualism, 39

democracy
  Americanization of concept, 92
  and corporatism, 99–100
  economic: Keynes's views, 22; proposal, 102
  and market, incompatibility, 76
demographic changes, 107–8, 148
demonstration effect, 41
Denmark, 3, 102
dependence, 46
De Rita, G., 152, 153
desertification, 164–5
destabilization, *see* political destabilization
developed countries, Myrdal's views, 18–19
development
  capitalism, 8–11
  dual interpretive polarities, 7–8
  end of, 77, 79; European societies, 89–90
  growth without, 76
  human, 26, 44
  and industrialization, 42–4
  Keynes's views, 22
  lagged, 40–2
  Marxist economists' views, 23, 24
  Mediterranean and European integration, 45
  models, 149–50
  Myrdal's views, 18–19
  policies, compatibility, 192–3
  polycentric, 26–7: from cooperation to co-development, 27–31; Europe's meso-regions, 133–4; material life, 16
Dini, Lamberto, 117
direct foreign investment, *see* foreign direct investment
diversity
  Mediterranean countries, 156–7
  genetic, 168–9
  Southern Europe and Scandinavia, 132–3
drugs trade, 5
dualism, 34–5
  accumulation process, 37–42

210　Index

dependence and exclusion, 46–8
European integration, 104, 105
origins, 35–7
political destabilization and worldwide apartheid, 48
Eastern Europe
economic marginalization and political destabilization, 74
nation-state, crisis, 72
productivity growth, 71
Scandinavia model, 3
see also socialist countries
East-West relations, 3
economic growth
without development, 76
employment effects, 61–3
export-led, 38, 39
Keynes's views, 22
Myrdal's views, 18
polycentric development, 27, 29, 30
Querini's views, 45
Silva's views, 42–4
sustainable, 26, 44
economicism, 26
economic marginalization, 2, 35, 52
causes, 109–10
dependence and exclusion, 46–8
Eastern Europe, 74
European integration, 104–5, 106
European Union regional scenario, 136
impact on production systems, 111–16
Italy, 5
Maghreb, 125–6
political destabilization and worldwide apartheid, 48
qualitative factors, 109–11
quantitative factors, 107–9
Southern Europe and Scandinavia, 132
studies, 107–11
economic power and social classes, 117
education, 111

Mediterranean agricultural sector, 170–1
policies, 195–6
efficiency
economic, 128
and equality, interrelation, 82–3
of firms, 84
output, 128
triadic capitalism, 28
Egypt, 105, 177
electric-arc furnace, steel production, 181
electronics industry
machine tools, 183
organization, 63, 65: IBM, 67
employment and unemployment
dualism, 38
economic growth's effect on, 61–3
Keynes's views, 22
lagged development, 41
marginalization, 108–9
Mediterranean countries, 160
energy sources, 109
Engels, Friedrich, 4
England, 36
Enlightenment
absolute monarchies, 10
modernization, 20
Myrdal, 31n.6, 32n.6
environmental effects of capitalism, 22, 164–5
equality, 82–3
ethnology, 9
Eurocentrism, 27, 131–2, 152
European integration, 104–7
Americanism, 82–3, 91–2
Cold War legacy, 131
Eurocentrism, 132
marginalization: impact on production systems, 111–16; studies, 107–11
Mediterranean countries, 44–5
European Union
agricultural policies, 25
Black Sea countries, agreements with, 149
expansion, 44–5
industrial relations, 97

Index

Mediterranean co-development, 151–2
Mediterranean policy, 140
  members, 104–6
  rethinking, 130
  solidarity, 134, 135–6: Baltic Region, 137–8
  exclusion, 46–8
  exports, 88
  extrapolation, fallacy of, 90

fall-of-the-Wall strategy, 3
Fanon, F., 1
Far East, 8
Fascism, 92
financial cooperation policies, 196
Finland, 109, 112, 137
firms
  corporate strategies (1990s), 98–102
  corporatism, history, 90–2
  flexible specialization, 93–6
  functional socialism and functional capitalism, 102–3
  functional structure, 85–9
  and globalization, 84
  industrial relations (1980s), 96–8
  interest groups and political exchange, 92–3
  origin, 85
  ownership and management, 84–5
  and state in West, 89–90
fish industry, 172–3
Foa, Vittorio, 25
food industry, 178–9
Fordism, 93–4, 95–6
foreign direct investment (FDI), 57–61
  in Mediterranean countries, 193–5: industrial sector, 175
  in Morocco, 44
  by transnational corporations, 55, 57, 58, 175
Foucher, Michel, 150n.1
France
  agricultural sector, 110, 160, 161
  industrialization, 36
  industrial sector, 177, 183, 186
  investment in Morocco, 144
Fuà, Giorgio, 40–2, 44
full employment, 22
functional socialism and functional capitalism, 102–3
fundamentalism, 123, 125

game theory, 75
General Council for Fishing in the Mediterranean, 173
generalization, fallacy of, 90
General Motors, 63–4, 66
genetic diversity, 168–9
genetic engineering, 172
Germany
  and Baltic countries, 112, 113
  industrialization, 36
  manufacturing sector, 109
  solidarity: Baltic scenario, 137–8; Danube scenario, 139; EU regional scenario, 135–6
germplasm, 168–9
Gerschenkron, Alexander, 36, 48n.2
Giarini, O., 77
globalization, definition, 52–3
Glotz, Peter, 73
Gomez y Paloma, Sergio, 199n.1
Graziani, Augusto, 39, 136
Great Britain, 86, 161
Greater Europe concept, 130, 136, 147–50
Greece
  Balkan crisis, 146–7
  EC membership, 44
  industrial sector, 177
  lagged development, 40
gross domestic product (GDP), 63, 160
gross national product (GNP), 18, 61–3, 108
growth
  demographic, 107–8
  economic, *see* economic growth
guilds, 17, 90
Gulf War, 151, 155

Hamel, B., 124
Hirshman, Albert O., 36, 48n.2

Index

historical school, 36–7
history
 capitalism's revision of, 8–9
 end of, 70–4
Holland, Stuart, 80, 92
human development, 26, 44
humanism, 26
Hungary, 176

IBM, 63
imperialism, 27, 34
income distribution, 22
income policies, 93
industrial clusters, 176
industrial districts, 85
industrialization
 and development models, 42–4
 and European crisis, 74
 historical forms, 33–5
 polycentric development, 26, 27
 and steel industry, synonymity, 181
 waves, 36–7
industrial leasing, 194–5
industrial organization, 63–5, 66, 67
industrial relations
 1980s, 96–8
 1990s, 98–101, 102
 flexible specialization, 95
Industrial Revolution, 8
industrial sector, Mediterranean countries, 154–5
 co-development and new technologies, 176
 foreign and transnational investment, 175
 markets and production structures, 174
 objectives of cooperation, 177–83
 specialization and cooperation, 177
 technology transfer, 183–6
inequality, 35
Infante, Davide, 116, 199n.1
infrastructure, 142, 143
innovation
 agricultural sector, 163
 Danube regional scenario, 139
 technological, 78–9, 110:
  Mediterranean industrial sector, 176, 179–80, 183
 theories, 78
institutionalism, 91
institutions, 11–15
 Bretton Woods, 119
 debt problems, origins, 121
 fundamentalism, 125
 industrial relations, 97–8
 Mediterranean co-development, 155, 191–2, 196–8
 polycentric development, 29
 structural adjustment policies, 120, 121–3
 Western, 89–90
interest groups, 92–3
interest rates, 122
International Fund for Agricultural Development (IFAD), 163
internationalization, 54
 stages, 33–5
 Welfare State, 131
International Monetary Fund (IMF)
 debt problem, 121, 192
 role, 119
 structural adjustment policies, 122
investments
 Mediterranean and European integration, 45
 security, 184
 socialization, 102: Keynes's views, 22
Iraq, 67
Ireland, 40
Islam, 157, 158–9
Israel, 141, 170
Italy
 agricultural sector, 160, 161, 164, 172: modernization, 25
 anomalous position, 4–5
 Balkan crisis, 146
 bourgeoisie, 117
 Council of Economics and Labour, 197
 dualism theories, 37, 38, 40

Index

European integration, 105
Fascism, 92
functional socialism and functional capitalism, 103
industrial sector, 176, 177, 179, 183: technology transfer, 184–5, 186
lagged development, 40
Mediterranean co-development, 151, 152–3
Mezzogiornio, 4, 132
migration, 188–90, 191, 192
national state, formation, 86
patents, 110
research and development, 111

Japan
industrial clusters, 176
productivity growth, 71
scientific progress, 159
specialization, flexible, 95
Jessop, Bob, 93
joint ventures, 176, 186
Jordan, 177

Kapp, William, 21
Keynes, John Maynard, 22–3, 26, 35
Keynesian policies, 35, 128–9
Klinderberger, C.P., 38

labour force
flexibility, 101–2
Mediterranean countries, 148
labour market policies, 195
lagged development, 40–2
Lapps, 15
large-scale industry, 39–40, 42
Latouche, Serge, 1
leasing, industrial, 194–5
legitimacy, market, 75
Leibenstein, Harvey, 48n.2
Lewis, W.A., 37–8
Libya, 172, 177
lifetime of products, 77
livestock capital, 169–70
local capitalist firms, 86, 87
Loubergé, H., 77
lung enterprises, 40
Lutz, Vera, 38

Maastricht Treaty, 105
Machiavelli, Niccolò, 10
machine-tool industry, 182–3
mafia, 5
Maghreb, 125–6, 144, 160
management of firms, 84–5
manufacturing sector, 109, 177
marginalization, *see* economic marginalization
marine resources, 172–3
market
Braudel's analysis, 16–17
economy: 1990s, 74; and democracy, incompatibility, 76; innovation theories, 78; nation-state, attempts to overcome crisis, 73
forms, 11–15
Mediterranean countries, 174
marketing, Mediterranean agricultural sector, 166–7
Marshall, A., 70
Marshall Plan, 82, 83
Marx, Karl, 4, 25, 90–1
Marxist economists
capitalism, 23–6: adaptability, 17
inequality, 35
Myrdal, 31–2n.6
social and political contract, end of, 77
Marshraq, 160
material life, 15–16
Mauritania, 172
Mediterranean countries
co-development, 151–5: agro-food systems, 160–73; culture and religion, 155–60; industrial systems, 174–86; migrations and labour market, 186–91; policies and institutions, 191–8
development models, 149–50
diversity, 133
European integration, 44–5
Greater Europe, 147
infrastructure, 142, 143
interface, 141–2

214 Index

marginalization, 111: agro-food trade balance, 110–11; demographic growth, 107–8; GNP, 108; impact on production systems, 113–16; technology, 110
production systems, population and migrations, 147–8
rural world, importance, 148–9
Silva's views, 42–4
solidarity, 134, 140–1: Danube region, 139
structural adjustment policies, 123–4
Mediterranean Forum, 197–8
Mediterranean Framework Programme, 198
mercantilism, 33–4
meso-corporatism, 92
meso-institutions, 97–8
meso-regional cooperation, 53–4
meso-regions, Europe, 133–4, 143–5
Mexico, 57
Mezzogiorno, 4, 132
micro-corporatism, 92
Middle Ages, 10
Middle East, 8, 146
migration, Mediterranean countries, 155, 186–7
agricultural sector, 165, 170
Charter of Extra-EC Immigration, 190–1
dynamics and causes, 187–8
profile and impetus, 188–90
modernization
Arab world, 157–8
and European crisis, 74
Marxist economists' views, 25
Mediterranean countries, 148–9
socio-economic formations, 14–15
underdeveloped countries, 19, 20–1
monarchies, 10
monetarist counterrevolution, 80–2
Morocco
agricultural sector, 162–3, 173
foreign investment, 144

industrial sector, 177
modernization, 148–9
structural adjustment policies, 125–6
multinational corporations, *see* transnational corporations
Myrdal, Gunnar, 1, 9
bourgeois and Enlightenment thought, 31–2n.6
developed countries, 18–19
poverty, vicious circle of, 35–6
underdeveloped countries, 19–21
Welfare State, internationalization, 131

national bourgeoisies, 117–18
national capitalist firms, 86–8
nation-state, crisis, 72, 73–4
neoclassical economics, 21, 35
neo-corporatism, 91–2
neo-Keynesian propositions, 128–9
Netherlands, 36, 110
new world order, 2–3, 48
Noble, David, 10–11, 50
nomads, 14
Non-Government Organizations (NGOs), 163
non-profit sector, 22
North Atlantic Treaty Organization (NATO), 80
Norway, 3
Nurkse, R., 36

oil industry, 181–2
origins of capitalism, 10
orthodox economy, 35
Ottoman Empire, 141
output
dualism, 39
efficiency, 128
national capitalist firms, 88
ownership of firms, 84–5

Paci, Massimo, 39, 74
Paggi, Leonardo, 82, 105
Palestine, 146–7
Palme, Olof, 3
Parboni, Riccardo, 73, 80

Index

participation
  changing concept, 100
  in international trade, 112, 113
Pasolini, Pier Paolo, 7, 15, 130
passive accords, 184
Pasolini, Pier Paolo, 130
patents, 110
Perna, Tonino, 49n.5
Perrone, Nico, 116n.1, 199n.1
Petrella, Riccardo
  co-determination, 29
  co-development, 27
  industrial organization, 63
  political destabilization, 48
  triadic capitalism, 107
petrochemical industry, 181–2
Poland
  GNP, 108
  industrial output, 125
  joint ventures, 176
  technology, 110
Polanyi, Karl, 74–5
policies, Mediterranean co-development, 155, 191–6
political destabilization, 2, 48, 52
  Balkan Crisis, 145
  Eastern Europe, 74
  foreign direct investment, 58
  Italy, 5
  Maghreb, 125–6
  marginalization, 46
  production organization, 66–8
  Southern Europe and Scandinavia, 132
  technological innovation, 79
polycentric development, 26–7
  diamond of, 27–30
  from cooperation to co-development, 27–31
  Europe's meso-regions, 133–4
  material life, 16
population distribution, 148
Porter, Michael, 32n.14
Portugal
  EC membership, 44
  fish imports, 172
  GNP, 108
  lagged development, 40
  technology, 110

post-Fordism, 93–4
poverty, vicious circle of, 35–6
privatization, 85, 122
process innovations, 78–9
product innovations, 79
production modes, 11–15
  dualism, 39–40
  marginalization's impact, 111–16
  Marxist economists' views, 24–5
  Mediterranean countries, 147–8, 149, 174
  national, 123
  polycentric development, 27–8
  transnational corporations, 65–6
profit-sharing plans, corporate, 102
property ownership, 14
public sector
  Braudel's analysis, 16–17
  polycentric development, 29–30
  role, 126–7
  structural adjustment policies, 122

Querini, Giulio, 44–5

raw materials, sources, 109
Reagan era, 3
real processes, 50–1
  globalization, 52–3
  internationalization, 54
  meso-regional cooperation, 53–4
  universalization, 51–2
reformism, 75, 80–3
regional conflicts, 80
regional development, 46–8
  policies, 195
Regional Mediterranean Consortia, 166
religion, 17, 157
Renaissance, 10
research and development (R&D), 111
  facilities, 110
  Mediterranean agricultural sector, 168
  policies, 195–6
'Rio Grande effect', 147–50

Romania, 152, 149
Rome, Club of, 77
Romeo, Rosario, 25
Rosenstein-Rodan, Paul, 48n.2
Rossi-Doria, Manlio, 25
Rostow, Walter, 36–7, 48n.2
Russia
  intelligentsia's theories, 9
  solidarity: Baltic scenario, 133, 137–8; Danube scenario, 139

salinization, 164
Salvati, Michele, 40
Saussay, P., 27, 29
Scandinavian model, 3
  cultural ethos, 138
  decentralization of Europe's infrastructure, 143
  elimination, 3, 4
  Eurocentrism and Westernization, 132
  failure, 21, 23
  nation-state, attempts to overcome crisis, 73
  neoclassical economics critique, 21
  solidarity: Baltic region, 137, 138; Danube region, 138–9
Schmitter, P.C., 91
science and capital, relationship between, 96
scientific progress, Arab countries, 159
self-sufficiency, 16
Sereni, Emilio, 24–5
shoe industry, 180
Shumpeter's Darwinism, 26
signorie, 10
Silva, Manuela, 42–4
slave trade, 33–4
small-scale industry
  dualism, 39–40
  lagged development, 42
  Mediterranean countries, 148
  technology transfer, 186
social and political contract, end of, 76–7
social cost approach, 21, 23
social democratic model, 73
social destabilization, 5
socialist countries
  crisis, 70, 71
  elimination, 3–4, 46
  firms, ownership and management, 85
socio-economic formations, dynamics of
  capitalism, 15–26: and society, hypotheses on, 11–15
  development, 7–11: polycentric, 26–31
socio-economic indicators, 26
  see also gross domestic product; gross national product
soil fertility, 165
solidarity, four rings of, 130–41
Somalia, 66–7
Soviet society, 71, 112
Soviet Union, former, 176
Spain
  agricultural sector, 173
  EC membership, 44
  industrial sector, 177, 179, 183, 186
  investment in Morocco, 144
  lagged development, 40
  marginalization, 111
  specialization, 65–6
  flexible, 52, 93–6, 102
  Mediterranean countries: agricultural sector, 166; industrial sector, 177
SPRINT, 184–5
stability, monetary, 120
state
  Braudel's analysis, 17
  new political role, 124–5
  sector, *see* public sector
  Western, 89–90
steel industry, 80, 181
stock exchange, 194
strategic alliances, 65, 67
structural adjustment policies, 105, 114, 120
  effects, 122–3: Maghreb, 125–6; Mediterranean, 123–4
  stages, 121–2
subjectivism, 24

success, capitalism, 9
surplus, 24
Susan, George, 121
sustainable growth, 26, 44
Sweden
  dynamism and mobilization, 71
  economic democracy movement, 102
  manufacturing sector, 109
  Scandinavian model and Olof Palme, 3
  technology, 110
Sweezy, Paul M., 23
Syria, 165, 170

taxation, 184
Taylorism, 95–6
technological determinism, 26
technology
  choice, 79–80
  end of development, 77
  gap, 41, 79
  industrial organization, 176
  innovation, 78–9, 110: theories, 78; types, 78–9
  Mediterranean agricultural sector, 168
  Mediterranean industrial sector, 174, 176, 179–81, 183: transfers, 179, 183–6; transnational investment, 175
  meso-regional co-development, 143–5
  social and political contract, end of, 76
  specialization, flexible, 96
  telecommunications industry, 64, 67
  textile industry, 179
  theoretical tools, 50–1
  globalization, 52–3
  internationalization, 54
  meso-regional cooperation, 53–4
  universalization, 51–2
third sector, 32n.8
Third World
  Bretton Woods institutions, 119

debt problem, 121
  foreign direct investment, 57
Thurow, Lester C., 70–1
Tobin, James, 81
Tolstoi, Leo, 9
Toyota, 66, 68
trades unions
  corporatism, 100–1, 102
  dualism, 38, 39
  functional capitalism, 103
  history, 90–1
  specialization, flexible, 95
transnational banks, 55
transnational corporations (TNCs), 87, 88–9
  competitive strategies, 53
  corporatism, 99
  foreign direct investment, 55, 57, 58, 175
  industrial organization, 63–4
  main offices and branches, distribution, 161–2
  political destabilization, 66–8
  production organization, 65–6
  socio-economic formations, 13
  technology transfers, 185–6
  triadic capitalism, 54–5, 56
Treuner, Peter, 150n.1
triadic capitalism, 2, 54–6
  corporate strategies, 98
  European studies, 106–7
  foreign direct investment, 57, 58, 59, 60–1
  globalization, 52
  Italy, 5
  marginalization, 35, 46
  Marxist economists' views, 24
  neo-corporatism, 92
  production modes, institutions and market forms, 13, 28
  world trade, 61, 62
Tunisia
  agricultural sector, 162, 164–5, 172
  structural adjustment policies, 126
Turatto, Renzo, 199n.1
Turkey
  development models, 149

industrial sector, 177
lagged development, 40
manufacturing sector, 109
Mediterranean scenario, 141
polycentrism, 133
'two-thirds society', 73

underdeveloped countries, 19–21
unemployment, *see* employment and unemployment
United Kingdom, 135–6
United Nations (UN)
  Development Program, 26
  International Fund for Agricultural Development (IFAD), 163
  regional conflicts, 80
United States of America
  EU regional scenario, 135, 136
  Islamic world, control and containment, 133
  productivity growth, 71
universalization, 51–2

value added, 24
venture-capital funds, 194
Vianello, Ferdinando, 40
voluntary sector, 32n.8

wages, 127
welfare state
  corporatism, 99
  crisis, 46, 74, 75, 76
  end of history, 70, 71
  internationalization, 131
  Italy, 4
  Myrdal's vies, 91
  national bourgeoisies, 118
  Scandinavian model, 3
  solidarity among EU countries, 135
  'two-thirds society', 73
Westernization, 131–2
Winslow, C.E.A., 36
working class, 118
World Bank
  debt problem, 121, 192
  role, 119
  structural adjustment policies, 122
world-economies, 53–4
world trade, 61, 62

Yourcenar, Marguerite, 9
Yugoslavia, former
  crisis, 145–6, 151
  GNP, 108
  industrial sector, 177